I0752612

IMAGES
of America

PROVINCETOWN
VOLUME I

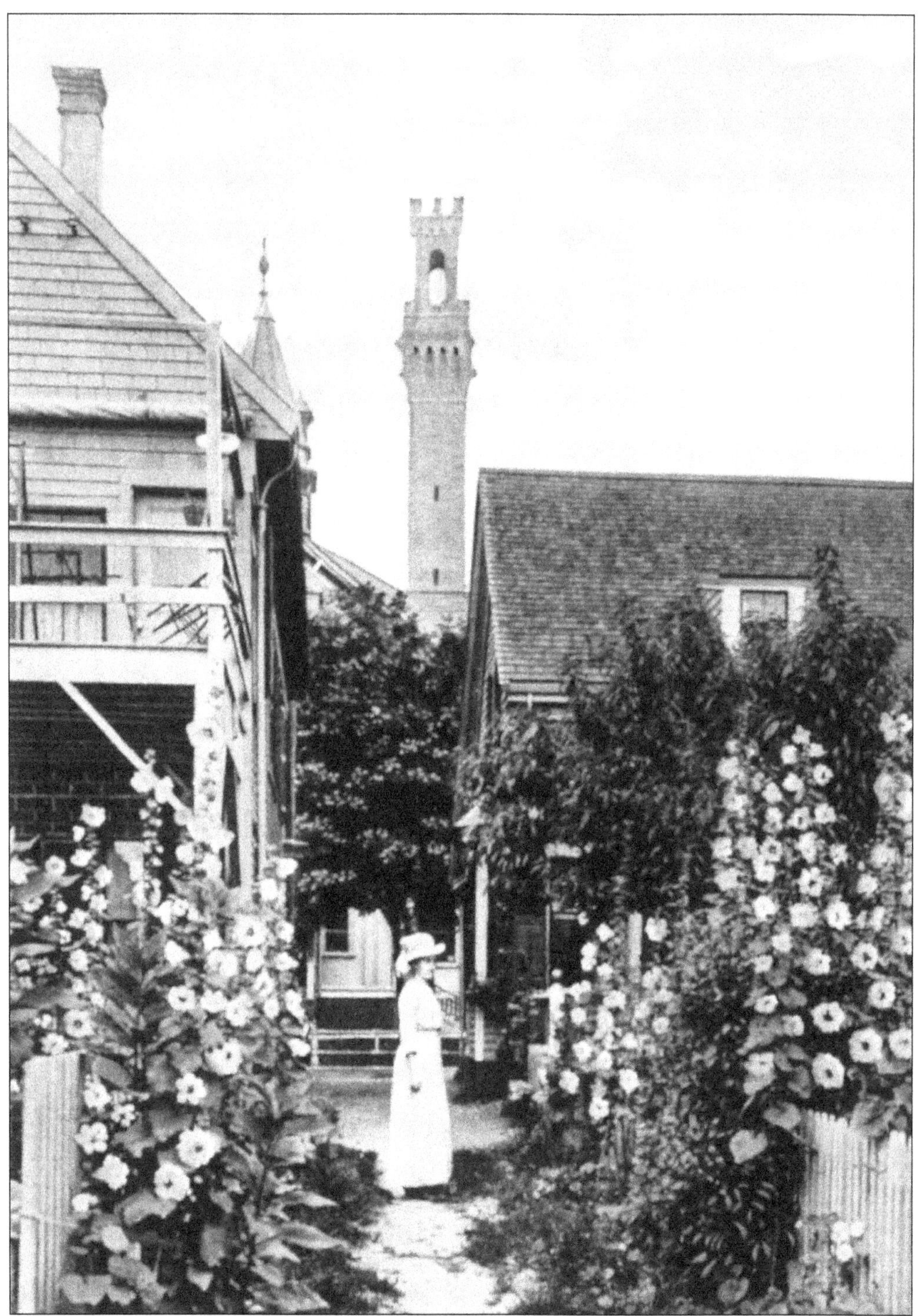

Hollyhock Lane (c. 1915 postcard published by H.A. Dickerman & Son, Taunton, MA). Two of Provincetown's most familiar landmarks, the town hall and the Pilgrim Monument, soar as do the abundant hollyhocks printed in polychrome on this charming postcard. The sandy walkway across from the town hall now has a board gate to prevent public access to the water.

IMAGES
of America

PROVINCETOWN
VOLUME I

John Hardy Wright

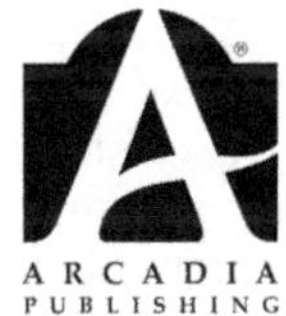

ISBN 978-1-5316-6015-4

Published by Arcadia Publishing
Charleston, South Carolina

For all general information contact Arcadia Publishing at:
Telephone 843-853-2070
Fax 843-853-0044
E-mail sales@arcadiapublishing.com
For customer service and orders:
Toll-Free 1-888-313-2665

Visit us on the Internet at www.arcadiapublishing.com

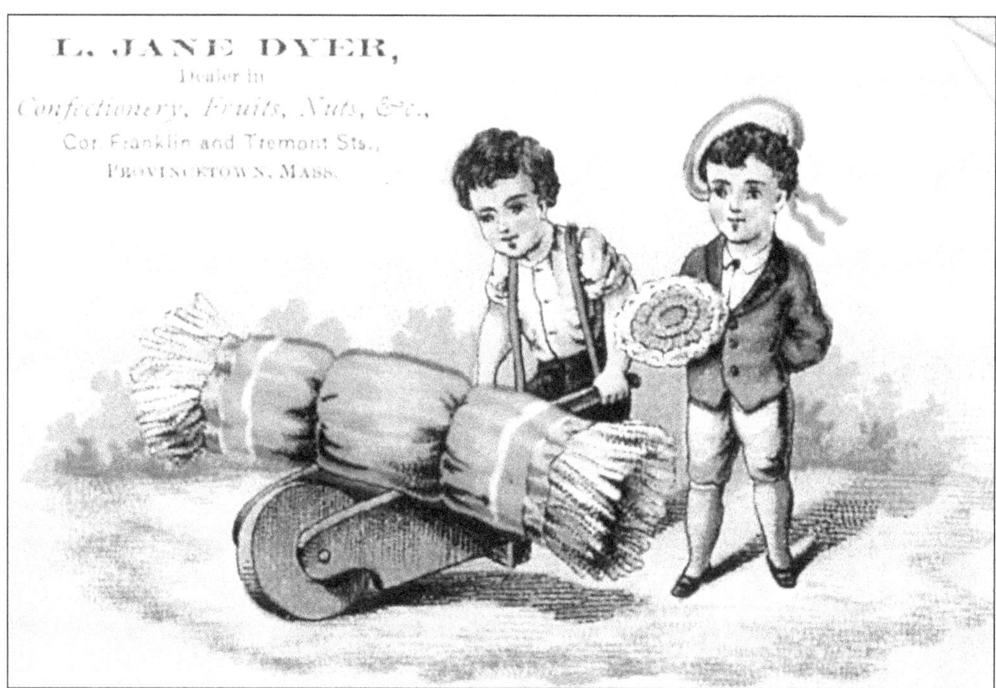

Trade card used by L. Jane Dyer, corner of Franklin and Tremont Streets (c. 1885). Miss Dyer may have had her confectionery and fruit shop in what is now Perry's Liquors at 1 Tremont Street. She also operated a dining room around this time in the center of town on the harbor side of Commercial Street near Standish Street (see p. 52). (Private Collection.)

Contents

Acknowledgments

Several individuals were very helpful in exchanging ideas about the history of Provincetown as it relates to this book, and I would like to thank Jack Barnett, Howard M. Bushnell, Ken Conrad, William Fitzpatrick, Robert F. Gilbert, Manuel J. "Cul" Goveia, Kenneth Gregory, Patricia Hallett, Stephen W. Hayes, Frederick Hemley, Peter B. Little, Bonnie Steele McGhee, Bryan McMullin, Eugenia A. Rogers, Dr. Andrew and Mrs. Brenda Selwyn, Joseph F. Schier, Stephen J. Schier, Skip and Arpina Stanton, Daniel Towler, Napi Van Dereck, and Emery Warner. Special thanks go to new friends Elena Curtis Hall, a perspicacious Provincetown native, and to James Cote for his fancy footwork in identifying views that befuddled the author. Individuals associated with institutions also deserve credit, and they include Debra deJonker-Berry (director, Provincetown Public Library); Reverend John A. Raposo (St. Peter the Apostle Church); Jeffory Morris (curator, Pilgrim Monument & Provincetown Museum); Susan Greendyke Lachevre (art collections manager, Massachusetts Arts Commission); John K. Roderick (president, Seamen's Bank); and James Zimmerman (photography archivist, Provincetown Art Association and Museum).

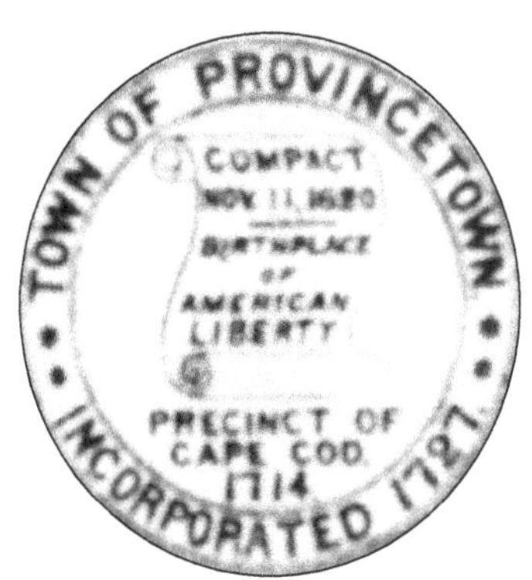

Introduction

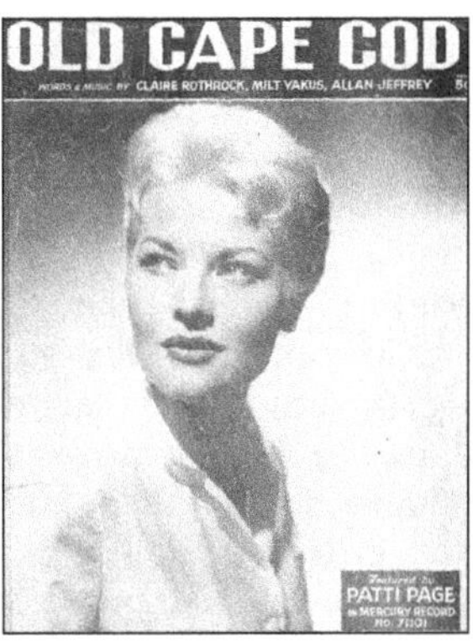

If you're fond of sand dunes and salty air,
Quaint little villages here and there;
You're sure to fall in love with old Cape Cod.
If you like the taste of a lobster stew,
Served by a window with an ocean view;
You're sure to fall in love with old Cape Cod.
Winding roads that seem to beckon you,
Miles of green beneath the skies of blue;
Church bells chiming on a Sunday morn',
Remind you of the town where you were born.
If you spend an evening, you'll want to stay,
Watching the moonlight on Cape Cod Bay;
You're sure to fall in love with old Cape Cod.

(Female vocalist Patti Page recorded this very popular song in 1956. The words and music are by Claire Rothrock, Milt Yakus, and Allan Jeffrey, and it was copyrighted by George Pincus & Sons Music Corporation.)

Marked by majestic and awe-inspiring **sand dunes** and very **salty air**, and certainly one of the most popular of the **quaint little villages here and there**, Provincetown, a magical spot located at the very tip of **old Cape Cod**, reminds many former visitors of the town which they very easily either **fall in love with**, or hate.

Lobster stew, Portuguese fare, and continental cuisine are **served by a window with an ocean view** in charming restaurants, many converted from stately Yankee sea captains' homes, and others from fish warehouses and shanties.

Two parallel, somewhat **winding roads**—Commercial and Bradford Streets—**beckon you** and thousands of summer vacationers and day-trippers who love to browse for souvenirs in shops and art galleries on the street so named for its mercantile businesses, and repose there or in guest houses on the street named in honor of the Pilgrim Colony's second governor, William Bradford.

Miles of green trails with scrub pine and bushes laden with bayberries and rose hips attract bicyclists, horseback riders, runners, and walkers, and those who prefer a narrated dune buggy ride to the simpler pursuits. Sun worshipers and shell collectors seek tanned bodies and unusual former nautical residences **beneath skies of blue** at Herring Cove and Race Point Beaches.

During the mid- to late nineteenth and early twentieth centuries, many church bells were **chiming on a Sunday morn'**, but fires destroyed several of these houses of worship, and others were razed or converted to new uses as dictated by changing times.

A home**town** atmosphere pervades Provincetown, especially during the fall and winter months when many seasonal storefronts are boarded up, chimneys exhale swirling smoke from homey fireplaces, and the summer gypsies have moved to warmer climes in search of other employment. Many residents enjoy the quiet off-season best of all, since there are far fewer people and even fewer automobiles and motorcycles to circumnavigate.

To **spend an evening** in Provincetown can be very special for newly marrieds, lovers—both straight and gay—and single straight, gay, and lesbian individuals, some of whom seek to find the love of their life on a crowded dance floor, in a cruise bar, or perhaps on the benches in front of the 1886 town hall.

Watching the moonlight flicker off anchored fishing and sailing vessels in the harbor was and is a romantic experience and provided creative inspiration for numerous authors and playwrights such as Norman Mailer, Eugene O'Neill, Mary Heaton Vorse, and Tennessee Williams, and for actors such as Bette Davis and Ann Harding (the incomparable Miss Davis performed in some plays at The Barn at 29a Bradford Street).

Daylight, however, with the atmospheric effects of sunlight on the harbor, is what drew artists here, beginning in the late nineteenth century. Charles W. Hawthorne, a Maine native, is credited with initiating art classes in Provincetown when he founded the Cape Cod School of Art in 1899. Many famous artists who work in different styles, "Sunday painters," and other creative people still find unique forms of inspiration in the picturesque port with which **you're sure to fall in love**.

Author's notes: Volume I of this pictorial history of Provincetown relates to the town's architecture and social history; Volume II will cover harbor views, whaling and fishing, art and artists, authors and playwrights, entertainers, and alternative lifestyles. Images in each chapter of this book are arranged according to street numbers (with some variations due to changes in numbering), with Commercial and Bradford Streets appearing first, followed by perpendicular and tertiary streets and lanes in a left-to-right format. Some postcards are printed with awkward or abbreviated titles, often hastily composed by the publisher or photographer; these titles appear as is in this book, with the deletion of repetitive information such as "Provincetown, Mass." and "First Landing Place of the Pilgrims," etc. Images not credited in a courtesy line are from the author's collection.

One

Historical Background

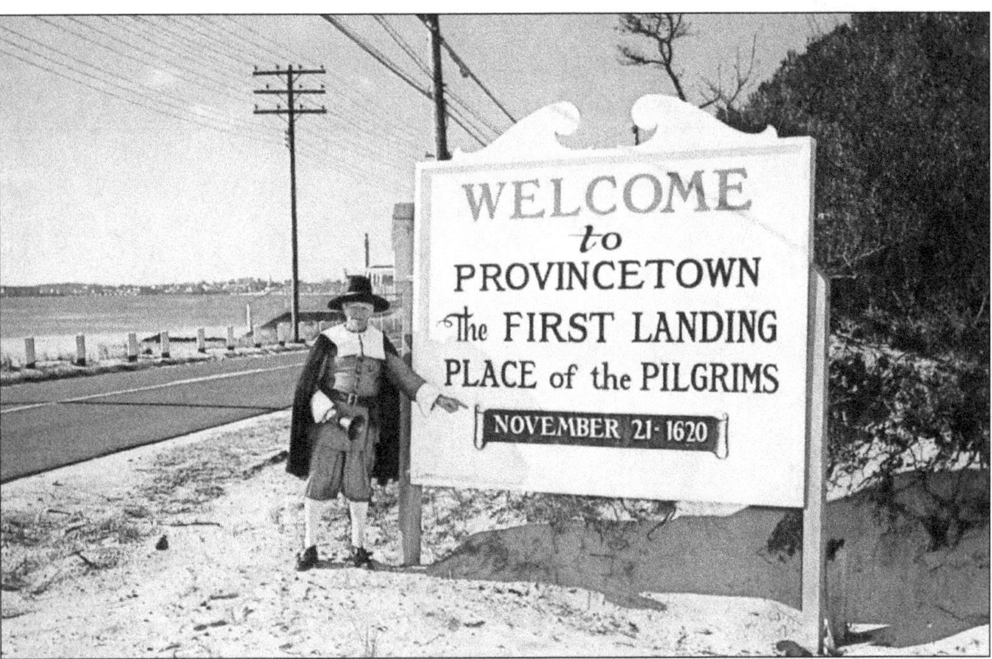

Welcome to Provincetown (c. 1945 postcard published by Cape Cod Photos, Orleans, MA). A former and larger Colonial-style wooden sign near Snail Road—the first entrance to Provincetown off Route 6—welcomed visitors to town as does Town Crier Arthur Snader, dressed in Pilgrim-style garb and holding the familiar large bell, the symbol of his office. Mr. Snader points to the sign that identifies the date of the Pilgrims' landing; however, most scholars say the historic event occurred on November 11, 1620 (Old Style calendar). The Pilgrim Memorial Monument, seen in the background between the two utility poles, is located exactly in the center of town and can be reached by continuing along the shore on Route 6A (which leads onto Bradford Street), or by taking the Conwell Street or Shank Painter Road exits off Route 6, which flank the imposing monument.

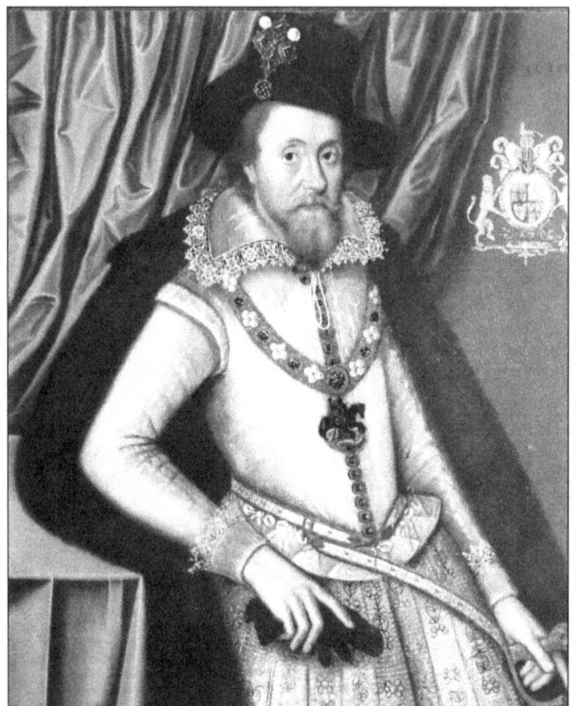

King James I (1566–1625). The resplendent Scottish-born monarch James I, son of Mary, Queen of Scots, was not a figure of great majesty—he was small, awkward, and had a speech impediment. Initially, James preferred Catholics to Puritans. During his reign, which began in 1603, the king's famous threat, "I will make them conform, or I will harry them out of the land," prompted the Separatists (Pilgrims) to leave England in the hope of finding a more tolerant home in America.

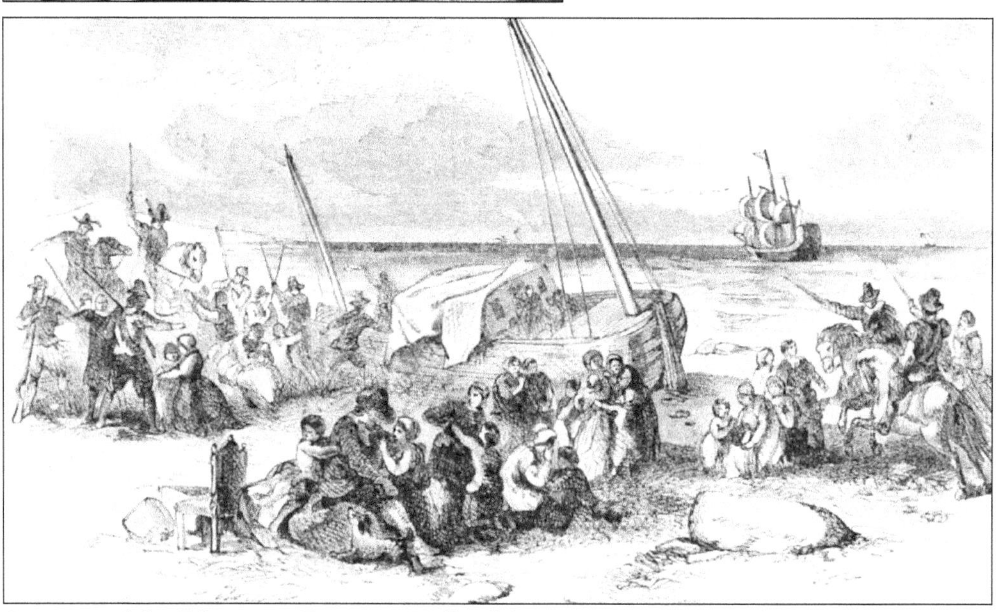

***Attempts of the Pilgrims to Escape to Holland* (c. 1905 engraving in the *Illustrated Pilgrim Memorial*).** "Scarcely had the first boat-load, consisting mostly of men, been taken on the ship they had engaged, when the party on the shore was surrounded by an armed band of horse and footmen, and made prisoners . . . and to crown their distresses, the captain . . . hastily weighed anchor, hoisted sail, and was soon a mere speck on the horizon. The agony of those on board was intense, but still more deplorable was the case of the fugitives on shore, most of them women and children. After being hurried from one place to another . . . they were suffered to escape and join their relatives in Holland."

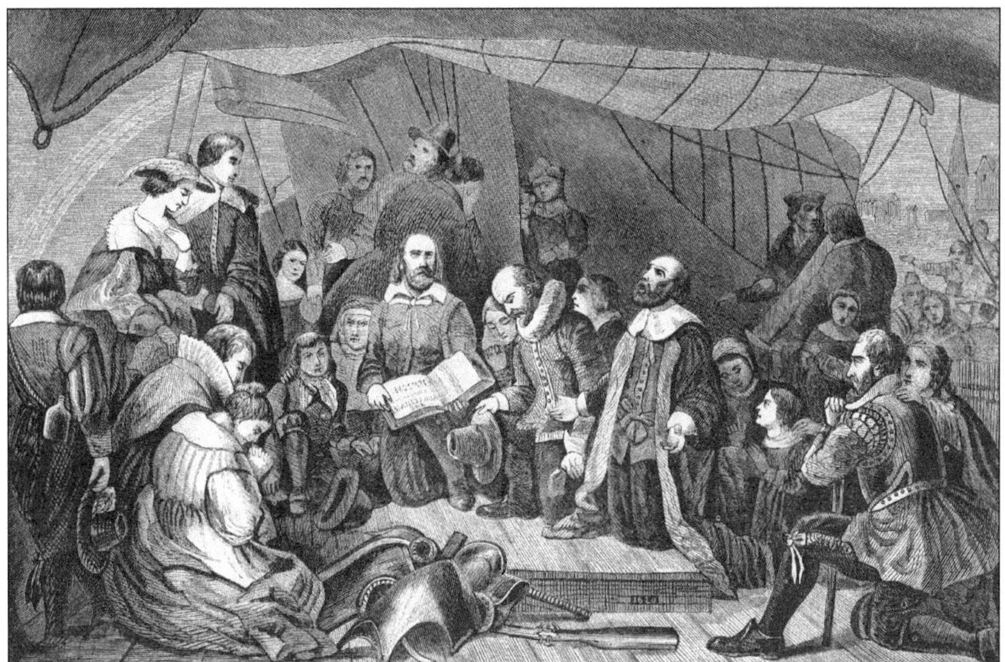

***Embarkation of the Pilgrims at Delft Haven* (c. 1900 engraving after the painting by Robert W. Weir in the United States Capitol).** " 'When they came to the place,' wrote William Bradford, 'they found the ship and all things ready. . . . The next day, the wind being fair, they went on board, and their friends with them, when truly doleful was the sight of the sad and mournful parting . . . their reverend pastor . . . commended them with most fervent tears to the Lord and his blessing; and then, with mutual embraces . . . they took their leave of one another—which proved to be their last to many of them.' "

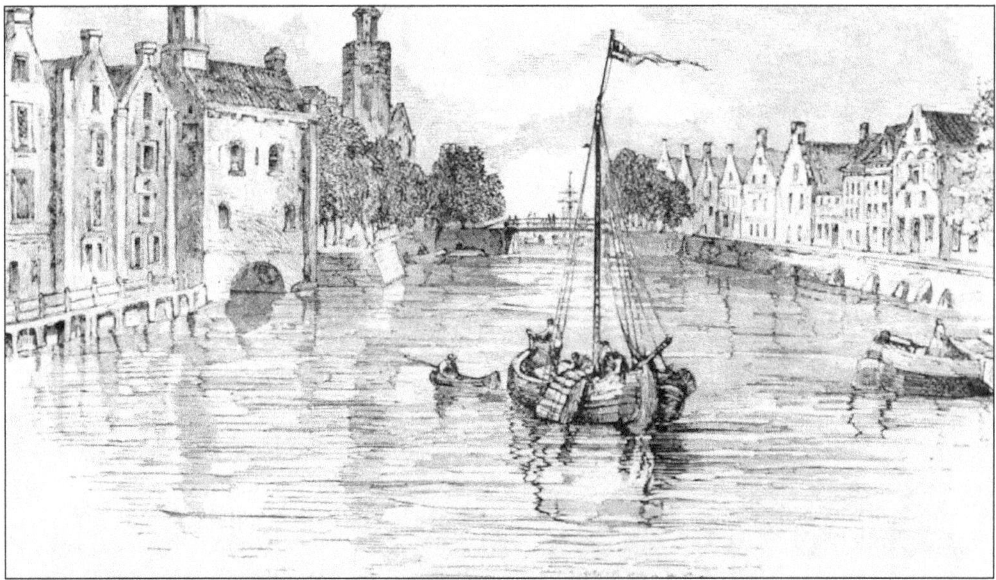

***Delft Haven* (c. 1905 engraving in the *Illustrated Pilgrim Memorial*).** "The haven of the city of Delft, is about fourteen miles from Leyden, and is the port in Holland where the Pilgrims embarked for America, as represented in 'The Embarkation.' "

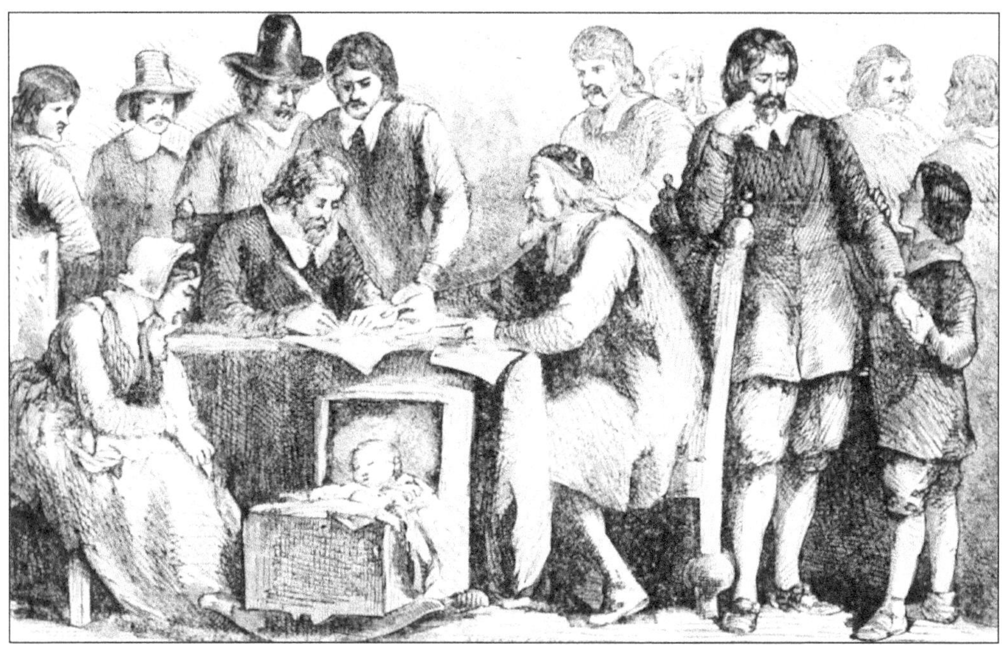

***The Signing of the Compact* (c. 1905 engraving in the *Illustrated Pilgrim Memorial*).** "Before landing, the Pilgrims entered into an agreement which served as the foundation of their government in their new home. It was drawn up in the cabin of the *May-flower*, and signed by the heads of families and such others as were considered of suitable age. . . . It commences in all the solemnity of an oath" and embodies a primitive form of republicanism which anticipated the Constitution of the United States. (See pp. 69–71).

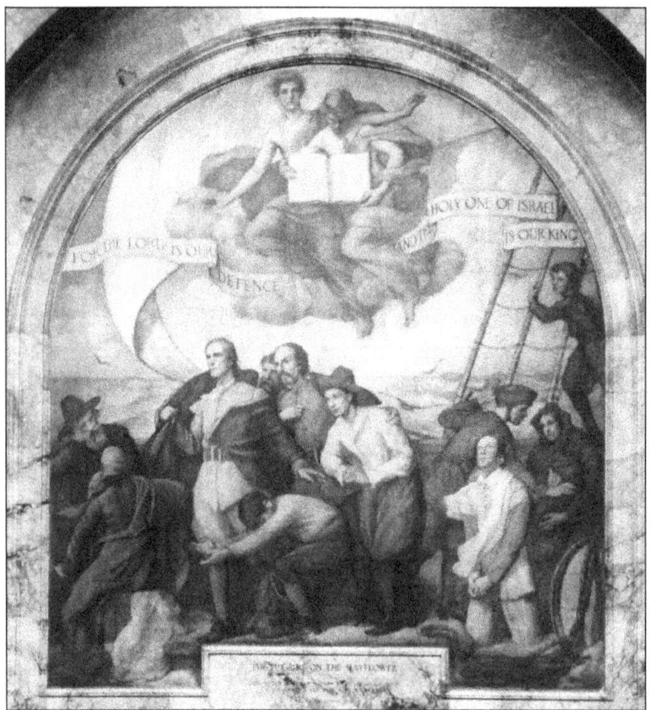

***The Pilgrims on the Mayflower*, mural by Henry Oliver Walker (1843–1929), 1902, Massachusetts State House.** Edward Winslow, one of the figures in this allegorical painting which is installed in Memorial Hall, was one of a few *Mayflower* passengers who later wrote about the passage to the New World. The observant Pilgrim noted that the harbor they encountered in Provincetown—but not known by that name to them—was "a good harbor and pleasant bay . . . wherein a thousand sail of ships may safely ride." (Courtesy Commonwealth of Massachusetts Art Commission.)

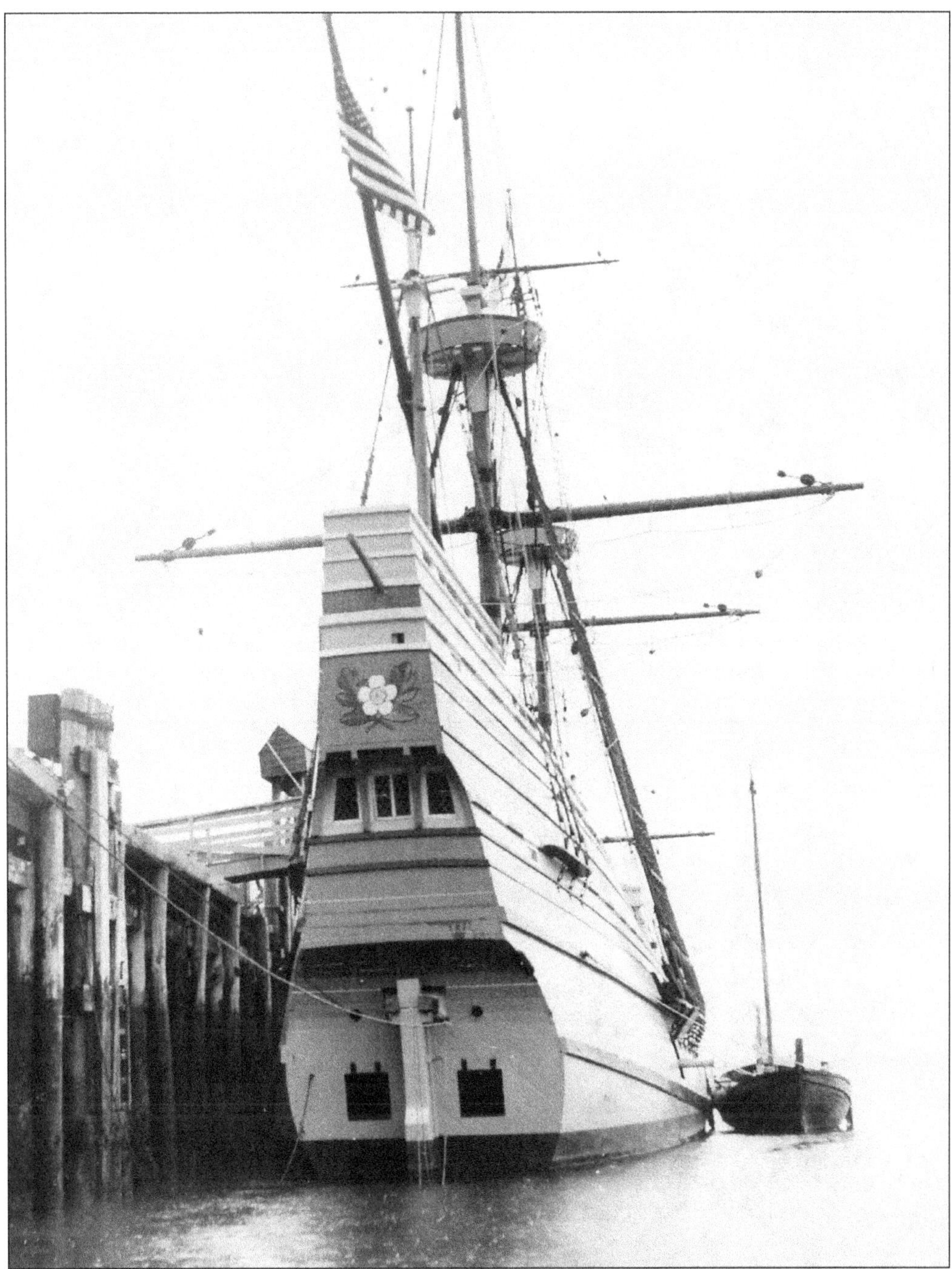

The *Mayflower II* at dockside, Plymouth, Massachusetts (c. 1960 photograph). The original *Mayflower* was a three-masted merchant ship just over 100 feet long and 181 tons burden. She had a crew of about 30 and carried 102 passengers on the sixty-six-day voyage to establish a colony in Virginia. Destiny changed the Pilgrims' course, however, and they dropped anchor off Long Point at the tip of Cape Cod. A reproduction of the *Mayflower* was launched from Plymouth, England, on April 20, 1957, and she arrived in Provincetown Harbor on June 12 en route to Plymouth, where she was berthed as a tourist attraction.

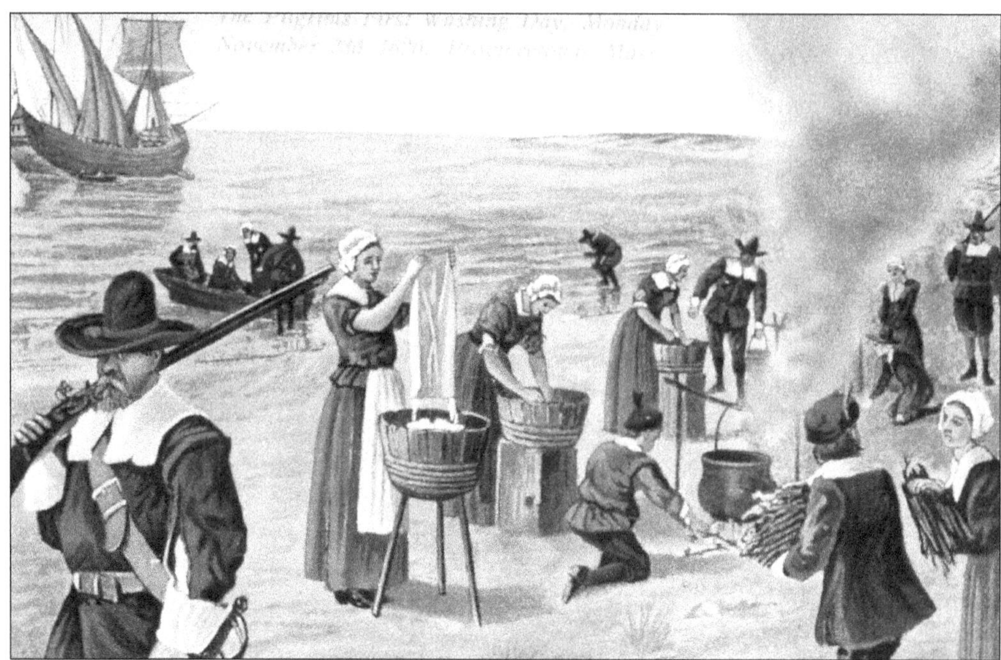

The Pilgrims First Washing Day (early-twentieth-century postcard published by I.L. Rosenthal, Germany). Pilgrim fathers assist Pilgrim mothers in washing "their lothsome cloaths" on what became the start of a lasting New England tradition—Monday washday!

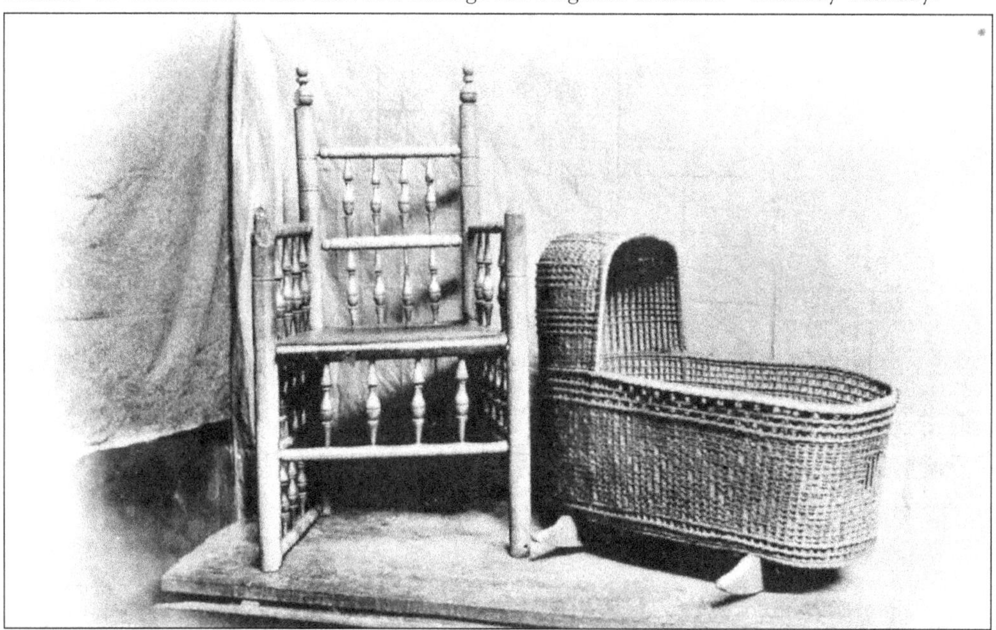

Elder Brewster Chair. Cradle of Peregrine White, Pilgrim Hall (early-twentieth-century postcard published by A.S. Burbank, Plymouth, MA). One of the earliest pieces of furniture made in America is this *c.* 1630–70 great chair, made of white ash with rows of turned spindles, which belonged to Elder William Brewster. The woven wicker hooded cradle was brought from Holland to America by William and Susannah White, whose son Peregrine was born on the *Mayflower* in Provincetown Harbor in November of 1620.

Two

Getting There

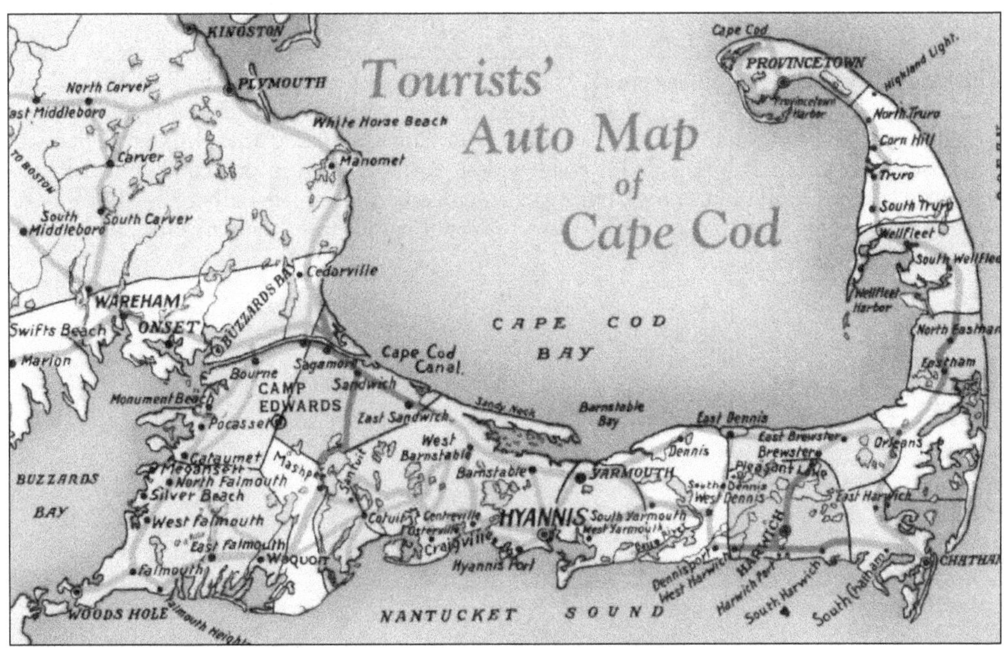

Tourists' Auto Map of Cape Cod (c. 1940 postcard published by E.D. West Co., South Yarmouth, Cape Cod). The oft-described configuration of Cape Cod's "bent elbow," or as Henry David Thoreau (1817–1862), the Concord, MA, essayist and poet penned "This bare and bended arm . . .," is easy to see in this printed linen-textured postcard. Most motorists take the direct approach, Route 6, which starts at the Sagamore Bridge over the Cape Cod Canal—this route runs 58 miles to Provincetown. Route 6A is the scenic way, favored by those who enjoy the small towns for their architectural and natural charms. The distance from Boston to Provincetown is about 120 miles (55 by ocean travel), and the distance from New York City is about 290 miles. Provincetown encompasses an area of 8.35 square miles, and the township is bounded by the Atlantic Ocean on the north and east, by Provincetown Harbor on the south, and by Cape Cod Bay on the west.

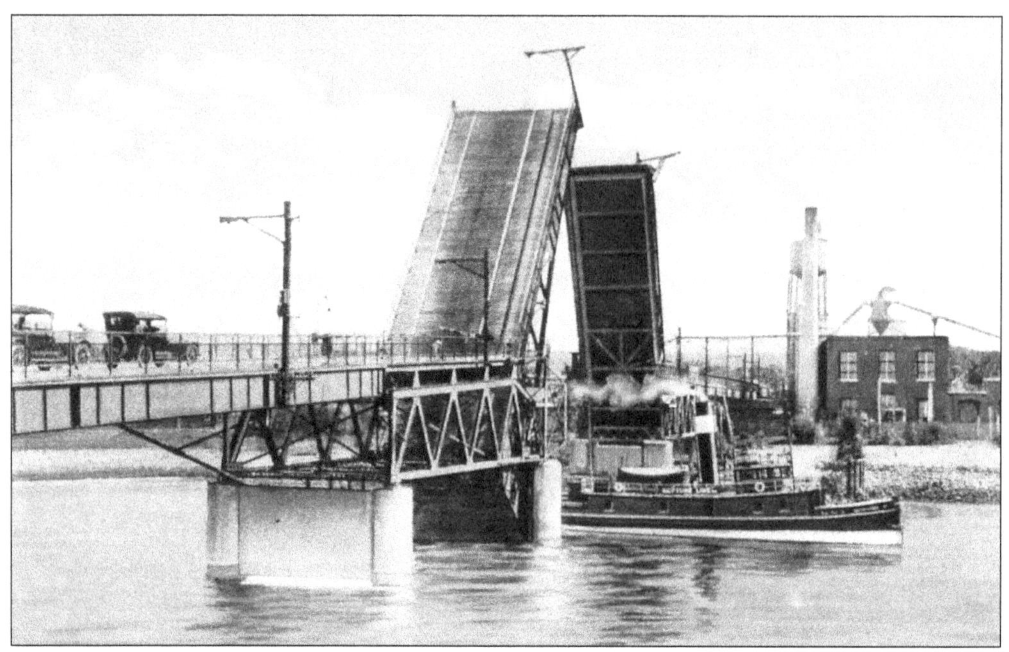

The Bridge, Cape Cod Canal, Sagamore, Mass. (c. 1925 postcard published by E.D. West Co.). A Neptune Lines steamboat is shown passing through the drawbridge that predated the monumental structure built 1933–35 at Sagamore. The Cape Cod Canal extends 8 miles from Sandwich to Buzzards Bay, and it is the widest sea-level canal in the world. The toll-free waterway cost $33 million and took five years to construct; it was officially opened in July of 1914. The canal protects commercial and recreational vessels from the dangerous outer cape with its swift currents.

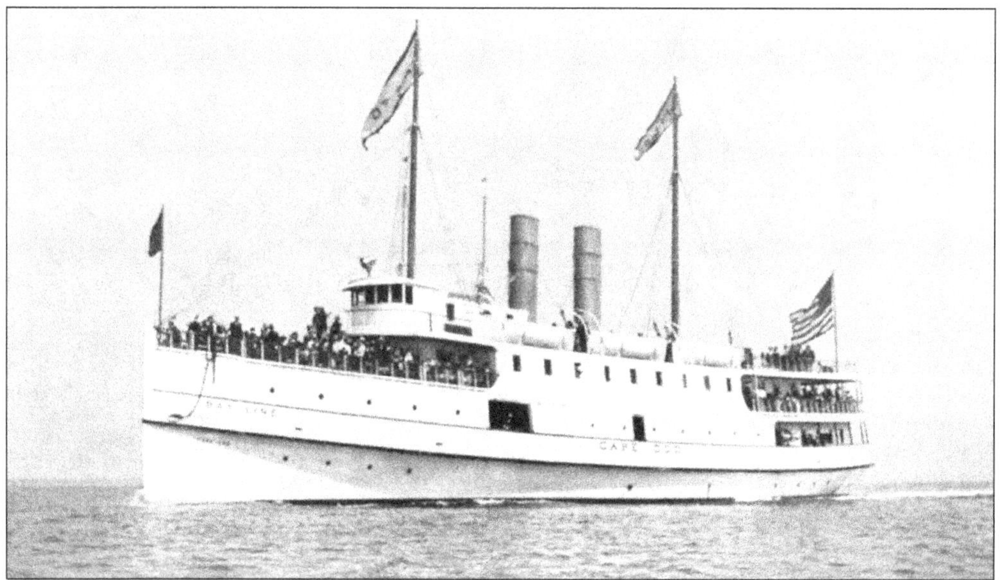

The *Cape Cod* (1898 photograph by The Perry Pictures Co., Malden and Boston, MA, and New York). In 1842 steam packets first started regular trips (but not excursions) between Boston and Plymouth; they later traveled between Boston and Provincetown at least thrice weekly. The Bay Line's *Cape Cod* replaced the steamer *Longfellow* in 1902.

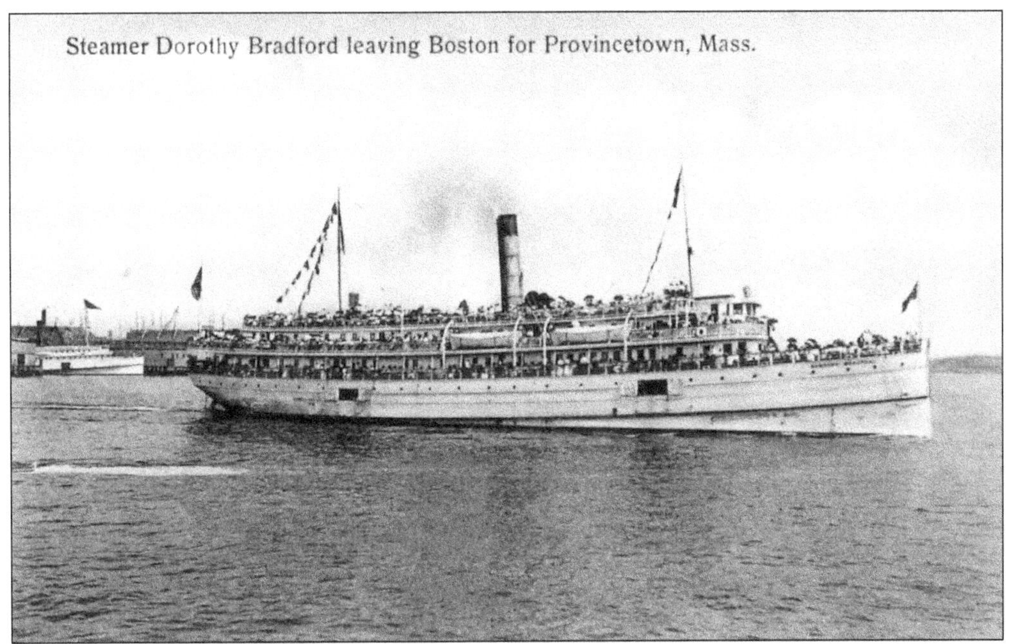

Steamer *Dorothy Bradford* leaving Boston for Provincetown (c. 1915 postcard published by *The Provincetown Advocate*, hereinafter referred to as *The Advocate*). Larger and faster than the *Cape Cod*, the *Dorothy Bradford* took her maiden voyage in 1910. She was named for Governor Bradford's wife, Dorothy May, who either drowned or took her life while the *Mayflower* was in Provincetown Harbor. A confusing but humorous sign on the *Dorothy Bradford* stated: "Passengers are not allowed in or outside the lifeboats."

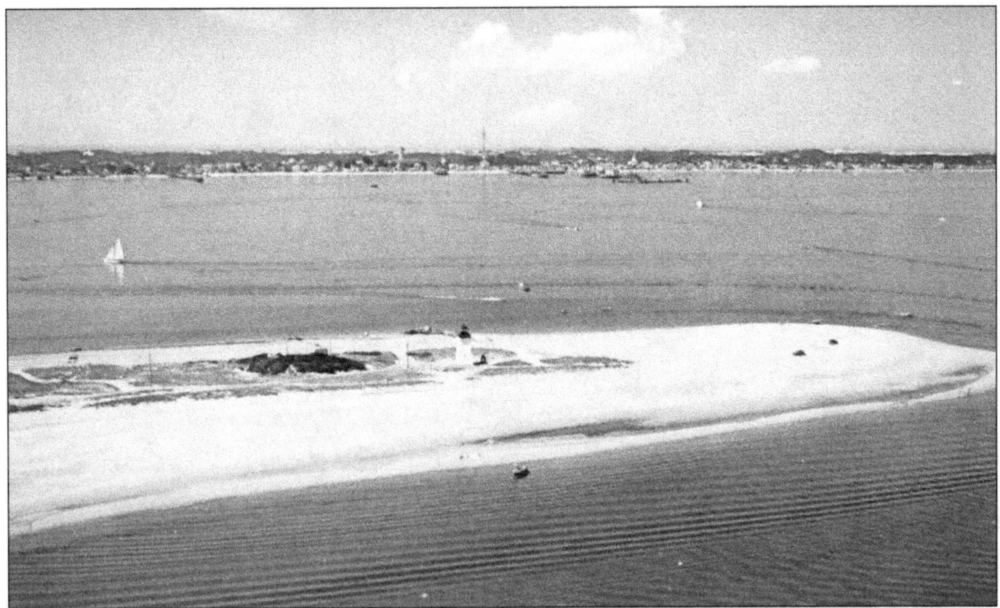

Aerial View of Long Point Light (c. 1970 postcard published by J. Lazarus, Hyannis, MA). Long Point Light, one of three lighthouses on the tip of Cape Cod, was constructed in 1826. A feeling of excitement almost always overcomes tourists when they finally round the sandy spit and see the panorama of Provincetown.

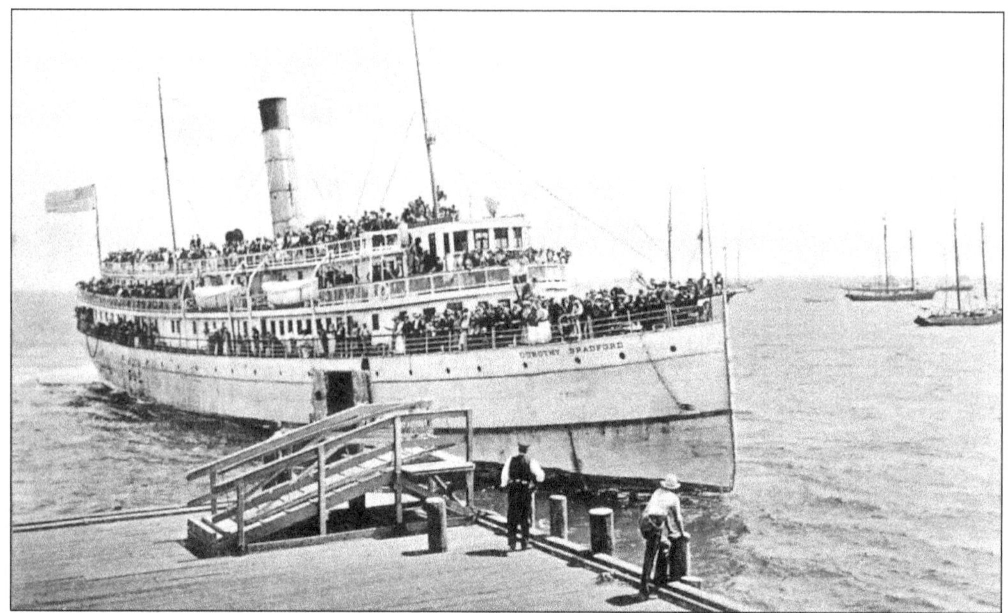

Steamer *Dorothy Bradford* Arriving at Provincetown (c. 1915 postcard published by *The Advocate*). In operation through the late 1930s, the *Dorothy Bradford* was owned by the Cape Cod Steamship Company, and she sailed from Long Wharf in Boston. On busy weekends well over one thousand passengers enjoyed dancing, refreshments, and relaxation (for those who secured staterooms). The one-way fare in 1931 was $1.75; the excursion, or round-trip, fare was $2. Today, as in days of yore, the vessel leaves Boston at 9:30 am and Provincetown at 3:30 pm.

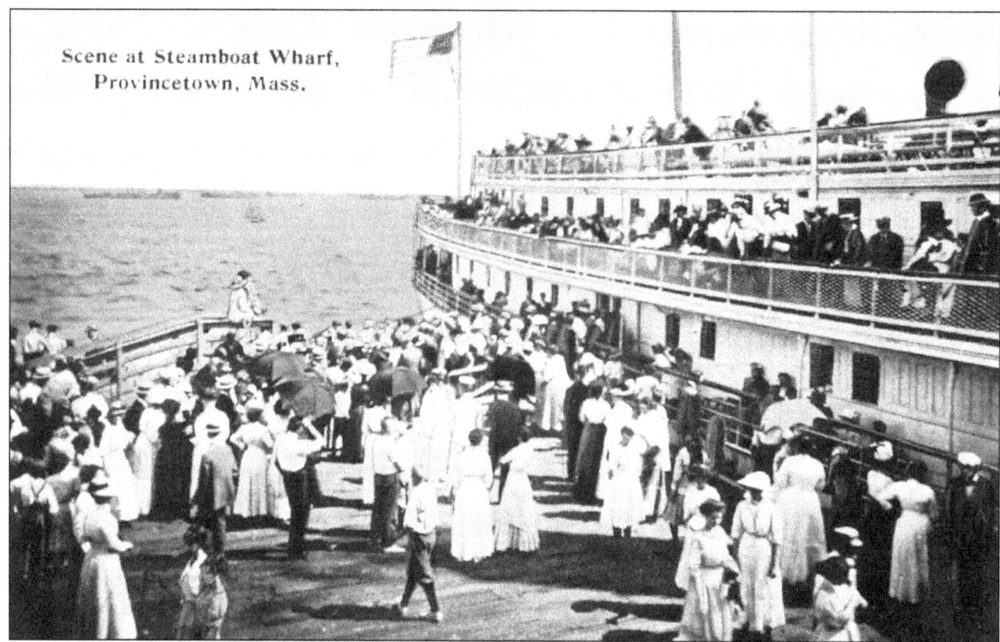

Scene at Steamboat Wharf (c. 1910 postcard published by Tichnor Bros., Inc., Boston, MA). Other excursion vessels well known to passengers of the past included the *Acorn*, *Governor Cobb*, *Express*, *Naushon*, *New Brunswick*, *Northern Light*, *Olata*, *Romance*, *George Shattuck*, and *Truth*.

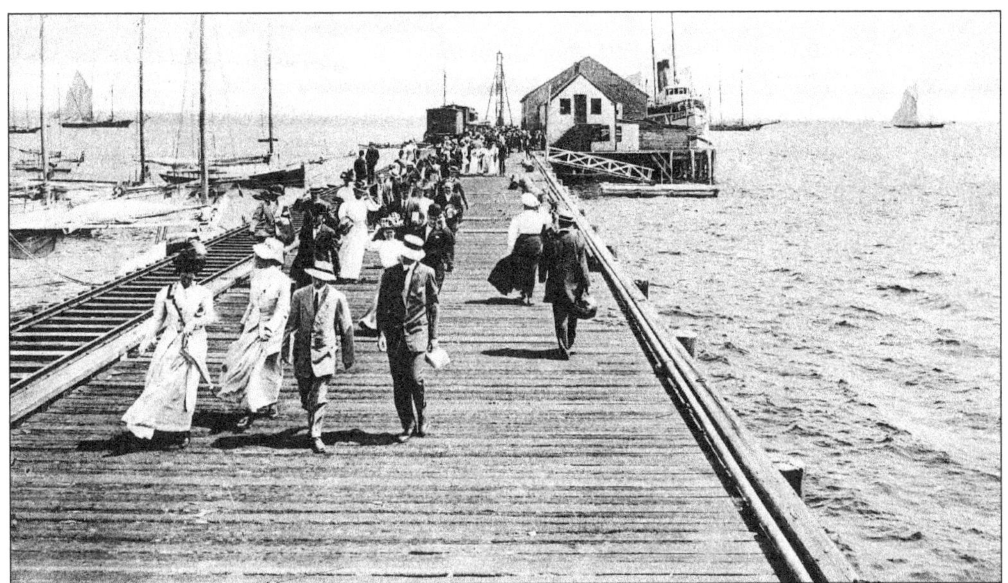

Arrival of Steamer *Cape Cod* (c. 1909 postcard published by *The Advocate*). The sender of this greeting noted that Railroad Wharf was "where we arrived July 22, '09." The first wharf was built along the harbor around 1835. Bowley's Wharf was the name of one of the first to be constructed (c. 1849), and it later was known as Steamboat Wharf. The Old Colony Railroad Wharf, shown here, was extended in July 1873 to include a double set of railroad tracks and docking space for vessels. Warm people and iced fish could then be shipped from there by train on regular schedules.

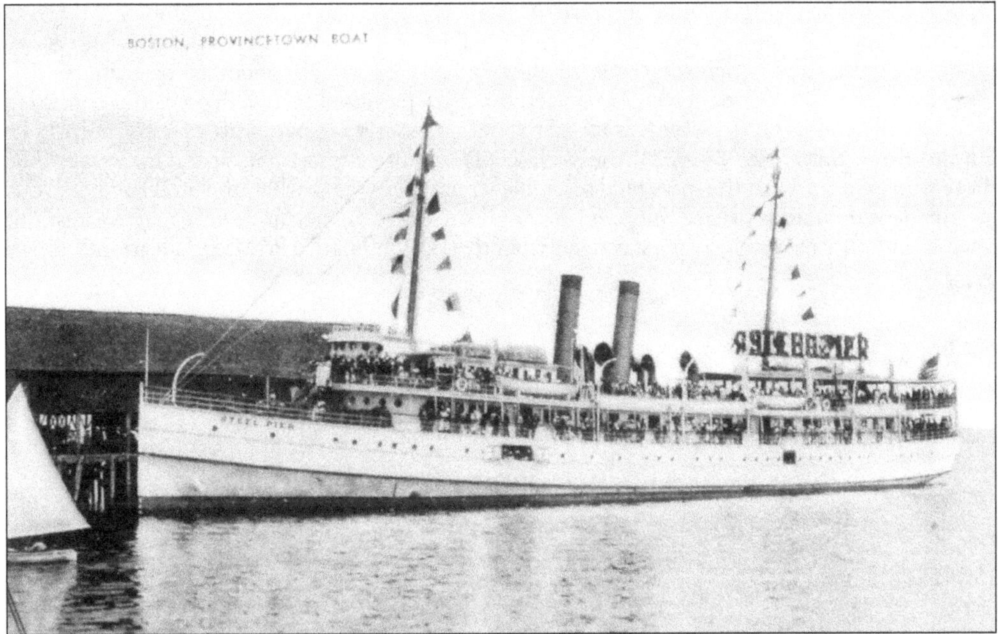

The *Steel Pier* (c. 1940 postcard published by The Cape Cod Post Card Co., Provincetown). While the ship is docked, people peer through its lower deck windows. The sleek, two-masted, double-smokestacked steamer was emblazoned with large letters that could be read from port or starboard.

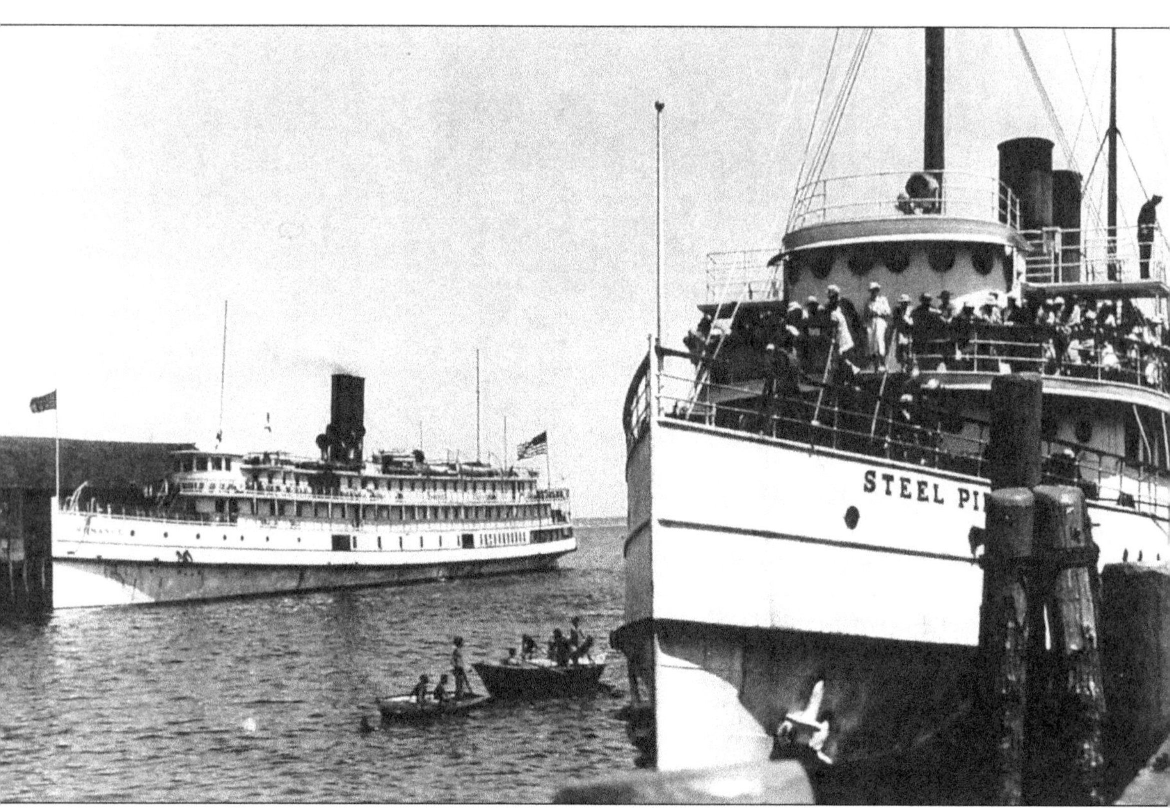

Diving for coins (c. 1935 photograph). At least three generations of amphibious, bronzed youngsters awaited amused tourists who threw coins for them off the ferries or wharves. A similarly amusing and somewhat related note written on a contemporary postcard stated: "Greetings from Cape Cod. Haven't forgotten the fish I promised you. Will go fishing some day soon." Shell vendors on the wharf also tried to persuade tourists to part with their coins. In 1946 Edward Rowe Snow (1902–1982), the prolific Massachusetts maritime historian, wrote, "For those who participate in the mad, wild scramble which takes place when the *Steel Pier* pours out its impatient thousands in June, July, and August, Provincetown must indeed appear as a bustling town intent only on serving the passengers from the Boston boat." (Private Collection.)

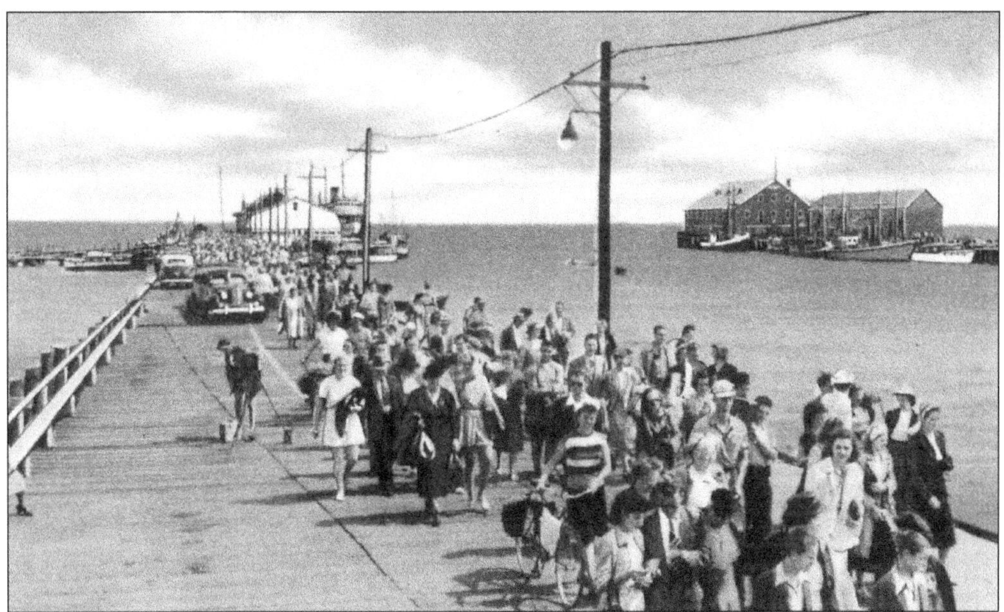

Crowds landing from the Boston Boat down pier (late-1940s postcard published by The Mayflower Sales Co., Provincetown). A local photographer and a bicyclist stand out in the throng about to enjoy an abbreviated afternoon ashore. The wharf with buildings at the right is now known as Fishermen's Wharf; in the past it has been called Frank Joseph's Wharf, Monument Dock, and Sklaroff's Wharf.

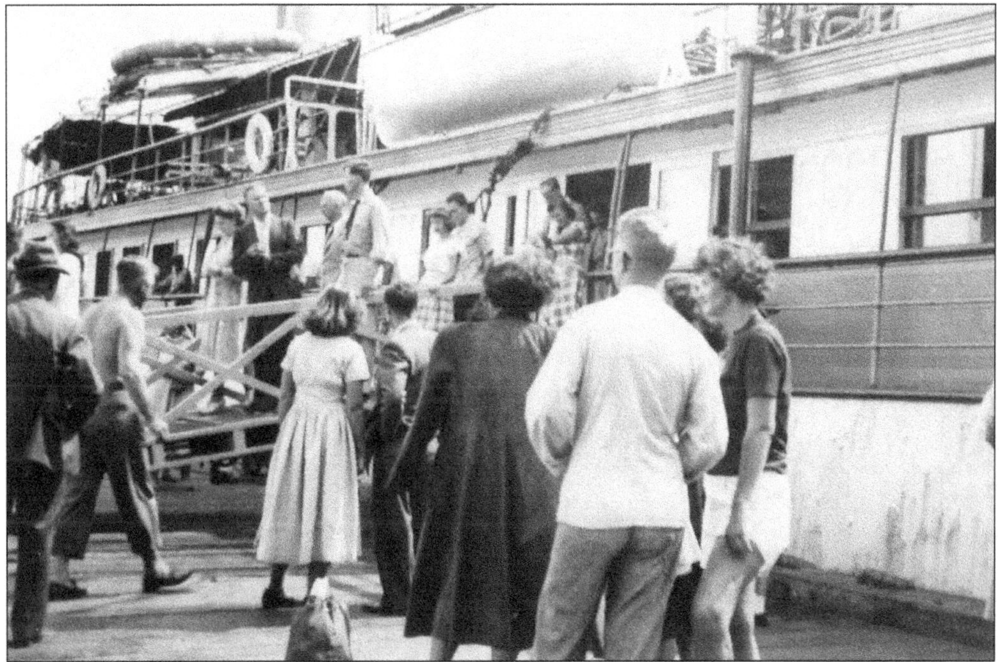

Disembarking from the *Steel Pier* (c. 1955 photograph). When the author was a boy in the 1950s, William H. McKown was captain of the M.V. *Boston Belle*; the friendly gentleman autographed a booklet called a *Souvenir of Cape Cod*, the occasion of which is still a strong memory.

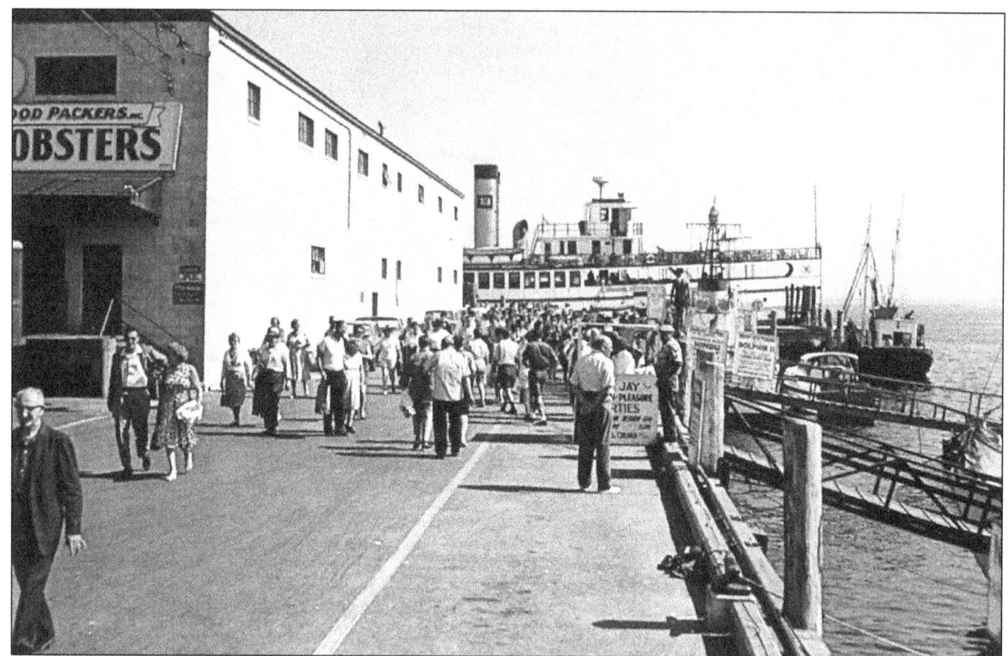

Boston boat landing at Town Pier (c. 1961 postcard published by The Mayflower Sales Co.). During the summer season tourists who had developed sea legs could go deep-sea fishing aboard the *Dolphin III*, or take a harbor tour aboard the schooner *Hindu*.

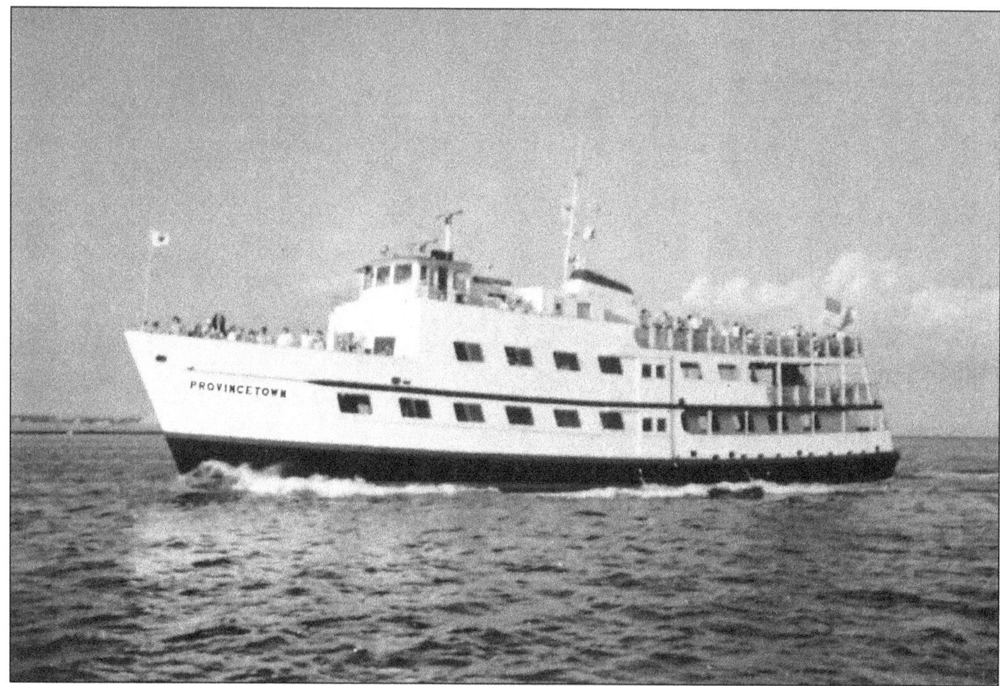

M.V. *Provincetown* (c. 1970 postcard published by Tichnor Bros., Inc.). The streamlined ferry made "daily cruises to Cape Cod during summer. Sailing from historic Long Wharf, Boston. Live band, Food & Grog always on hand. Bay State, Spray & Provincetown Steamship Co."

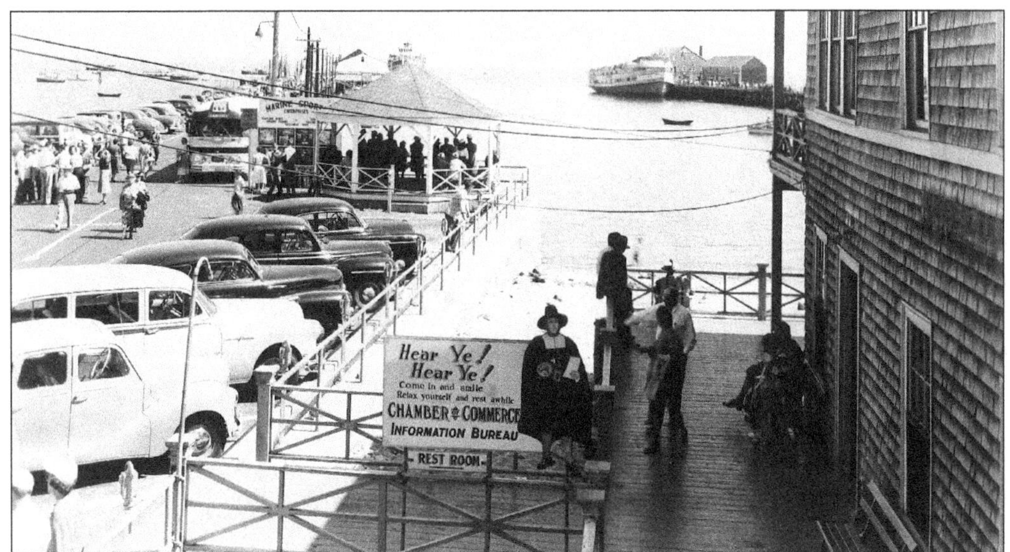

The head of MacMillan Wharf (1950 photograph). A chartered bus is dropping off tourists by a pavilion near the shingled chamber of commerce building. The once familiar walking and talking town crier has taken the form of a painted wooden cutout. A bronze tablet mounted in granite at the head of the wharf was dedicated to Provincetown's most famous native son—Donald B. MacMillan. It depicts a two-masted vessel somewhere in the frozen Arctic and is inscribed "MacMillan Wharf/a tribute to/Donald B. MacMillan R. Adm. U.S.N.R./for outstanding achievement in the field of arctic exploration." (Courtesy Seamen's Bank.)

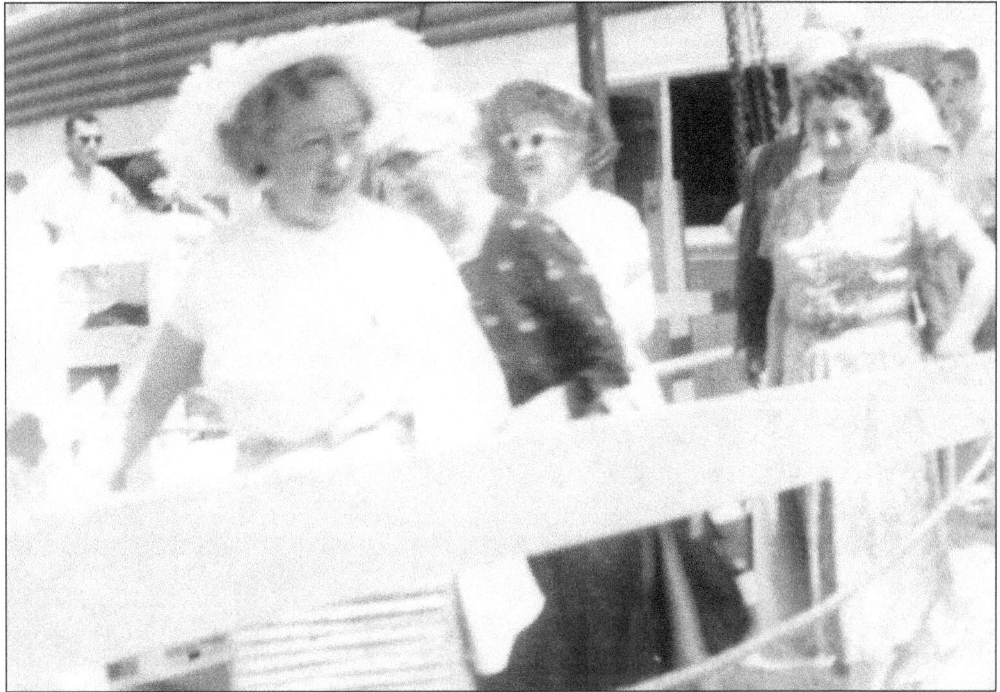

Disembarking from the M.V. *Provincetown* (c. 1965 photograph). A fashionably dressed lady in white leads other passengers down the gangplank for an afternoon of sightseeing and shopping in town. (Courtesy Warner Collection.)

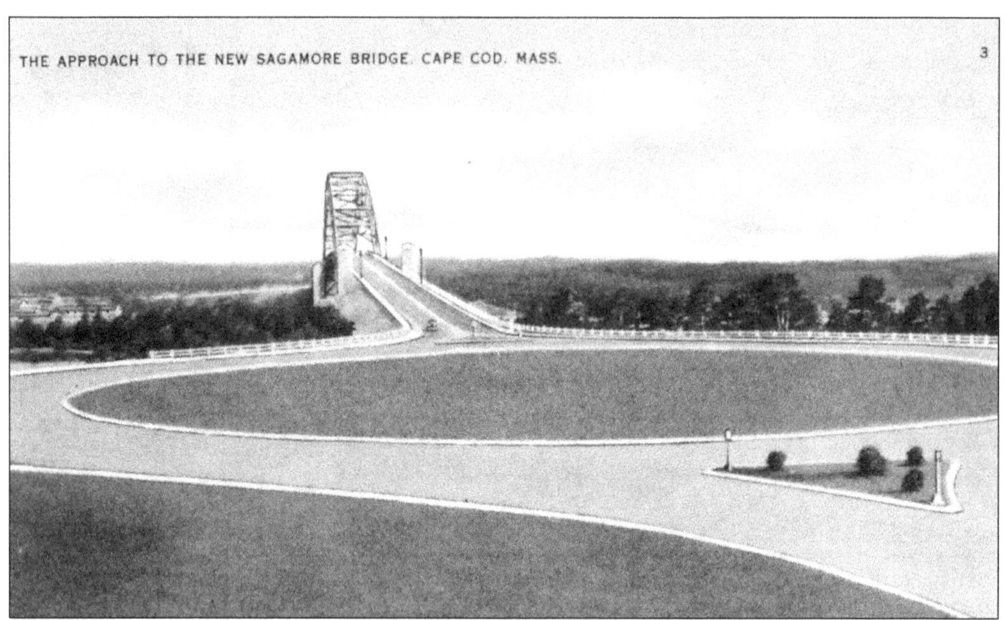

The approach to the new Sagamore Bridge (c. 1936 postcard published by Tichnor Bros., Inc.). Although one inevitably encounters traffic at the rotary and on the Sagamore Bridge today, this artist's view includes only one automobile! Built between 1933 and 1935, the Sagamore Bridge is 1,833 feet long and has a central span of 135 feet. The width of the arch is 500 feet and the maximum height of the steel work is 270 feet above sea level. Bus service to Provincetown was begun in the early 1940s with three daily buses making connections to New York City trains and the Providence, RI, boat.

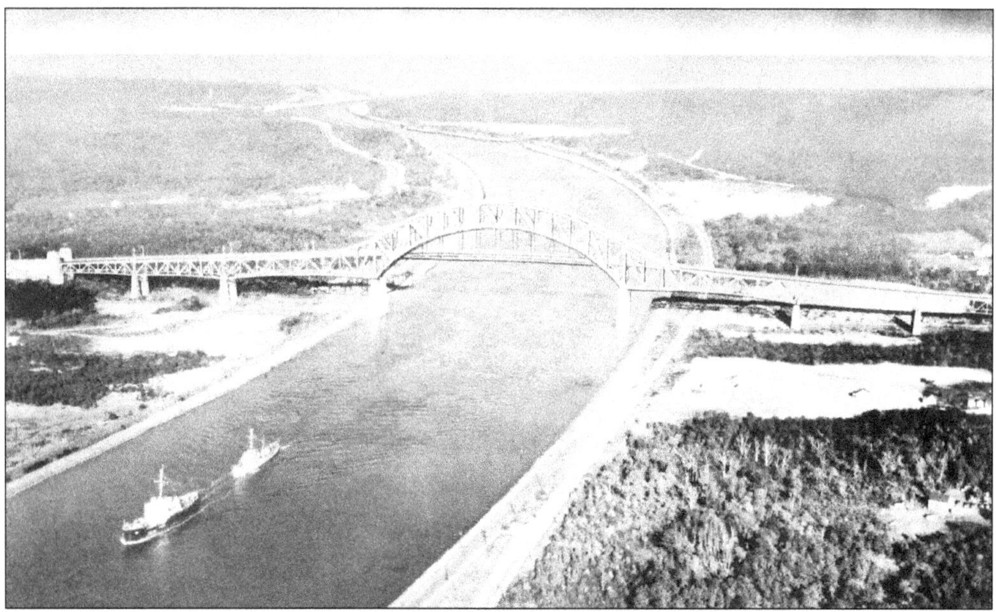

The Bourne Bridge (c. 1940 photograph). "This bridge was completed in 1935 at an approximate cost of $1,500,000. Length 2,684 feet; central span 135 feet above high water; width of arch 500 feet; maximum height of steel work above sea level 270 feet." The Bourne Bridge is 851 feet longer than its parallel rival, the Sagamore Bridge.

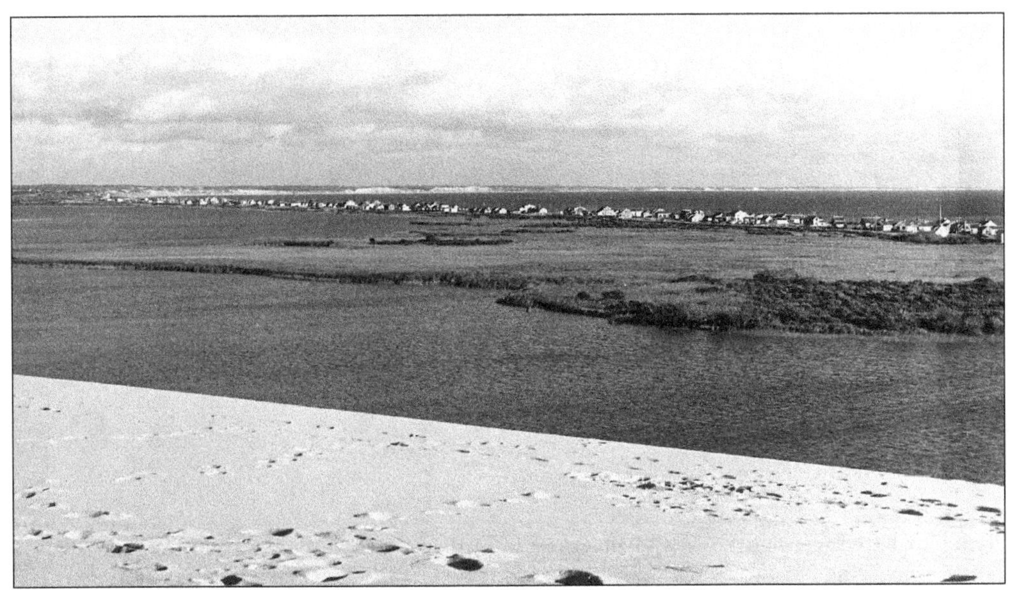

The entrance to Provincetown along Beach Point, North Truro (c. 1956 photograph by Cyril J. Patrick). The photographer was standing on a dune overlooking man-made Pilgrim Lake when he took this sweeping view of summer cottages. Pilgrim Lake was created in 1869 by the closure of the East Harbor inlet from Cape Cod Bay; the lake provides for ice boating in the winter and fishing in the summer. In the eighteenth century the King's Highway was laid out around the sand dunes of the harbor for stagecoach travel. By 1922 the state road reached Provincetown, and the Mid-Cape Highway was constructed in the mid-1950s. (Courtesy Seamen's Bank.)

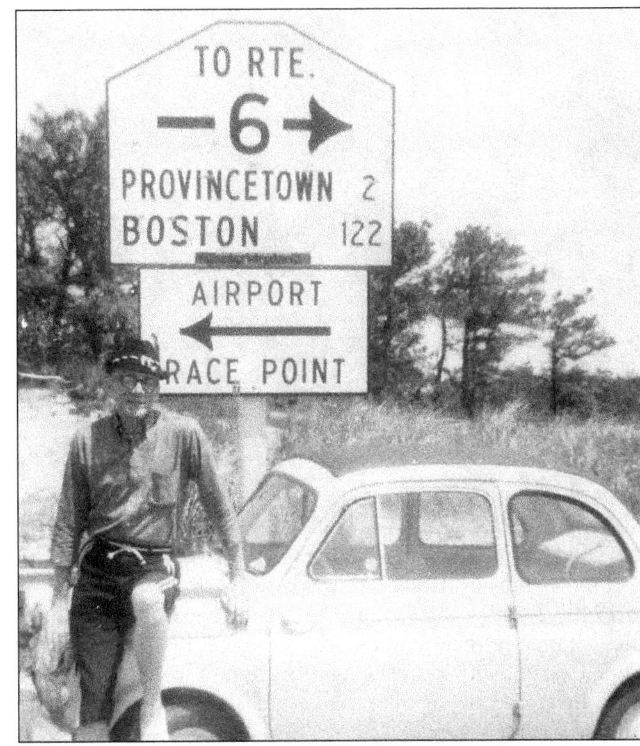

Almost there! (1961 photograph). Emery Warner, a Lynn, MA, resident and leather industry worker, has parked his dependable Fiat by road markers near Provincetown, and strikes a jaunty pose for his shutterbug friend. (Courtesy Warner Collection.)

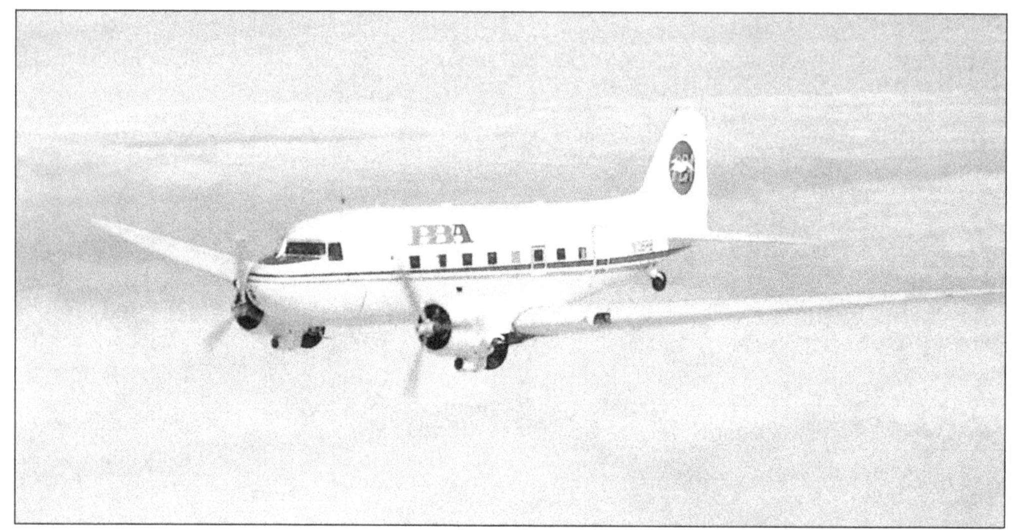

Flying to Provincetown (c. 1970 postcard published by Bromley & Co., Boston, MA). This twin-engine Douglas DC-3 airplane was owned by the Provincetown Boston Airline, and it was one which made regular flights from Boston's Logan Airport to the small airport in Provincetown between 1948 and 1988. At one time the one-way fare was $8.50 per person. John C. Van Arsdale Jr., who founded the airline company, was also one of the captains; the term "shuttle" originated as a result of the initial flights operating on demand.

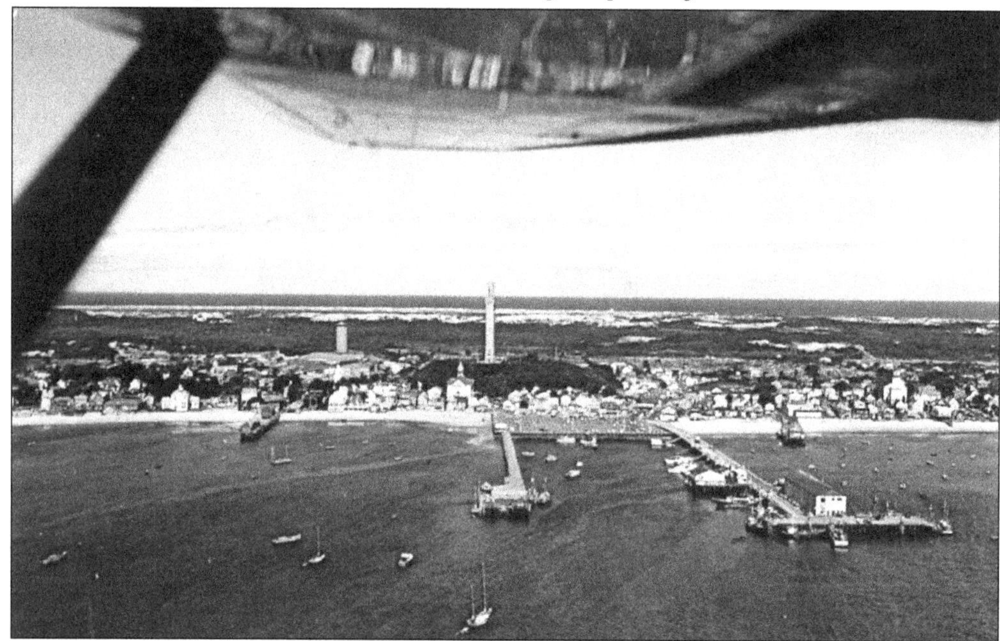

Aerial view of the town's center (c. 1970 postcard published by Cape Cod Photos). Cape Cod chronicler Edward Rowe Snow wrote the following about a 30-minute flight to Provincetown in 1946: "By now we were 3,000 feet in the air, veering out across Massachusetts Bay. There in the distance far below, its sandy shores outlined against the blue ocean, lay my destination—Cape Cod . . . with almost every location of importance visible from our plane half a mile in the air. The great bridges over the Canal, the fire towers, Pilgrim Monument, Highland Light, all seemed to urge us on."

Three

The Town Center

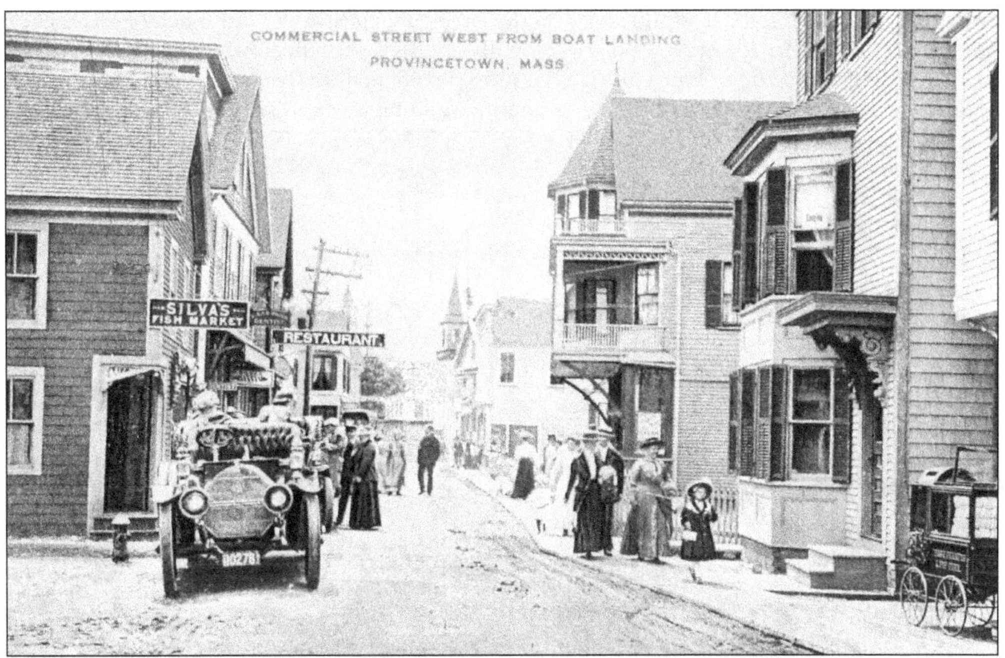

Commercial Street West from Boat Landing (c. 1907 postcard published by The New England News Co., Boston, MA). Well-heeled tourists walk along the plank sidewalk on the land side of busy Commercial Street, while others congregate around their elegant, new touring cars on the harbor side, near the intersection of Standish Street. Victorian-period projecting door hoods, balconies, and bay windows contrast with plain gable-ended buildings which changed almost yearly from residences to businesses. Fresh fish could be purchased from Silva's Fish Market by the town's residents, or by restaurateurs to be served that day to the town's visitors. Restaurants, a dentist's office (Dr. Wager's), and "Wippich the Jeweler" advertised their businesses with various trade signs, and a vintage popcorn wagon tempted passersby with packaged treats of fresh peanuts and popcorn.

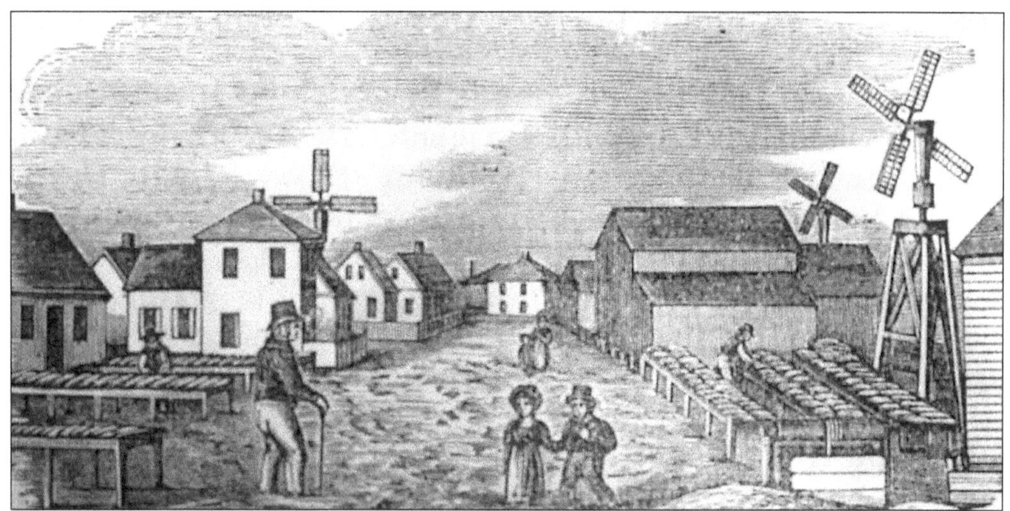

***View in the Village of Provincetown* (1839 wood engraving).** The street depicted in John Warner Barber's "cut" is Commercial Street, a narrow, irregular road that runs approximately 3 miles. The historian-artist noted that the houses on the street "are mostly one story in height, and, with their out-buildings, stand along on the street, apparently without much of an effort at order or regularity." In 1839 the population was about 2,049. Provincetown was incorporated in 1727 after it separated from Truro in 1714. In 1748 the population was "reduced to two or three families," but by 1776 there were thirty-six families residing in about twenty homes.

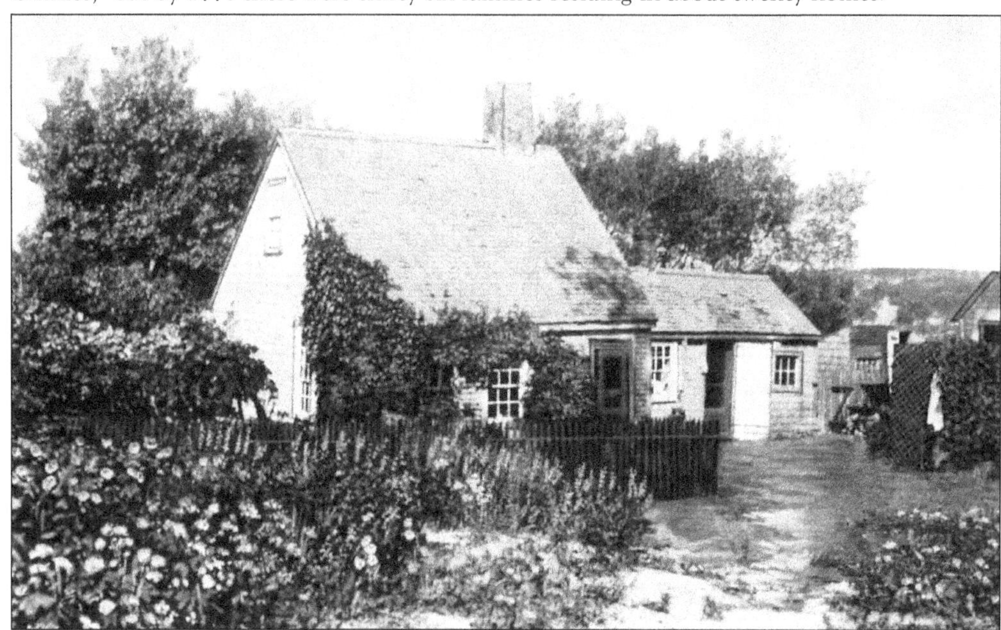

"Oldest House" (c. 1917 postcard published by H.A. Dickerman & Son). A questionable title of "Oldest House, Provincetown, Mass.," accompanies this image of a Cape Cod structure thought to have been situated on King's Way off Pleasant Street until recently. Varieties of the Cape Cod house appear in town; some have one and one-half stories and others are gable-roofed with three, four, or five windows. More two-story houses dating to the Federal period abound than in other Cape towns. Clapboards and shingles were the favored house covering, and small-paned, sliding sash windows add to the charm of these small, indigenous dwellings.

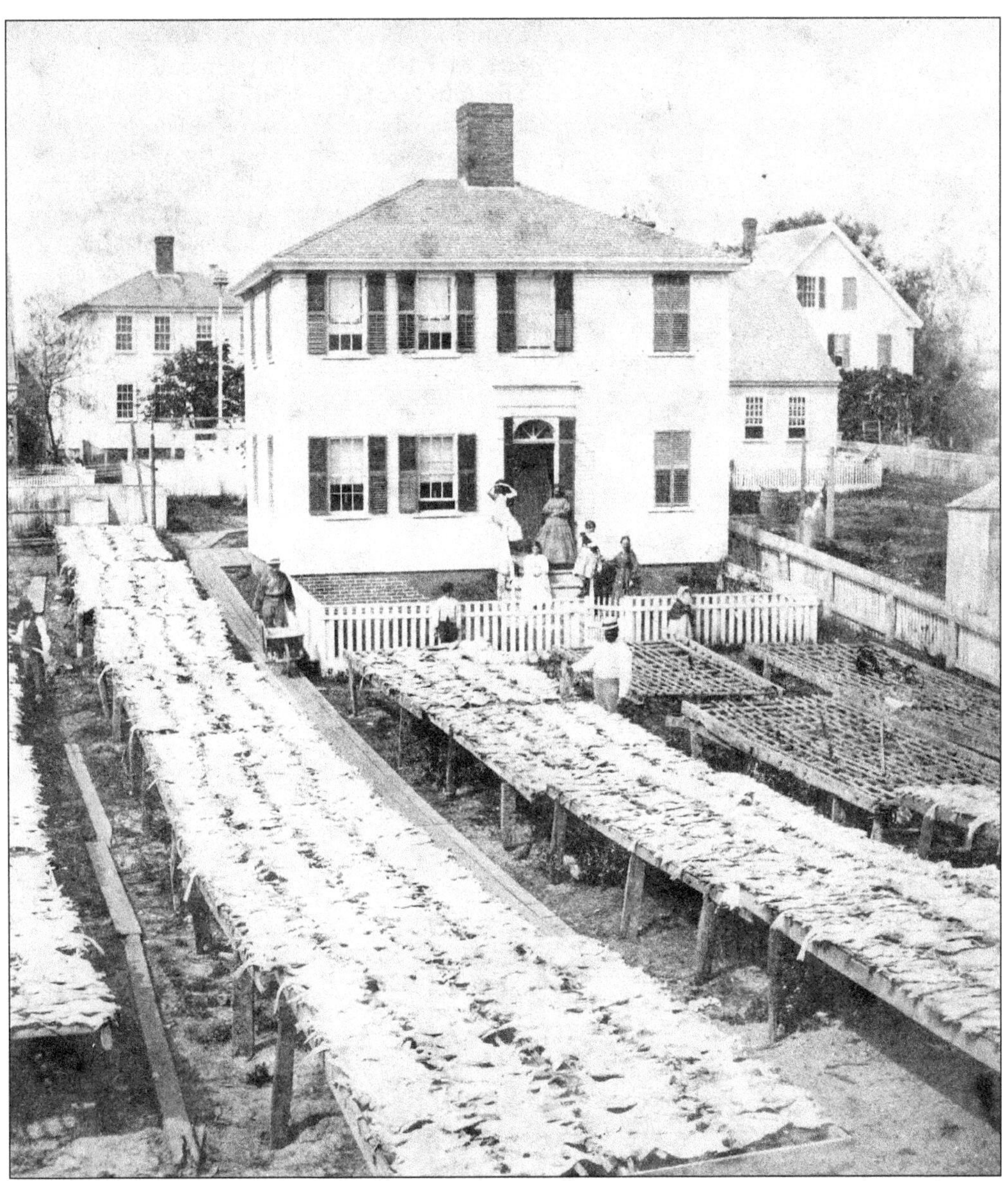

Making fish (c. 1885 stereopticon view taken by George H. Nickerson). Long rows of halved codfish curing in the sun and air on fish flakes dominate this view of a house identified as being in Provincetown. Most of the female members of the family are inside the small, fenced-in front yard. Henry David Thoreau, who made three walking trips on Cape Cod between 1849 and 1855, wrote, "a great many of the houses here were surrounded by *fish-flakes* close up to the sills on all sides, with only a narrow passage two or three feet wide, to the front door; so that instead of looking out into a flower or grass plot, you looked on to so many square rods of cod turned wrong side outwards." The occupation of "making fish" involved the turning over process, which Thoreau wrote was "the principal employment of the inhabitants at this time."

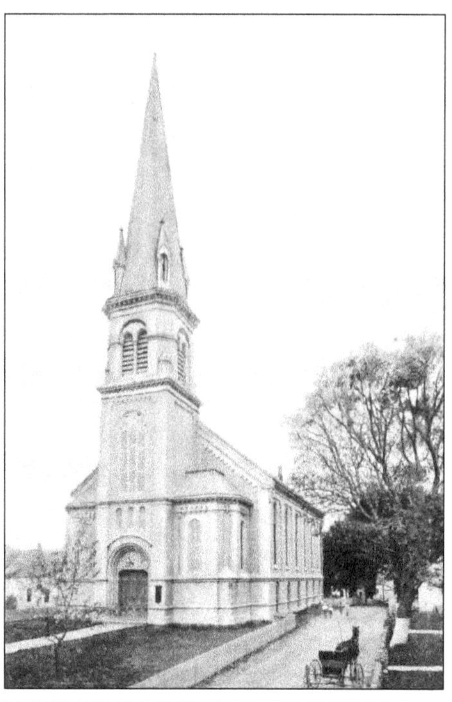

Centenary M.E. Church, 170 Commercial Street (c. 1905 postcard published by *The Advocate*). The Methodist Society was incorporated in 1811 and this structure was built in 1866 so that brethren near the West End of town could have their own house of worship. The new, arch-shaped entrance and the tapered octagonal steeple with gilded ball finial that reached 165 feet heavenward cost the society $40,000. A lightning bolt caused the fire that destroyed the church on March 14, 1908.

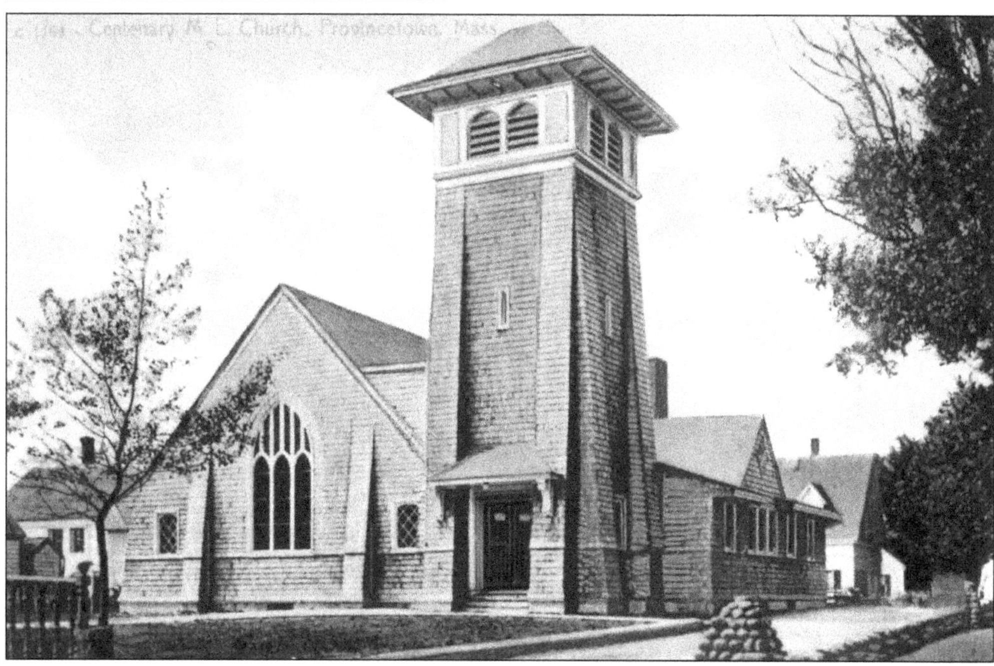

Centenary M.E. Church, 170 Commercial Street (c. 1910 postcard published by *The Advocate*). The second edifice of the Centenary Methodist Episcopal Church was built around 1910 on the same site at the corner of Winthrop Street. The shorter, Shingle Style structure had a tapering bell tower with an integral entrance at the right side in contrast to the central entrance location of the previous church. This building was razed about forty years later (around 1948) when it and the land were acquired for the construction of the First National Bank of Provincetown.

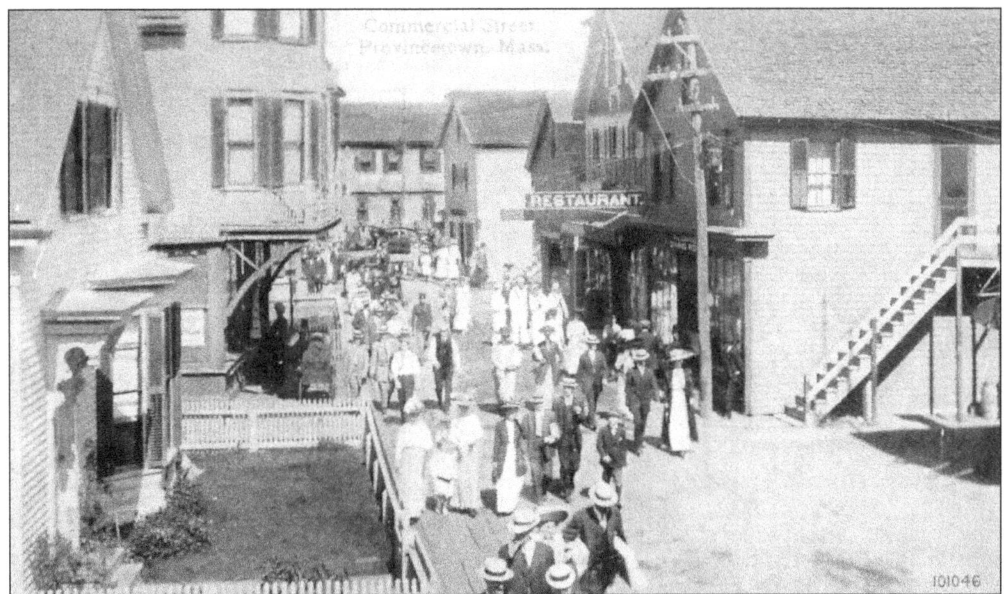

Commercial Street looking east towards Standish Street (c. 1915 postcard published by H.A. Dickerman & Son). A group of sailors walk among well-dressed people strolling the town's main thoroughfare. Meals, or merely an ice cream cone, could be purchased in the restaurant or store in the foreground. Miss Elizabeth Livingston offered treat-hungry tourists "FRO-JOY" ice cream at her 409 Commercial Street shop in 1931.

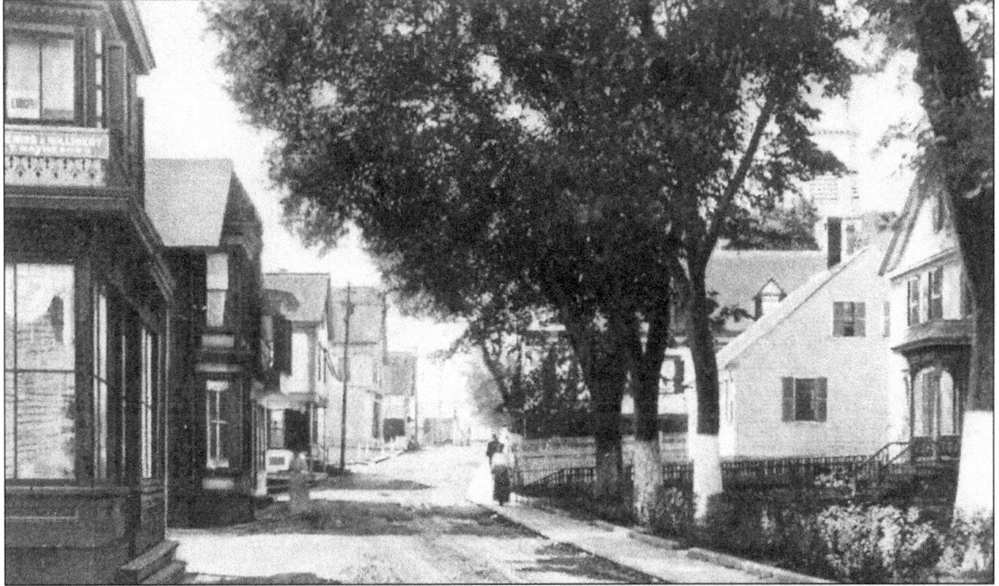

Commercial Street looking west from the Court Street area (early-twentieth-century postcard published by *The Advocate*). Shade-producing elm trees cool these nineteenth-century houses, many of which have first-floor shops. The plank sidewalk was laid out on the land side of the street, and people, then as now, have to hop, skip, and jump between buildings on the harbor side. The Misses Mamie S. and Jessie T. Matheson ran a millinery, fancy goods, and souvenir shop in the front part of the house at the far left, which was purchased in 1882 by their father, William Matheson, who owned Steamboat Wharf behind the building.

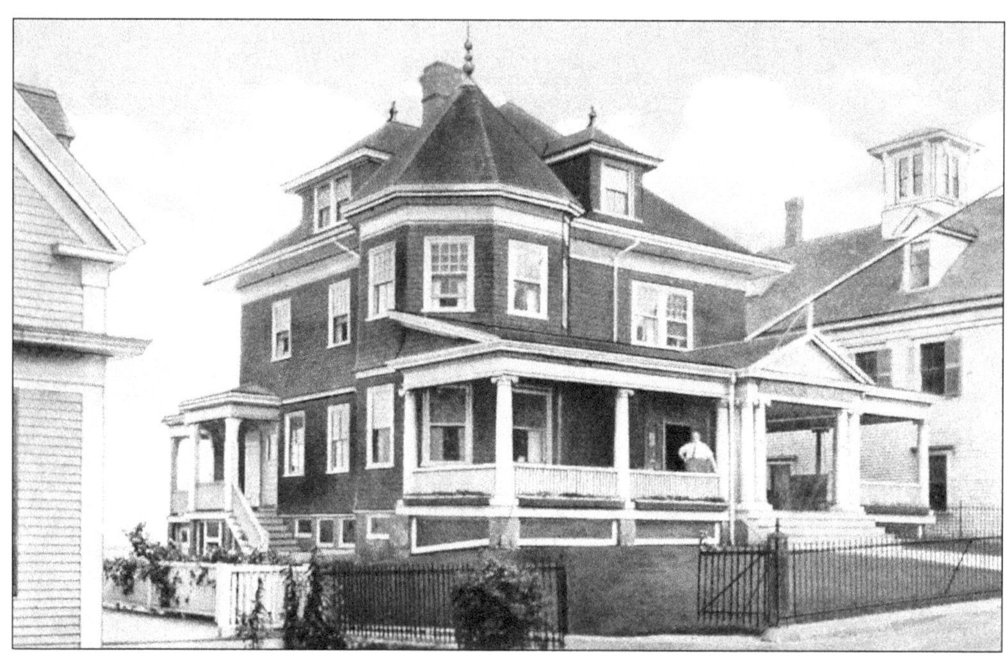

Anchor and Ark Club, 175 Commercial Street (c. 1940 postcard published by E.D. West Co.). This *c.* 1870 turreted and columned-porch Queen Anne-style house opposite Winthrop Street became the Anchor and Ark Club, which was established in 1935. The architectural integrity of the building has been maintained, and it has been known as the Anchor Inn for several decades.

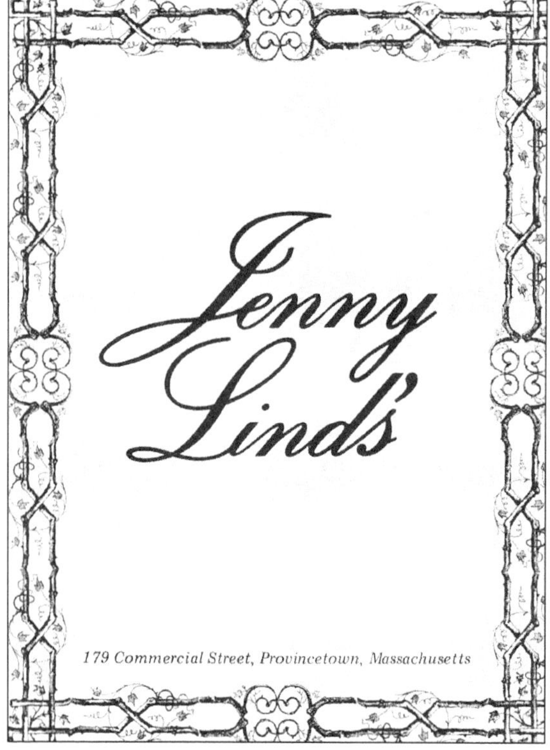

Jenny Lind's menu cover (c. 1977). Breakfast was served at the trendy restaurant from 9 am to 3 pm and included "complimentary drink: Bloody Mary, Cape Codder, Champagne or Juice. Also, your choice Lyonaisse potatoe or cottage cheese, & toast." Popular breakfast specials were "The 'Madame Butterfly' Morning After—two eggs any style with choice of bacon, sausage, linguica, or smoked ham" for $3.75, or "French Toast 'Manon'—our double cut french toast served golden brown, either plain or with fresh strawberries and/or with whipped cream" for $2.50 and $2.95 respectively. (Courtesy Howard M. Bushnell.)

United States Post Office, 211 Commercial Street (c. 1941 postcard published by the Town Crier Shop, Provincetown). This Georgian-style brick government building was constructed in 1932 near the end of Herbert Hoover's term as president. The cornerstone indicates that Ogden L. Mills was secretary of the treasury, and that James A. Wetmore was the acting supervising architect. The building is noted for its "strong design of assertive character executed in appropriate materials and detailed in a bold and sensitive direction."

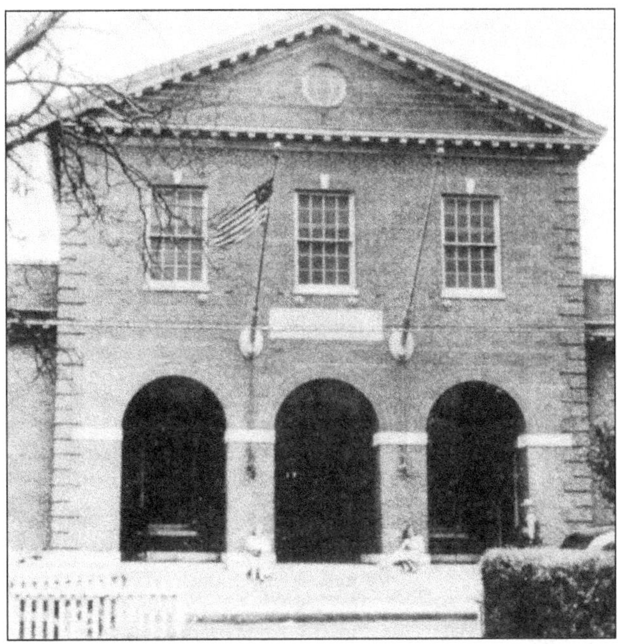

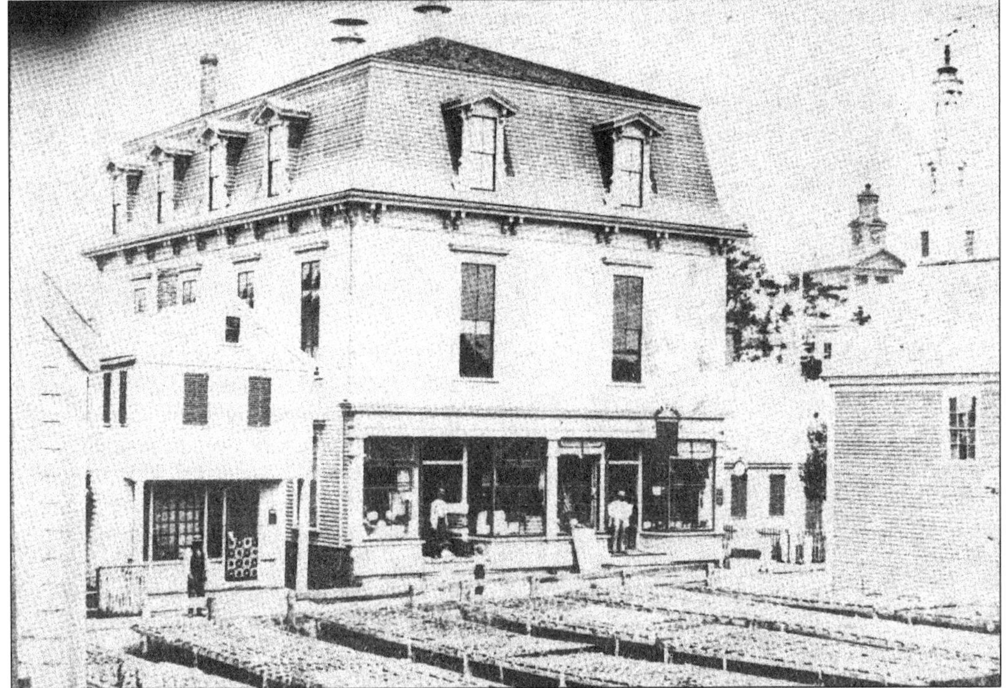

Drying fish opposite Masonic Hall, 224 Commercial Street (c. 1875 photograph). The "making" of fish on flakes stopped in town around 1912, thus purifying the air for all. The old Union House was the site of the hall built in 1870 for King Hiram's Lodge of Free and Accepted Masons, whose charter was signed by Paul Revere. The town's second newspaper, *The Advocate* (founded 1869), noted that it would have "a commodious public hall on the second floor, and the lodge room on the third floor. The first floor will be occupied by stores." The large structure was lowered one story in 1973. (Courtesy Seamen's Bank.)

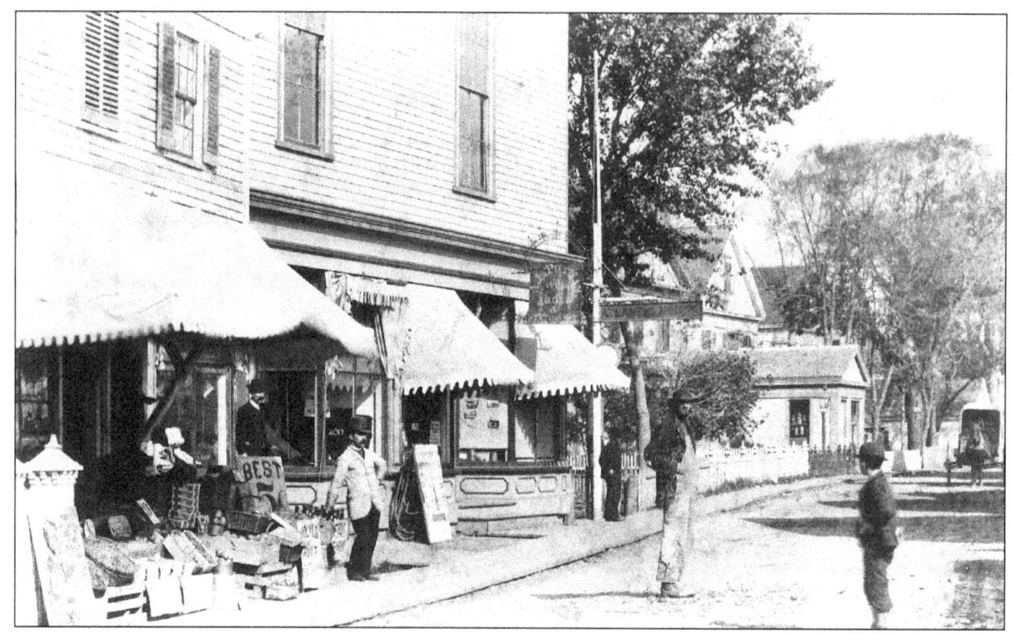

Commercial Street at the corner of Masonic Place (c. 1890 photograph taken by William M. Smith). Scalloped awnings protect produce in front of James P. Holmes's store (the caricature at the far left reads: "Take my word for it the fruit is ripe. Don't pinch."). To the right are the dry goods store of Hezekiah P. Hughes and A.J. Putnam & Co.'s book and stationery store (the latter two businesses were located in the Masonic Block). A tall man who may be "Mr. Reddington" stands in the street near the signs for the bookseller and the Atlantic House. (Courtesy Seamen's Bank.)

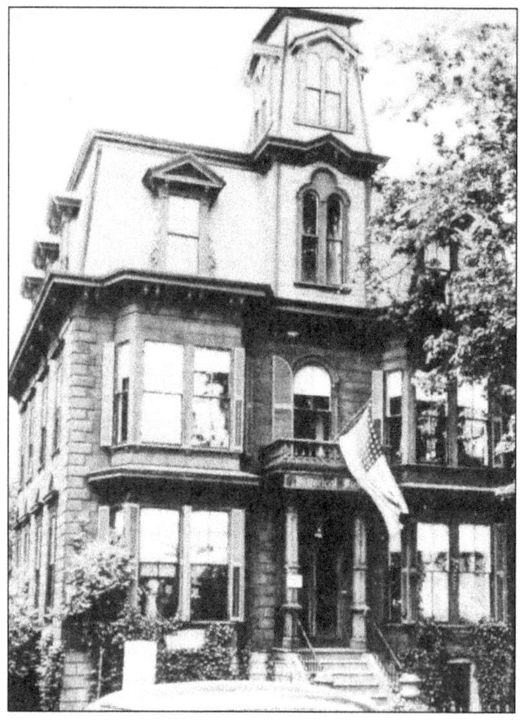

The Benjamin Lancy Mansion, 230 Commercial Street (c. 1940s postcard published by Town Crier Shop). Unfortunately only the upper two stories of Provincetown's most ostentatious house still reveal the past splendor of the 1874 Second Empire structure. Benjamin Lancy, an eccentric, wealthy merchant-ship owner, used a secret material to cover certain areas of wood to give it the appearance of brownstone. His strange children, who later lived in the basement of the house, tried in vain to discover the secret process. Before the building was converted to commercial purposes it served as the headquarters of the Provincetown Historical Society. (Courtesy Bonnie Steele McGhee.)

Universalist Church, 236 Commercial Street (c. 1923 postcard published by *The Advocate*). Congregationalism was the dominant religion in town up until 1833, when the Universalist Society was organized. Barnstable architect Benjamin Hallett designed the handsome 1847 Greek Revival house of worship, the steeple of which may have been inspired by a plate in Asher Benjamin's *The Country Builder's Assistant*, published in Greenfield, MA, in 1796. The oldest standing church in Provincetown, the Universalist church is shown flanked by residences built around the same time.

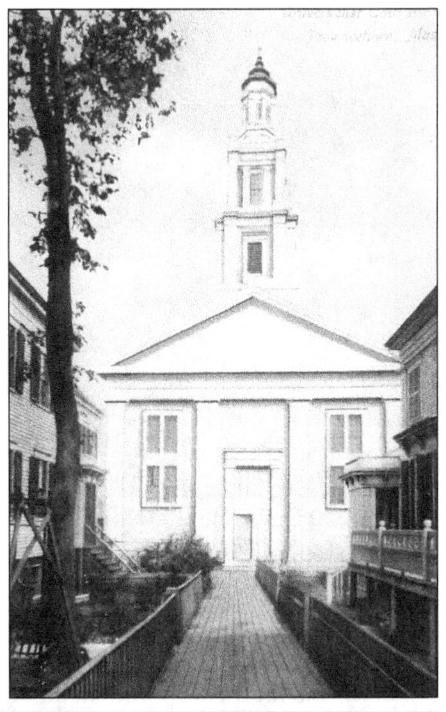

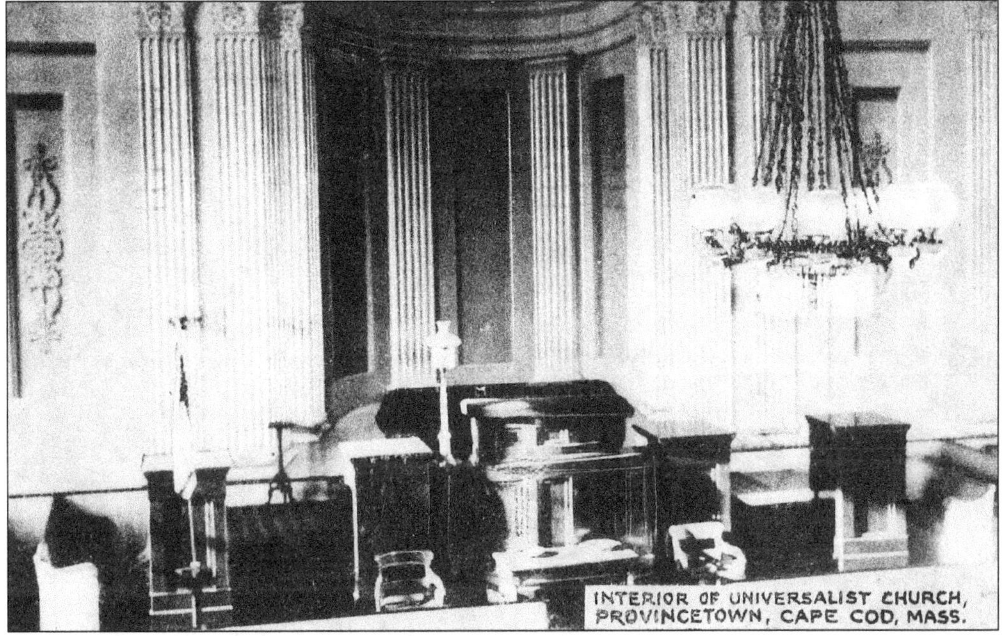

Interior of the Universalist Church, 236 Commercial Street (c. 1945 postcard published by The Collotype Co., Elizabeth, New Jersey, and New York). Wonderful trompe l'oeil decoration painted in egg tempera en grisaille around 1850 by Carl Wendte (1820–1848), a young German artist, graces the church's interior. An impressive mid-nineteenth-century Sandwich glass chandelier with cut glass globes and sparkling prisms lights the sanctuary. Provincetown's first bible was voted to be purchased at a town meeting on January 28, 1784; some town meetings were held in this church prior to the construction of the town hall in 1886.

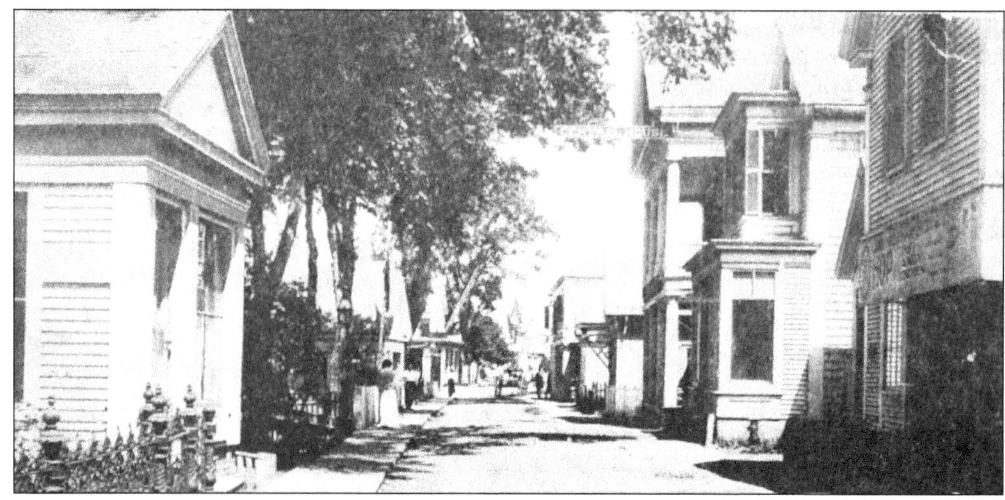

Commercial Street looking east (1900 postcard with illegible publisher's name). The county road was extended through town in 1835, making Commercial Street (often referred to as Front Street) a standard 22-foot width. Three years later, in 1838, federal and state grants provided the materials and money to lay a plank sidewalk along the land-side length of the street. Thoreau wrote that the inhabitants, many of whom refused to tread on the plank sidewalk, "could walk in the middle of the road without trouble even in slippers, for they had learned how to put their feet down and lift them up without taking in any sand."

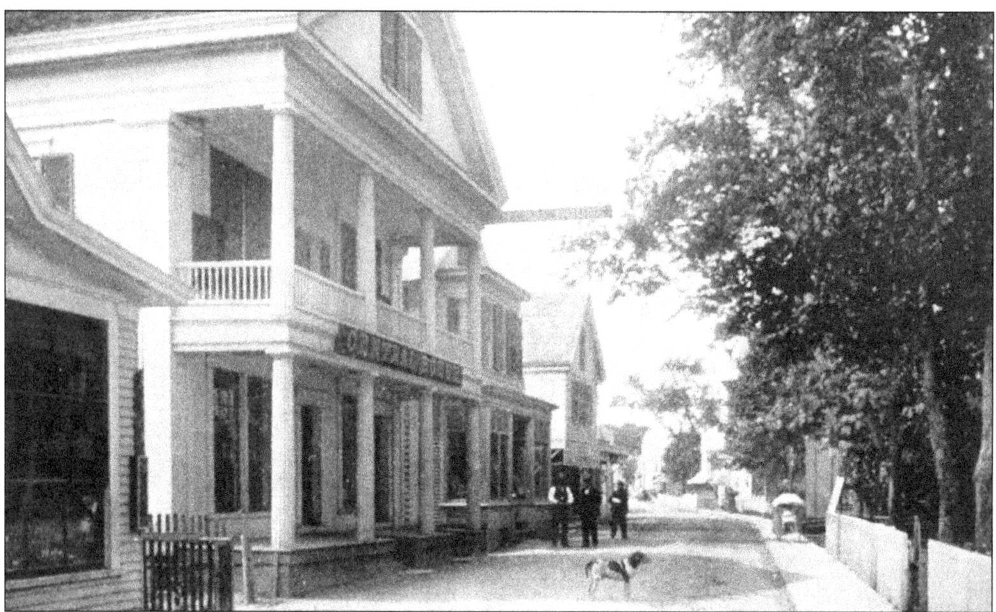

The Central House Hotel, 247 Commercial Street (1898 photograph published by The Perry Pictures Co.). Built in 1836 for Timothy P. Johnson, the Central House Hotel was used initially as a public hall for entertainment purposes. In 1882 H.H. Sylvester wrote, "experience tells the summer visitor that a vacation can be very pleasantly and profitably spent in Provincetown... The nights are just right for refreshing sleep, for from every point of the compass except due north the wind blows from off the water. If you wish, you can have fish for breakfast, dinner, and supper, freshly caught from the bay and cooked as only Provincetown cooks can cook them."

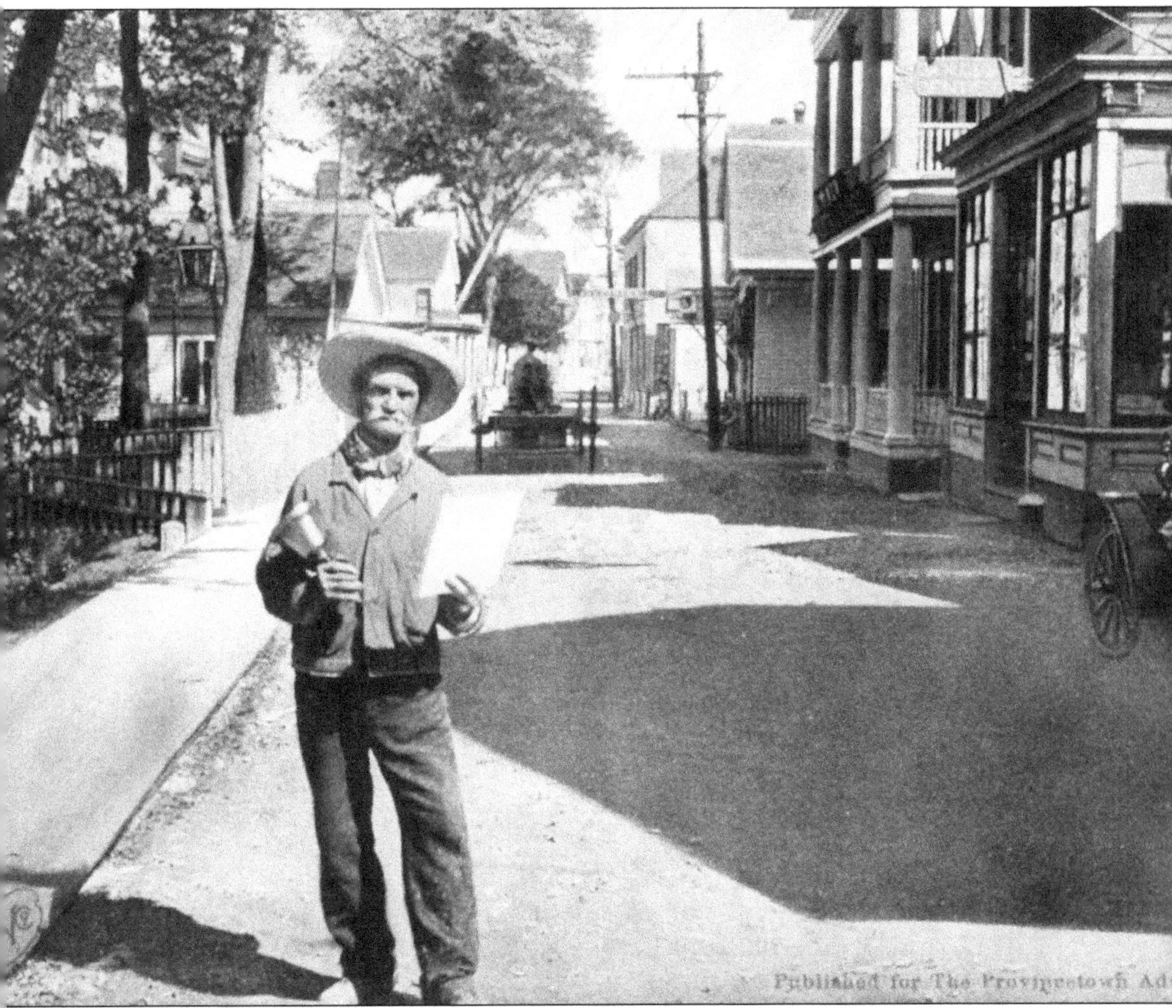

Town Crier George Washington Ready (c. 1906 postcard published by The Metropolitan News Co., Boston, MA). Dressed in everyday clothing, and usually depicted wearing a patterned scarf around his neck, George Washington Ready was one of the most colorful town criers. "Professor" Ready achieved national fame after he reported seeing a sea serpent a half-mile from the shore off Herring Cove in 1886. The message on the back of this postcard states: "This is one of the old customs still in vogue in this town. This is the main street: sidewalk on but one side of the street just wide enough for one team to pass another." Later generations who enjoyed the plank sidewalk "greatly regretted when lumber became so expensive that it was replaced by concrete" (around 1930).

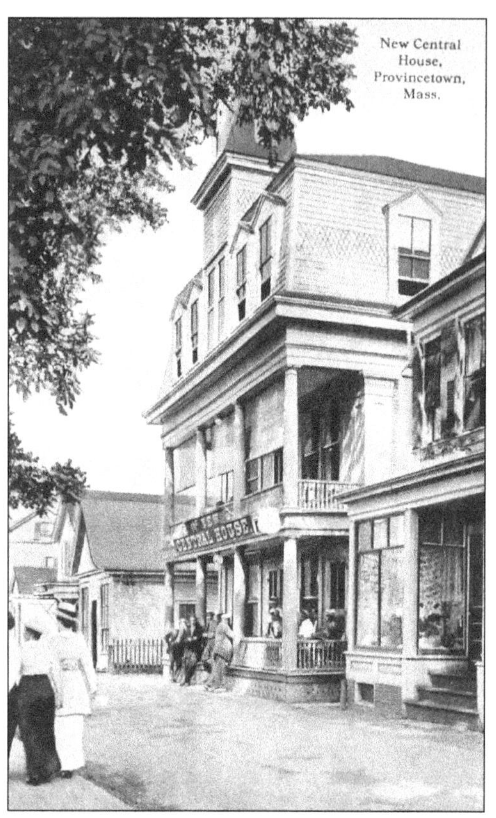

The New Central House, 247 Commercial Street (c. 1915 postcard published by C.T. Photochrom, Chicago, Illinois). After the Civil War the Central House Hotel was remodeled and enlarged by the new owner, Allen Reed. By 1903 a French mansard roof with dormers on all sides and a steeple changed the exterior appearance; additional bedrooms were added (bringing the total to about seventy-five), and so were billiard, pool, and smoking rooms. The popular hotel was then known as The New Central House; later names included The Town House, the Sea Horse Inn, and the current name, The Crown & Anchor Motor Inn.

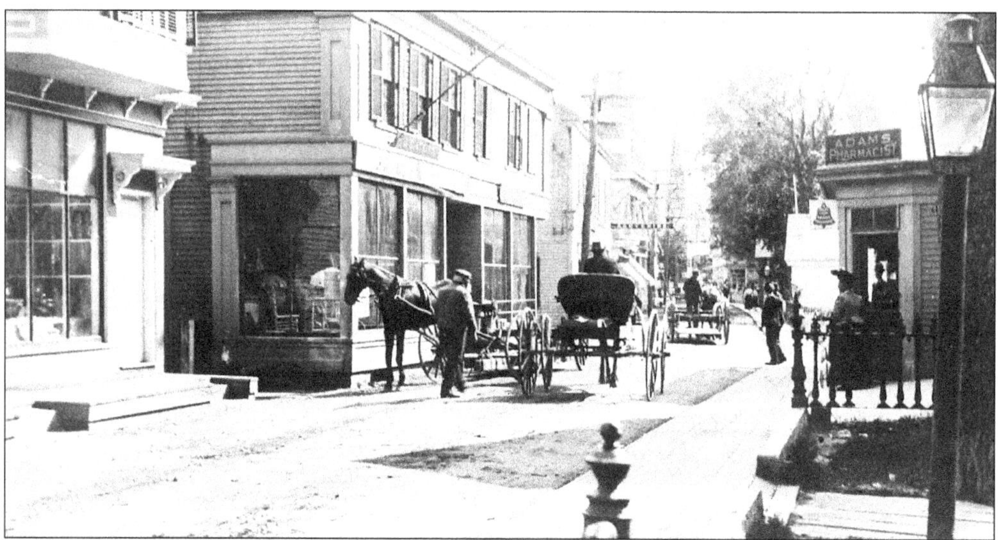

Commercial Street looking west towards Gosnold Street (c. 1905 photograph). The Greek Revival building in the middle of this view and the similar one only partially visible to the right were constructed between 1836 and 1858; they have been identified as early "wharf head" structures. J.E. Atkins's furniture store and the post office were located in the left building, as was the first telegraph office in town. The second floor is where the women's Nautilus Club has gathered for many years. The other horse-drawn conveyances pass the Adams Pharmacy, the oldest continuously operated drug store in Provincetown. (Courtesy Seamen's Bank.)

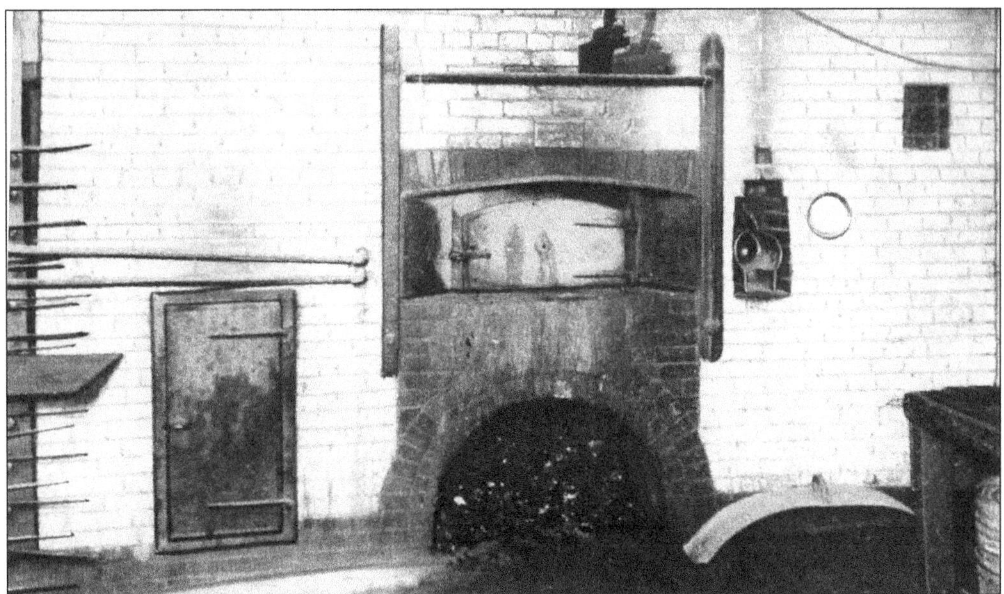

The Old Dutch Oven in Provincetown Bakery, 251 Commercial Street (early-twentieth-century postcard published by Tichnor Quality Views, Cambridge, MA). Bakeries in town began specializing in "Old World" edibles around the time Portuguese families began arriving in the mid-nineteenth century. In the early 1930s the bakery was located to the east of the New Central House. C.W. Burch Jr., the proprietor, saw to the quality of the breads, cakes, and pastries offered for the public's consumption.

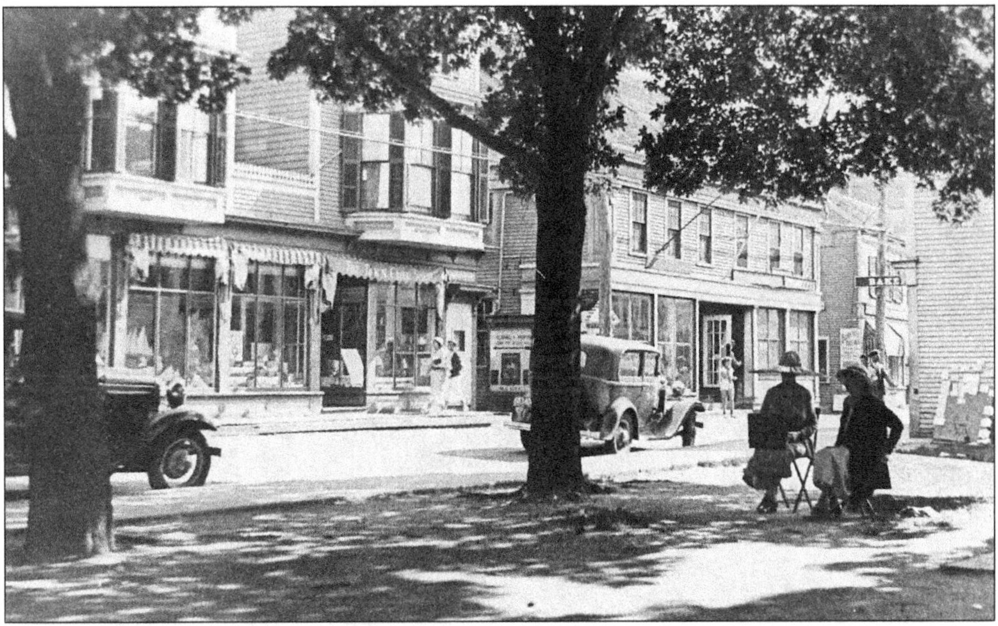

Commercial Street businesses opposite the town hall (c. 1925 photograph). A woman artist and her friend sit in the shady park across the street from nineteenth-century houses altered and adapted for commercial purposes. The two houses at the left with the in-fill section were built in the mid-1850s. Both were raised one story in the mid-1870s for Obadiah Snow & Son's fancy goods and household furnishings store. (Courtesy Seamen's Bank.)

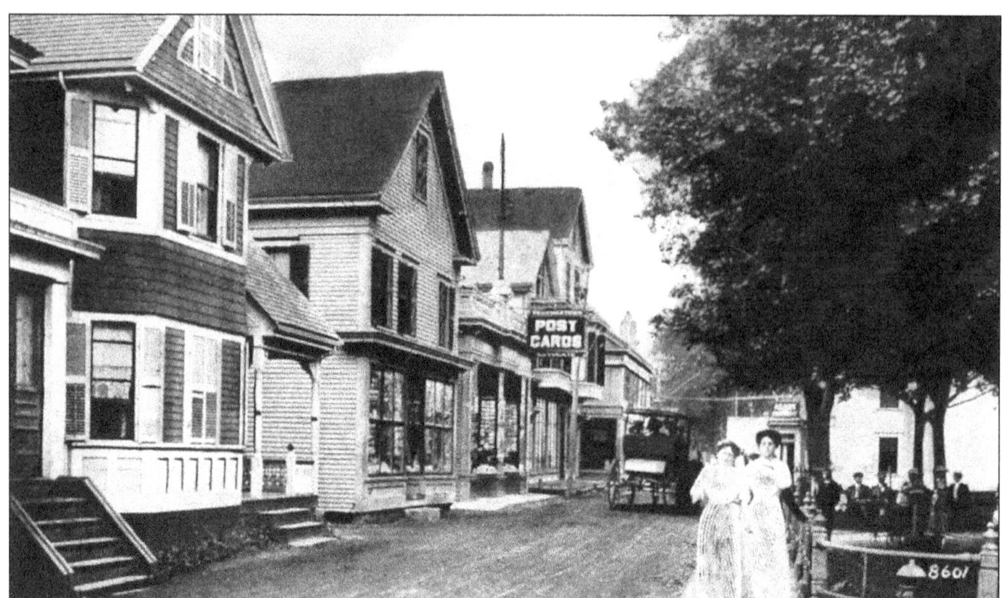

Commercial Street with Provincetown Advocate Building (c. 1915 postcard published by The New England News Co.). Some professionals and merchants located across the street from the town hall around 1890 included Jonathan Higgins, an attorney and counselor-at-law; D.A. Smith, a merchant tailor; and Mrs. Mary Young, whose specialty was "oysters served in every style." The Adams Pharmacy, at the corner of Gosnold Street, was the site of Samuel Rider's home, where the first Methodist sermon in town was delivered in 1793.

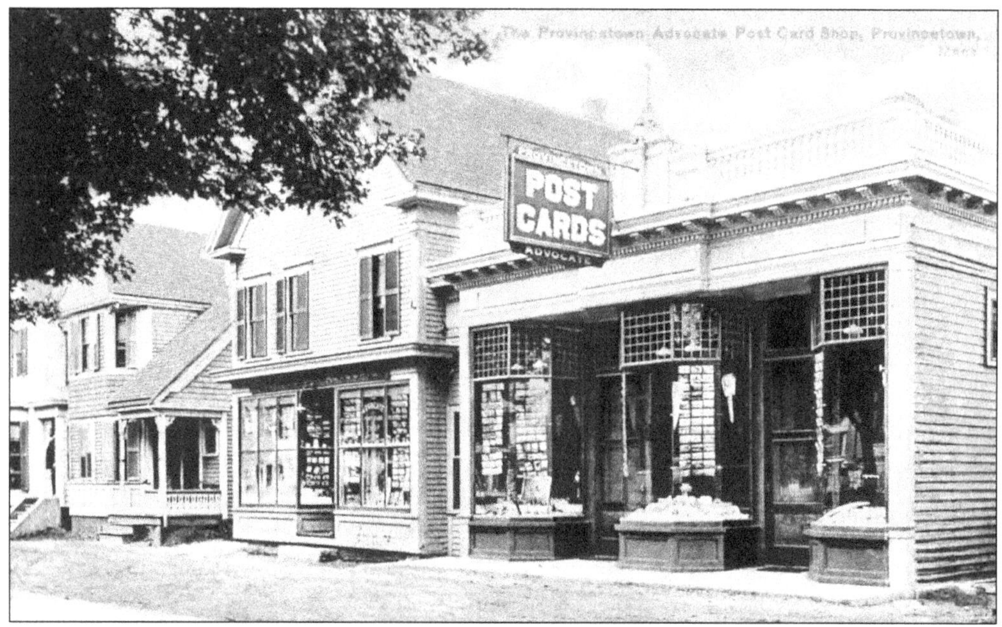

The Provincetown Advocate Post Card Shop, 265 Commercial Street (c. 1915 postcard published by *The Advocate*). An architecturally rich cornice and balustrade crown the one-story shop that catered to tourists. The canted corners accommodated two entrances and gave greater visibility to the rows of appealing postcards. Souvenirs and more postcards were also offered for sale next door in the building acquired by *The Advocate*.

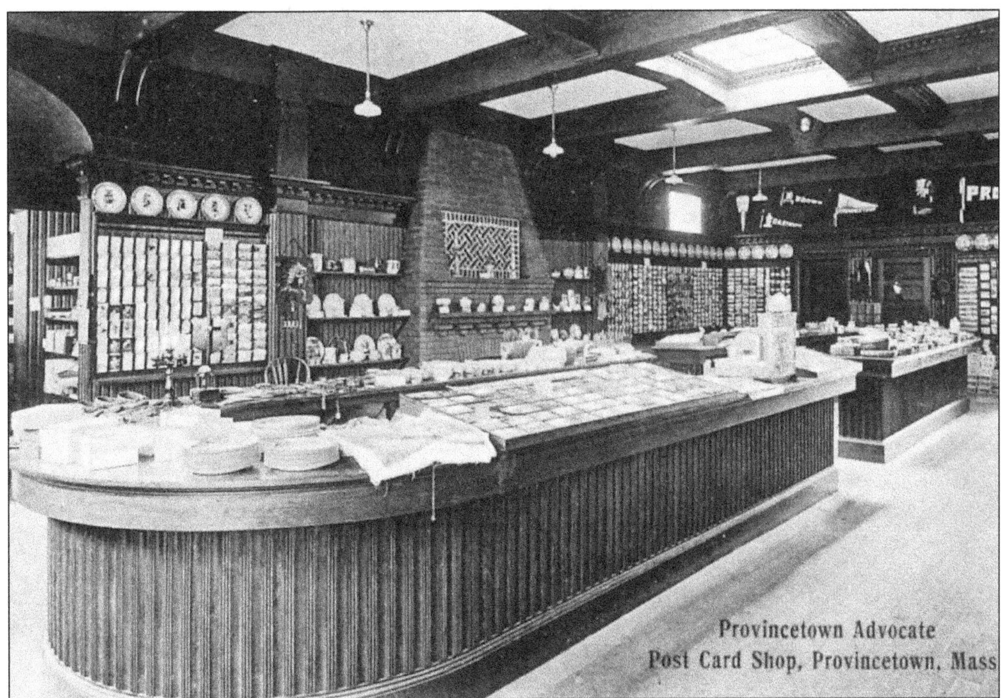

Provincetown Advocate Post Card Shop, 265 Commercial Street (c. 1915 postcard published by *The Advocate*). A professional architect undoubtedly designed the shop's formal interior in the Colonial Revival style as reflected through Edwardian eyes. Stacks and rows of commemorative plates—the always popular Wedgewood historical blue-and-white transfer plates printed with such scenes as the "Landing of the Pilgrims" and "Priscilla and John Alden," selling in the 25¢ to 35¢ range—were neatly displayed along with other souvenir bric-a-brac and town pennants for the burgeoning tourist trade.

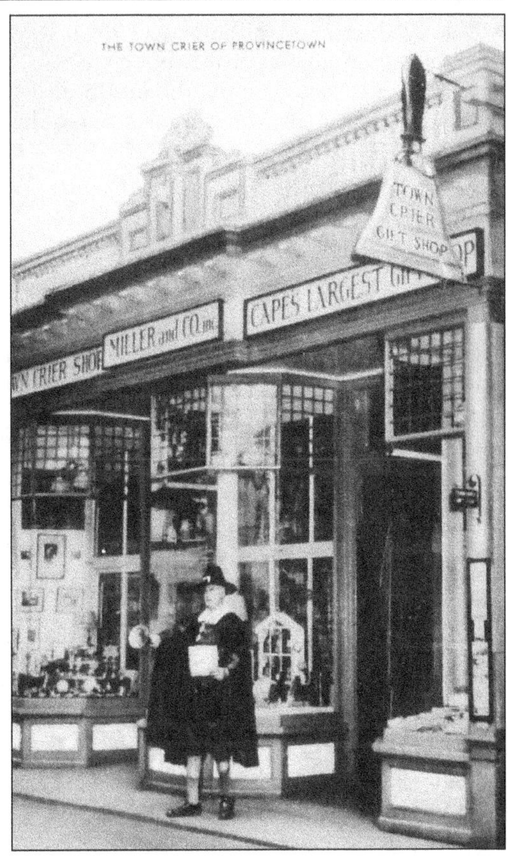

The Town Crier Gift Shop, 265 Commercial Street (late-1930s postcard published by The Town Crier Shop). The Town Crier Shop succeeded The *Provincetown Advocate* Post Card Shop, and according to its sign was the "Cape's Largest Gift Shop." Charles Walton, the gentleman dressed as a Pilgrim, was not one of the official town criers, but was hired to attract souvenir hunters into the shop.

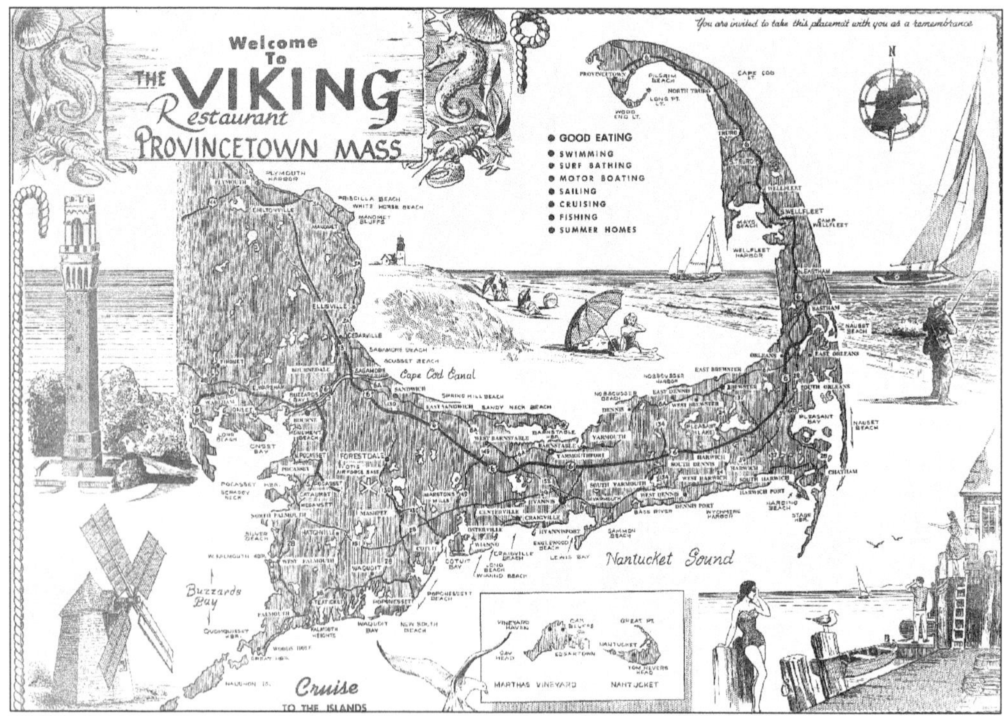

A Viking Restaurant place mat (1964). Restaurants with historic or distinctive names and good reputations always attract hungry diners. Located at 269 Commercial Street, the Viking Restaurant was owned during the mid-twentieth century by "Boozie" Silva prior to the period when "Billy Mac," Ina McFarlane's son, ran the well-patronized establishment.

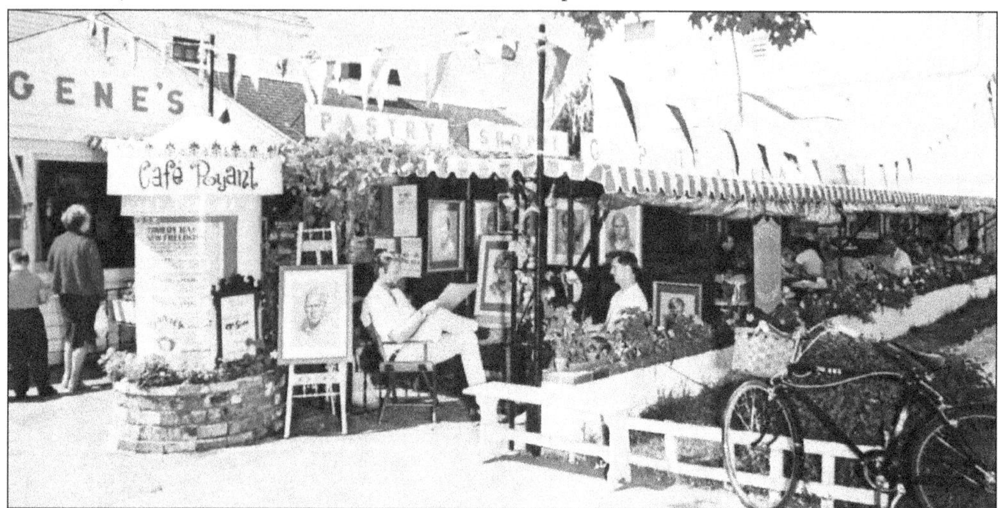

Café Poyant and Art Cinema, 256 Commercial Street (c. 1975 postcard published by Bromley & Co.). An art cinema was housed in the former Congregational church, and a sidewalk cafe with kiosk owned by Eugene Napoleon Poyant, one of the last town criers, gave this section of Commercial Street a Parisian ambiance. Portrait artist Harvey Dodd, a resident of Provincetown since 1959, is busy capturing the likeness of a tourist while surrounded by examples of his pastel portraits. The sender of the postcard noted that, "This is a favorite meeting place of many famous people."

Congregational Church, 256 Commercial Street (c. 1915 postcard published by *The Advocate*). Located to the left of the town hall (but unfortunately remodeled), the "Church of the Pilgrims," built in 1843, was the Congregationalists' fourth church in town. Timbers from the "Old White Oak" meetinghouse—built in 1793 near the site of St. Peter the Apostle Church on Prince Street—were used to construct this church. Congregationalism went into decline in Provincetown during the early nineteenth century, and some of the church's parishioners converted to Unitarianism.

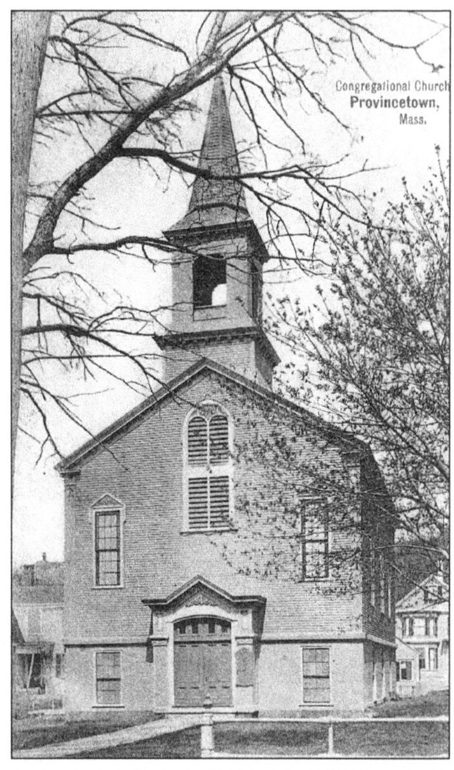

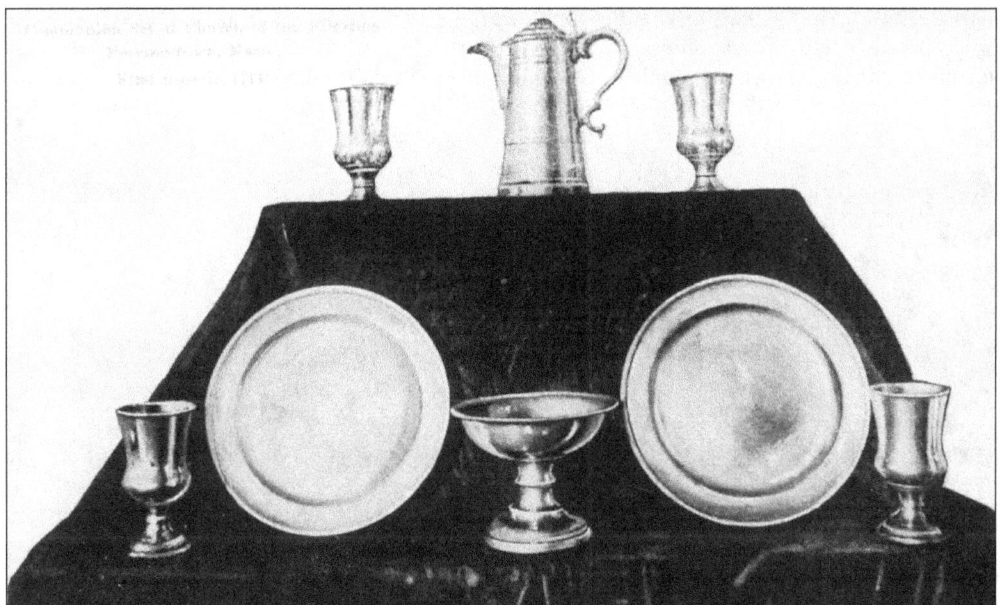

Communion set at Church of the Pilgrims, 256 Commercial Street (c. 1914 postcard published by *The Advocate*). Well-to-do townspeople usually gave money to their church in order to have communion pieces made to order; otherwise they donated individual family vessels for the formation of a service. Silver and pewter flagons, plates, and cups were standard forms; these pieces were undoubtedly transferred to another church or donated to a museum when the Congregational church was deconsecrated.

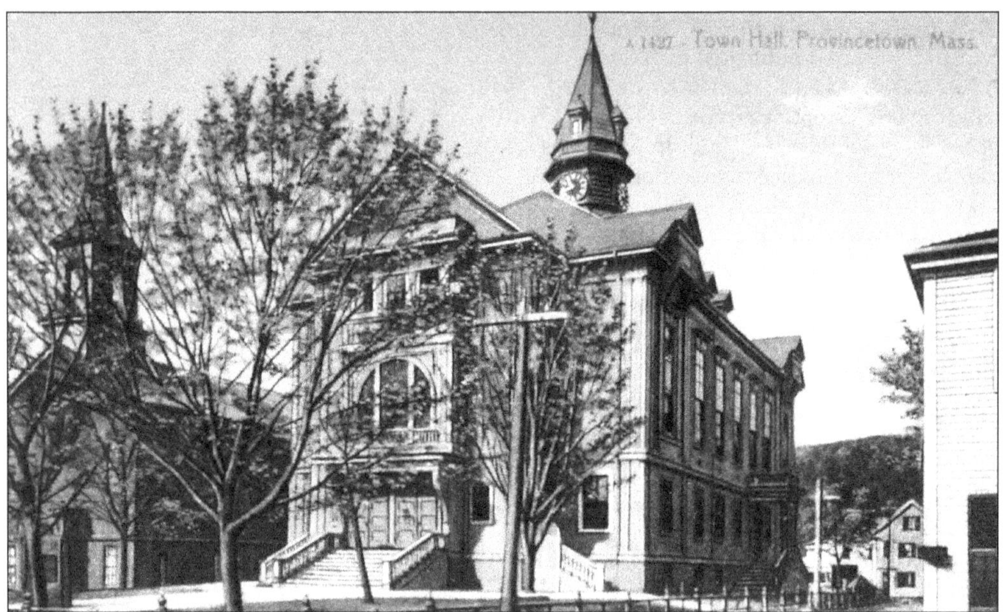

Town hall, 260 Commercial Street (c. 1915 postcard published by *The Advocate*). Provincetown's second town hall was built on the site of the home of the Reverend William Henry Ryder when that land was left to the town. Construction of the late-Victorian building began in September 1885, and it was dedicated on August 25, 1886. Governor George D. Robinson delivered an address, and musical entertainment was provided by the Puritan Band. A ball was held in the new structure at 9 pm, and fireworks were presented on Railroad Wharf. Town offices are located on the first floor, and a second-floor hall can accommodate one thousand people for various political or cultural events.

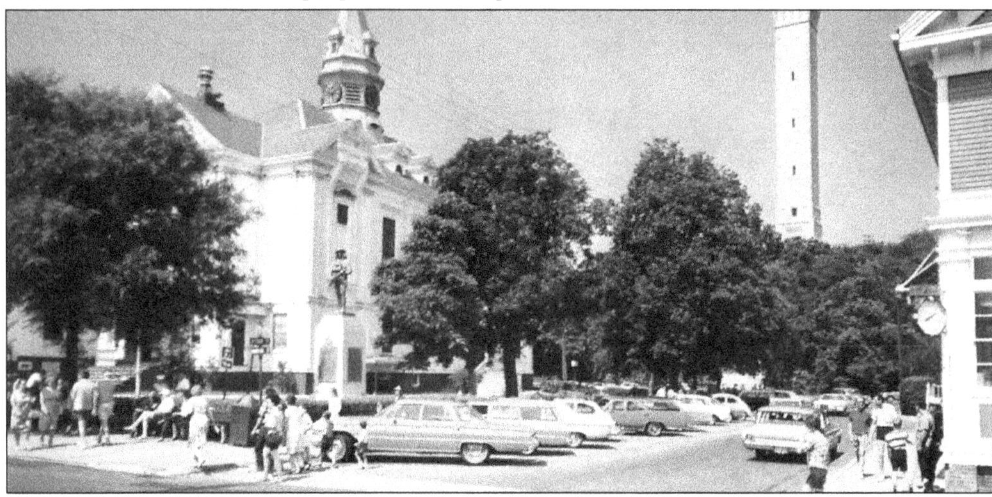

Corner of Commercial and Ryder Streets (c. 1964 postcard published by Bromley & Co.). In 1851 the Seamen's Savings Bank (the incorporated name) acquired the Italianate house at 276 Commercial Street and converted the first floor into their new headquarters. On the opposite corner of the street stands the World War Memorial, dedicated in 1928 to the three hundred Provincetown men who answered the draft call to "Save the World for Democracy." Only thirty-eight men were required to fill the quota; the names of the twelve heroes who died in the cause are listed on the memorial.

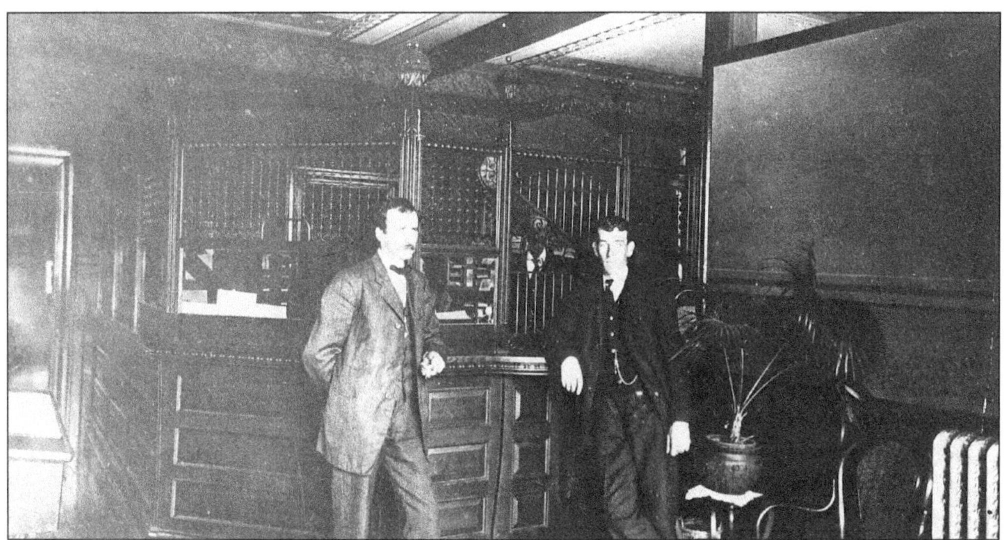

The Lobby of the Seamen's Savings Bank, 276 Commercial Street (c. 1910 photograph). The bank's Colonial Revival interior with its dark, raised panels, decorative woodwork, and stenciled borders is a far cry from the décor at the original location on Union Wharf in the West End (the bank was located inside a ship's chandlery and grocery store). Treasurer William H. Young (left) and Myrick C. Young lean against the teller's cage. (Courtesy Seamen's Bank.)

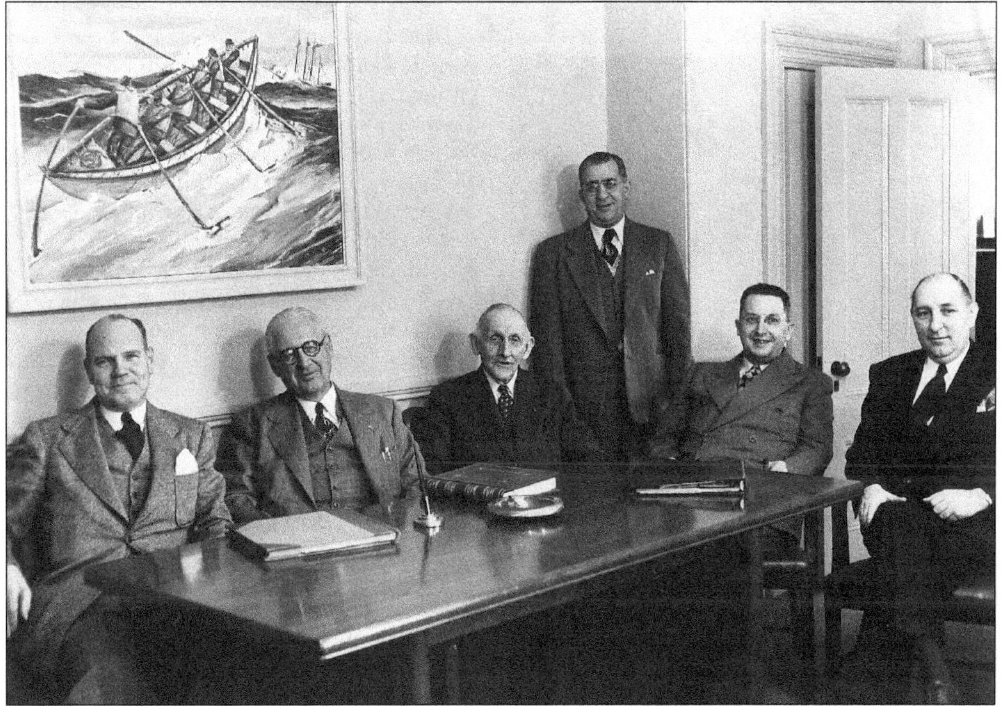

The Seamen's Savings Bank Board of Directors, 276 Commercial Street (c. 1951 photograph). An untitled 1942 marine painting by Swedish-born artist Charles Kaeselau is one example of the germane artwork collected by bank officials. Shown in the board of directors' room are, from left to right, John F. Rosenthal, Frank O. Cass, Thomas J. Lewis, William F. Silva, George F. Miller Jr., and Robert A. Welsh. (Courtesy Seamen's Bank.)

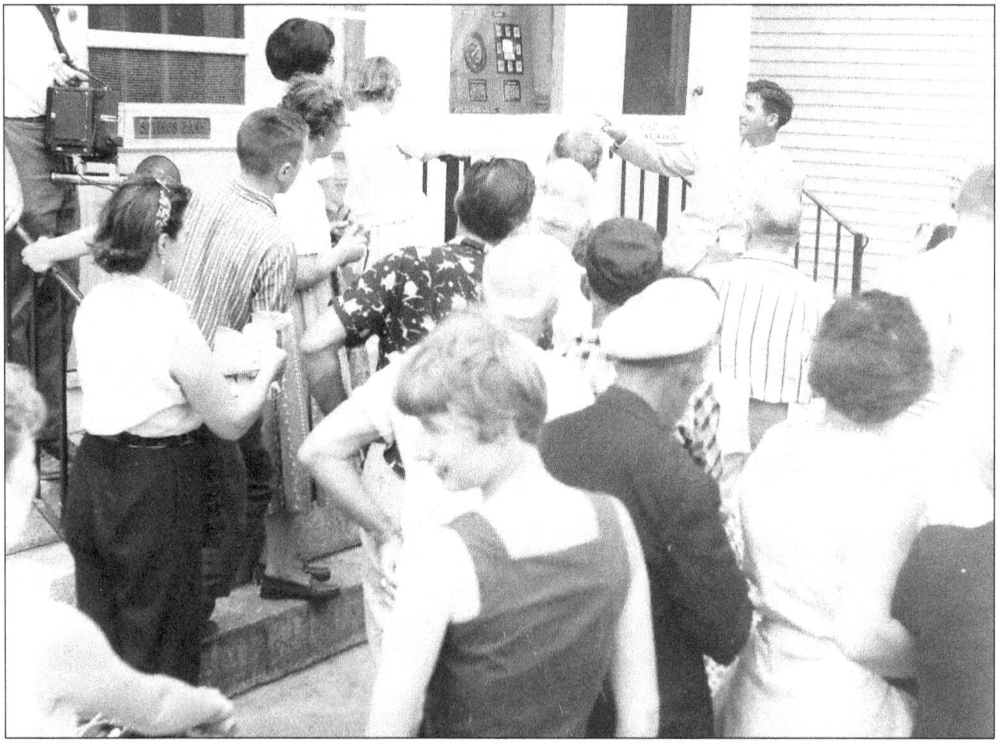

A meteorological explanation (c. 1962 photograph). Cape Cod resident Don Kent, a weather forecaster on Boston television station WBZ for several decades, points to a window display set up at the Seamen's Savings Bank. The young lady in the foreground is Marie Leonard Taves of Provincetown, an employee of the bank. Sivert J. Benson hung his insurance office sign on the building's right front door. (Courtesy Seamen's Bank.)

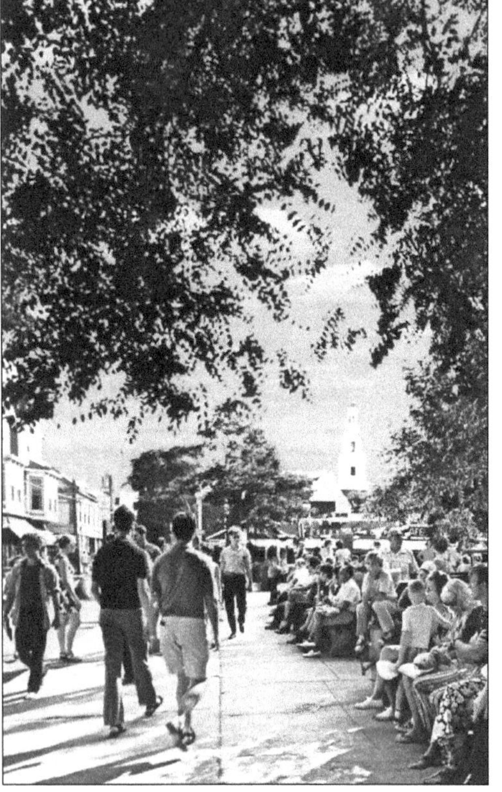

Benches in front of the town hall (c. 1970 postcard published by J. Lazarus). One of the most pleasant ways to spend time in Provincetown, day or night, is to observe the pedestrian parade, or to "watch the pass," as locals say in Nantucket. The people in this artistically manipulated postcard are probably waiting for the ferry to take them back to Boston.

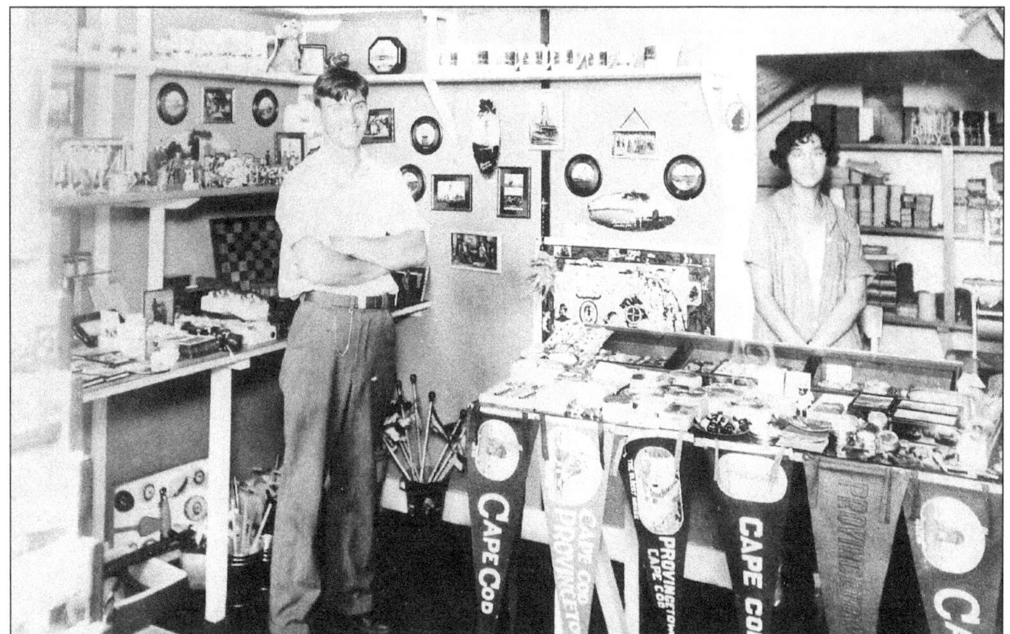

The Souvenir Shop, 286 Commercial Street (c. 1935 photograph). The handsome young couple, Preston Grant Hall and his Portuguese wife, Maria da Cruz Hall, ran this successful shop from the 1930s to the 1950s. They purchased their home, a former sea captain's mansion, at 396 Commercial Street in 1938, and ran it as the Preston Hall Guest House. Three years later a Boston newspaper columnist wrote that in Provincetown, "The souvenir shops fill to bursting and the hiss of frying fish and hot-dogs is drowned out only by the clinking of cash registers." (Courtesy Elena Curtis Hall.)

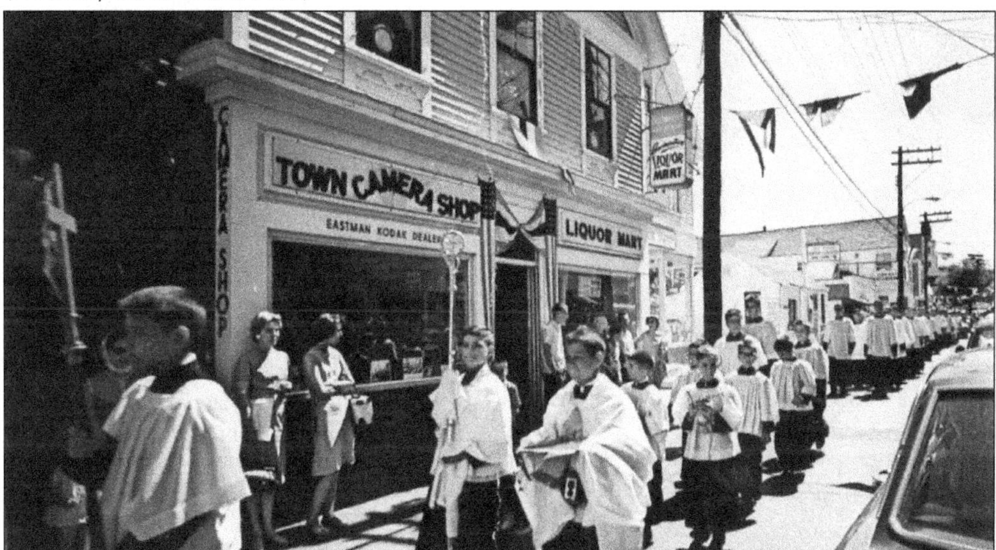

Altar boys procession to MacMillan Wharf (c. 1955 postcard published by Cape Cod Photos, Orleans, MA). A procession of altar boys from St. Peter the Apostle Church walks along Commercial Street toward the corner of Standish Street, where they will join hundreds of people at the end of MacMillan Wharf for the annual Blessing of the Fleet, which always occurs in late June.

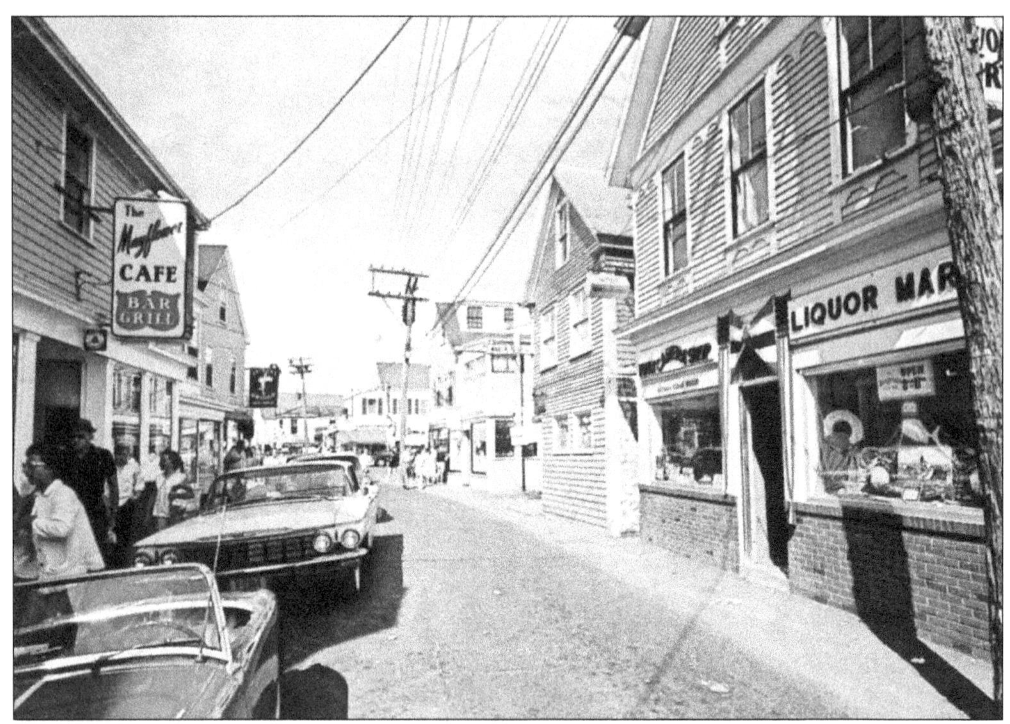

Commercial Street looking toward Standish Street (c. 1960 postcard published by the Town Camera Shop). The camera and photographic supply shop adjacent to the package store (formerly Perry's Liquors) published this view of one-way Commercial Street looking east with cars parked on one side and utility poles stationed on the other. A hastily written message on the reverse of the postcard states: "Down for a few days-have a cottage-lots of sights, beards, side-burns, everything."

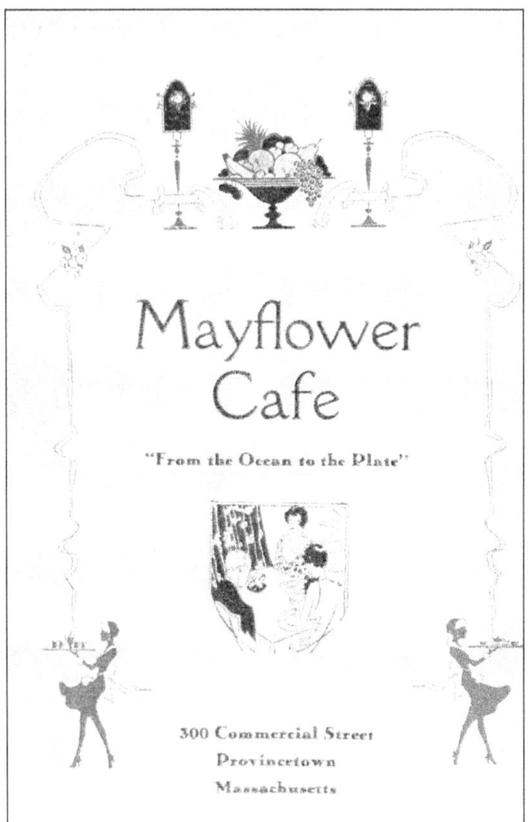

A Mayflower Café menu (1930s). The café's first menu featured a tasteful table setting with shaded candlesticks above a vignette of elegant diners dressed in the fashion of the period. Attenuated waitresses served traditional and popular ethnic food such as Portuguese kale soup, quahaug bisque, Wellfleet oyster gumbo, Cape Cod turkey (stuffed codfish), mackerel vinha d'alhos, sea clam pie, New England clam chowder, etc., along with the freshest Portuguese bread. (Courtesy Janoplis family.)

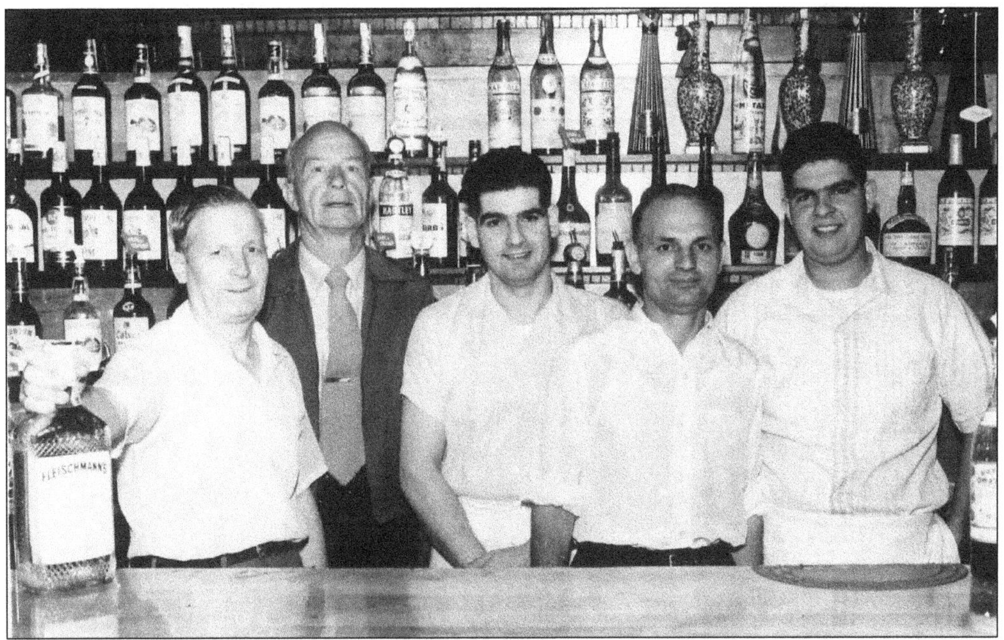

Behind the bar at the Mayflower Café, 300 Commercial Street (c. 1955 photograph). Brothers Mike and Sam Janoplis (at the left) opened the Mayflower Café, which is still family operated, in 1929. Anastos, a visiting relative from Canada, is flanked by the second-generation owners, sons Mike and Sam. Townspeople jocularly referred to the restaurateurs as "The Greeks." (Courtesy Janoplis family.)

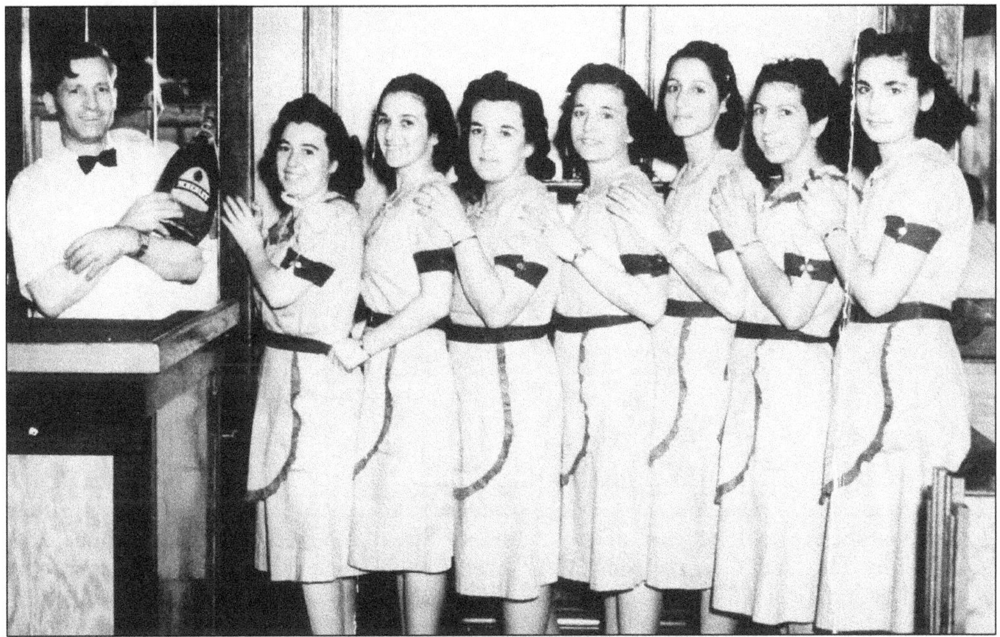

Mayflower Café waitresses, 300 Commercial Street (c. 1938 photograph). Cheerful, uniformed waitresses line up at the bar while bow-tied Mike Janoplis clutches a large bottle of whiskey. From left to right, the "girls" are Frances Peters, Mary Noons, Eleanor Sousa, Bee Packett, Mary Steele, Mary Roderick, and Sally Grice. (Courtesy Janoplis family.)

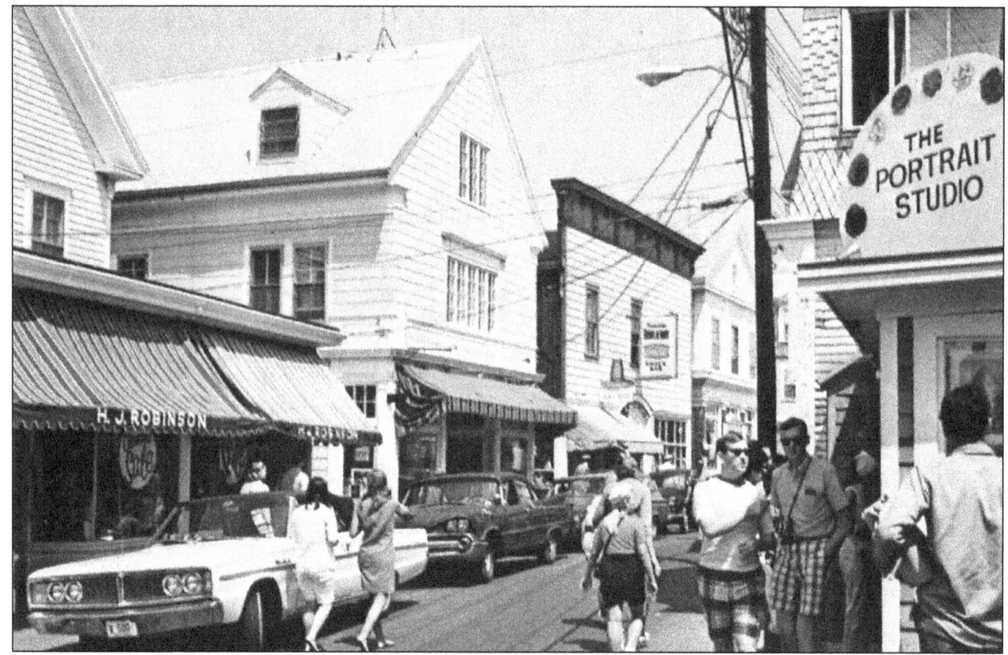

Commercial Street looking east near the Standish Street intersection (c. 1965 postcard published by Bromley & Co.). "P-town's" main street unfortunately started to get a honky-tonk appearance in the 1950s and '60s. A snack bar was located in the Bowl-A-Way at 288 Commercial Street in the 1880s false-front building.

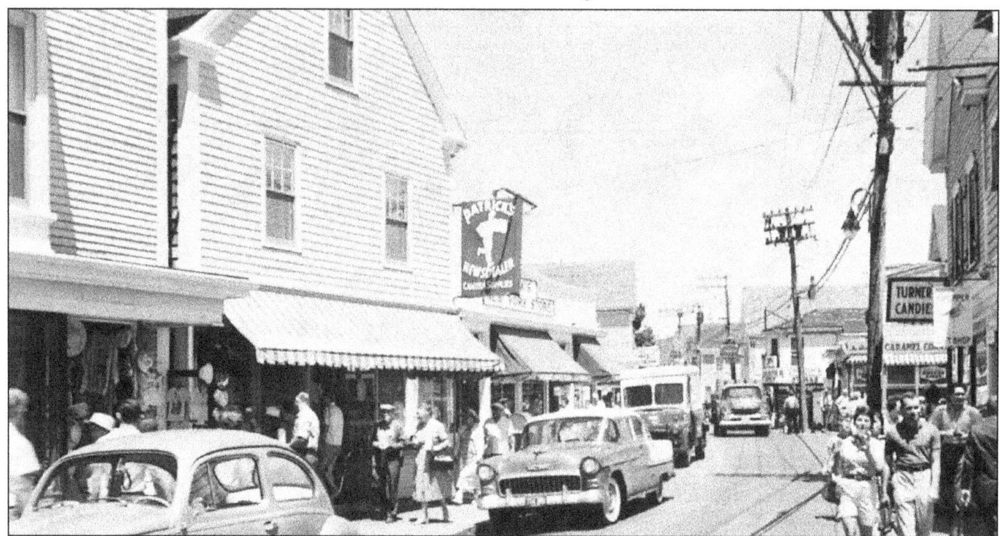

Commercial Street looking east at the Standish Street intersection (c. 1955 postcard published by The Slate Co., Hyannis, MA). Everyone bought local and national newspapers at Patrick's, and Lewis's New York General Store stocked bolts of fabric, thread, and jeans until around 1960. Candy and fudge, caramel corn, and ice cream fortified tourists as they searched for items of personal adornment such as Cape Cod T-shirts, sandals from Marrakesh, and distinctive fish-scale jewelry, sold by the Atlantic Coast Fisheries. Beach plum jelly—a popular souvenir and delicious alternative to strawberry jam—reminds people of Cape Cod when they spread it on toast at home.

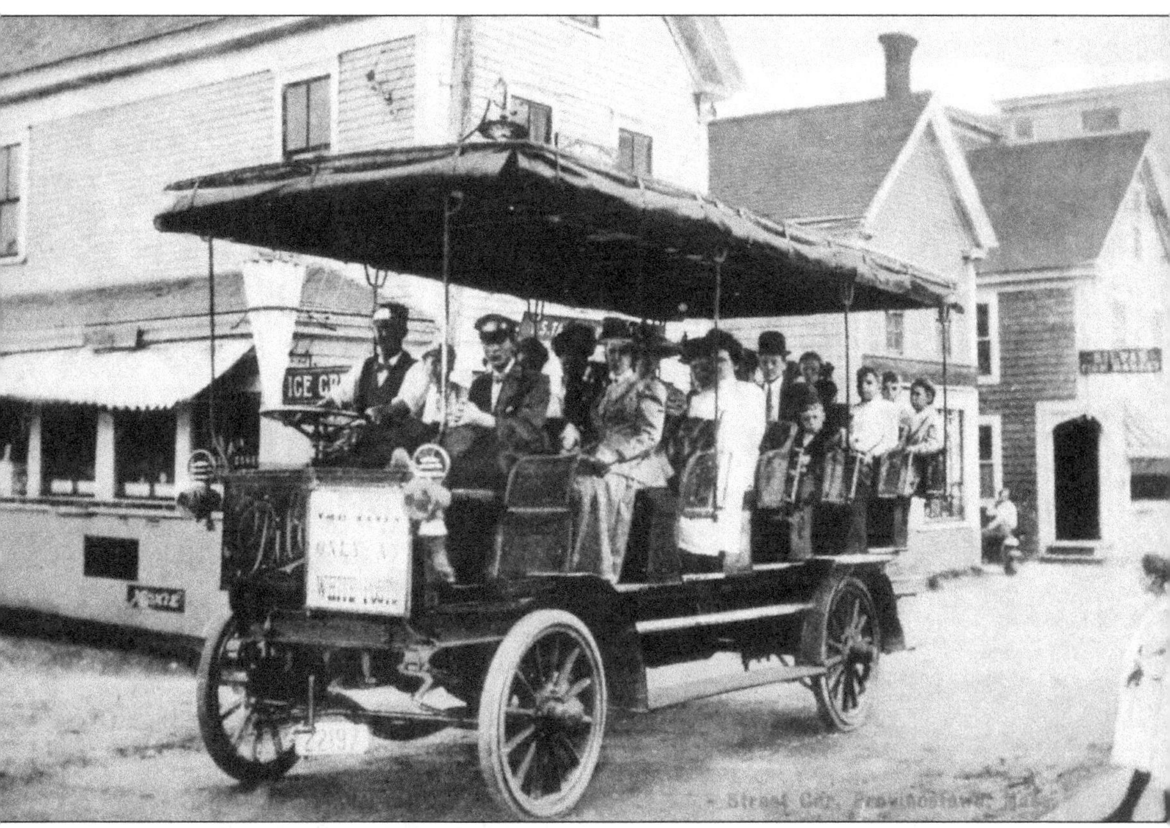

Street Car at the corner of Commercial and Standish Streets (c. 1910 postcard published by *The Advocate*). Known locally as the "accommodation," this early, open-air, motorized bus had an overhead protective canopy with flaps that could be lowered in foul weather. A one-way ride along the length of Commercial or Bradford Streets cost 5¢, and the accommodating drivers would stop here and there to do errands for townspeople. Bill Nickerson may have been the first driver in town; however, Josiah L. Young claimed he was "the town cabby" originally. The jovial Mr. Kendrick was a well-liked driver whose many Cape Cod stories delighted passengers. The accommodation pictured was the Pilgrim, one of the earliest vehicles of the type with hard rubber wheels. Will Taylor ran the ice cream and candy store on the corner for several decades.

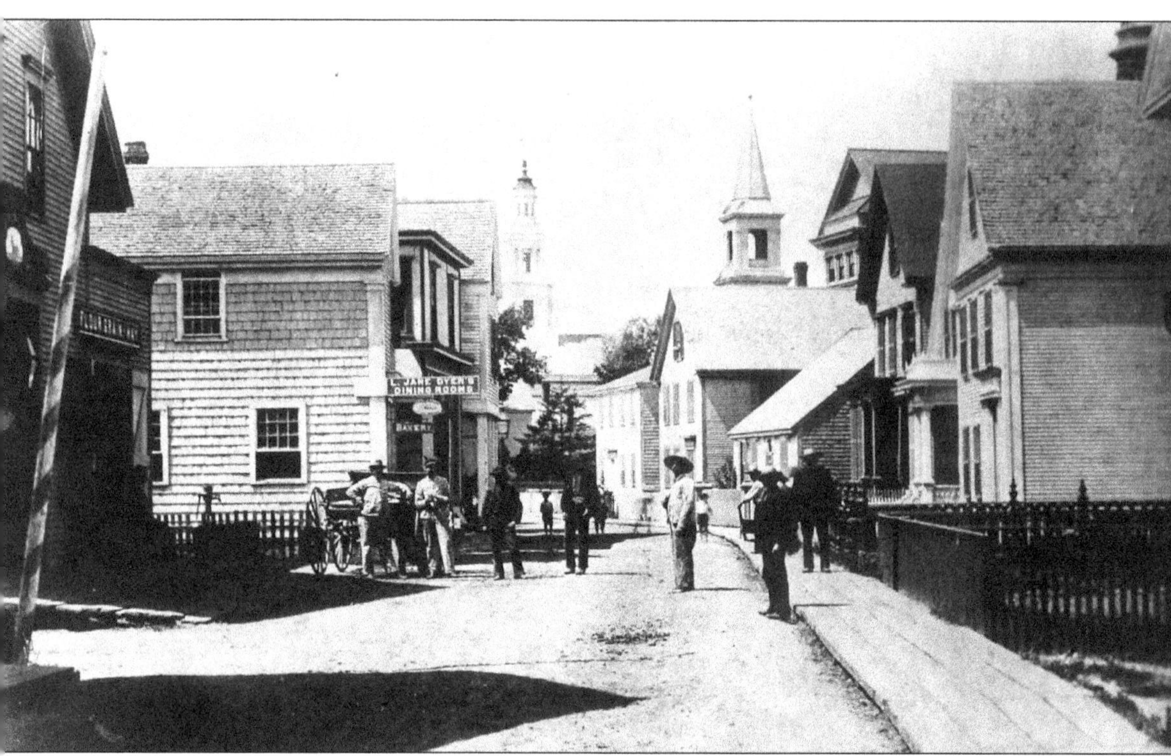

Commercial Street looking west toward Ryder Street (c. 1890 photograph). The public buildings and private residences on the right side of the street, which appear stacked architecturally, present an interesting chronological view of structures before commercial interests took over. The steeply pitched, typical Cape Cod house in the center is flanked by Greek Revival/early Victorian dwellings, and a hipped-roof Colonial house can be seen near the intersection of Ryder Street. Dominating the image, from left to right, are the steeples of the Universalist church, the Congregational church, and the gable-ended roof of the town hall. On the left side of the street, Samuel Knowles's Livery Stable (established in 1873) can be identified by the painted horse and provisions signs. Miss L. Jane Dyer's Dining Rooms and a bakery were located next door in the shingle-sided house. During the mid-nineteenth century, animals were not slaughtered in town; meat was brought from Boston on packet ships to be prepared in public houses and early restaurants. (Courtesy Seamen's Bank.)

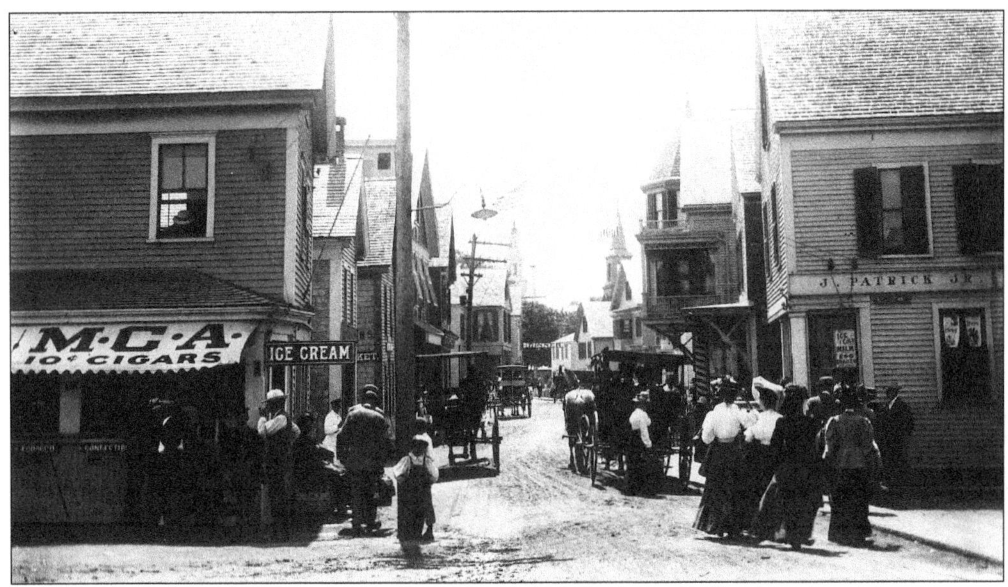

Railroad Square at the junction of Commercial and Standish Streets (c. 1910 photograph). Menfolk and boys cluster near the store offering "10¢ cigars and ice cream," while a group of women scurry towards J. Patrick Jr.'s newspaper store, perhaps for an egg shake (available in all flavors). The tall and unsightly telegraph poles were installed in 1855, and telephone lines were added in 1883; electricity replaced the oil-burning street lamps around 1904. During the census year of 1890, the 4,642 inhabitants gave Provincetown the highest quota of year-round residents of all towns on Cape Cod. (Courtesy Seamen's Bank.)

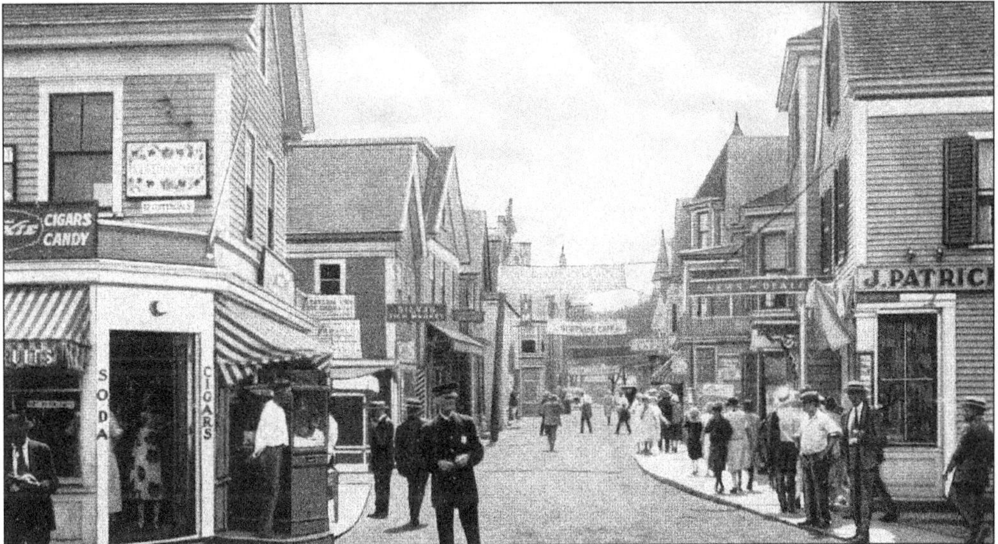

Commercial Street looking west from Standish Street (c. 1925 postcard published by E.D. West Co.). The large banner stretched across the street advertised "The Blue Lattice/ Fine Food Popular Prices." Some businesses located on Commercial Street in the late 1930s were The Ship's Wheel (where antiques could be "browsed" or purchased); the Harbor Vanity Shoppe (a beauty shop for "milady"); H.M. Malchman's, opposite the town hall (a practical and elegant men's furnishings store); and John A. Francis's real estate office (for those interested in buying Provincetown property).

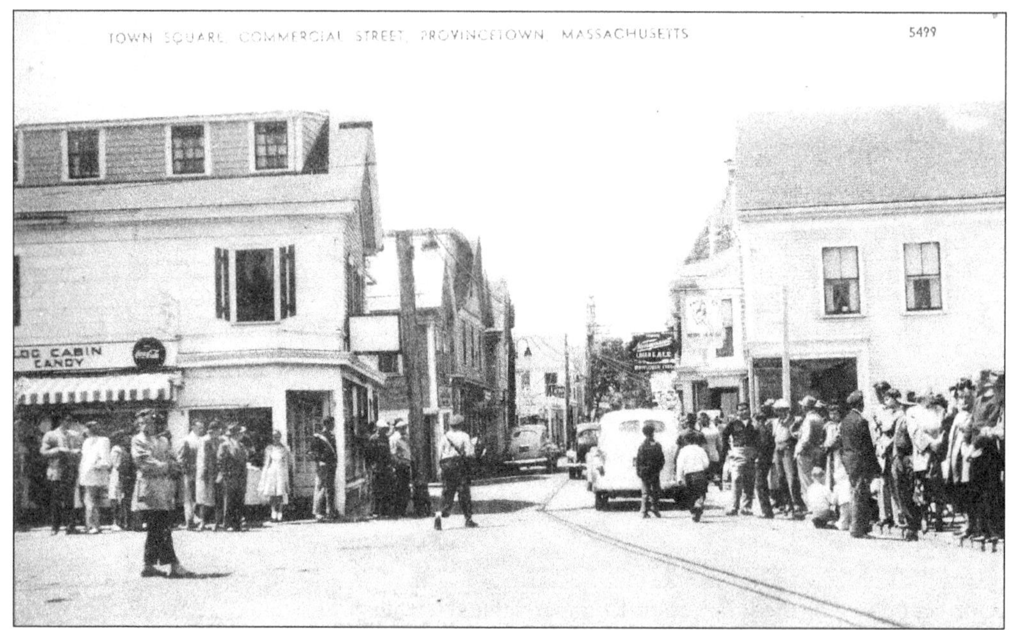

Town Square (c. 1940 postcard published by American Art Postcard Co., Boston, MA). The Mayflower Café featured a large, shaped hanging sign advertising Cape Cod's own "Famous Narragansett Lager & Ale," and a running newsboy was the trade sign for "Patrick's News Dealer." Both of the signs are located beyond the crowd of onlookers on the pedestrian-preferred side of Commercial Street at Town, or Railroad, Square.

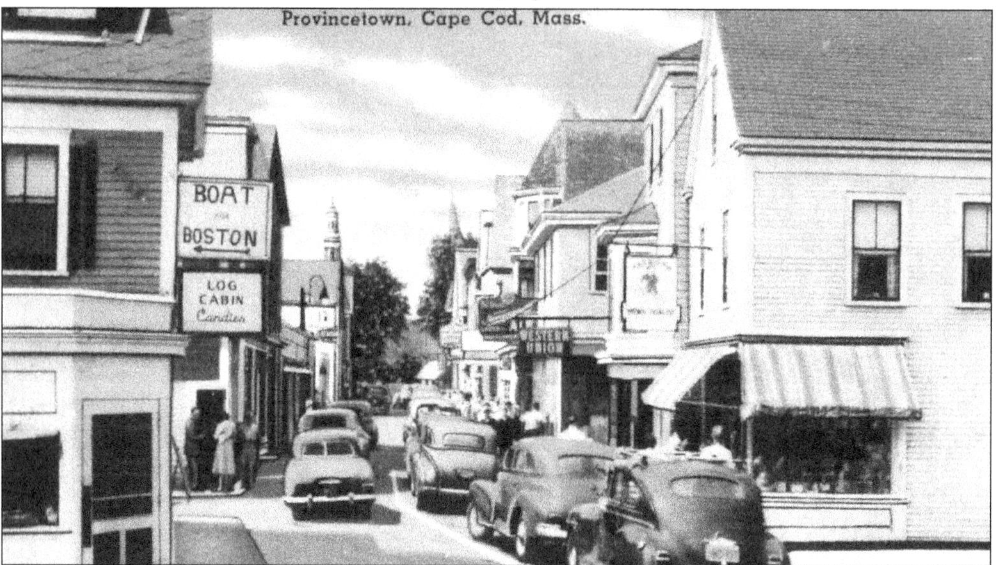

Commercial Street looking west (c. 1948 postcard published by The Mayflower Sales Co.). Two lanes of one-way traffic pass stores—"small and desperate trades," as described by local author Mary Heaton Vorse (1874–1966) in the 1940s—and restaurants displaying their respective services at the corner of Standish Street. In late July of 1940 fifteen hundred cars came into town within a two-and-a-half-hour period. Tourists who needed repair work done on their vehicles could contact Mayer's (which also featured a new car showroom) on parallel Bradford Street.

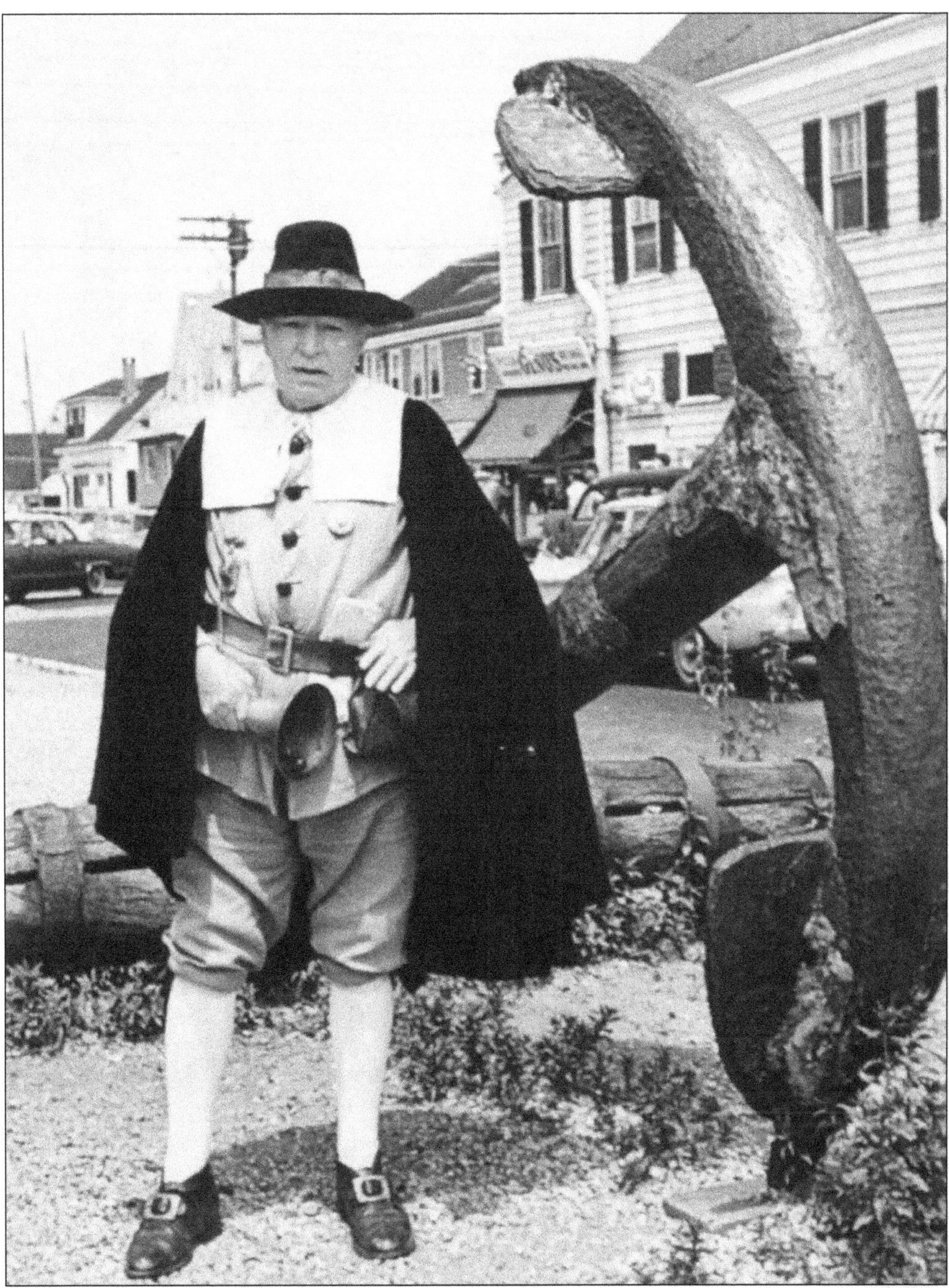

The Town Crier at Lopes Square (c. 1962 postcard published by Cape Cod Photos, Orleans, MA). Arthur Snader, a sculptor, stands by an exceedingly large, wrought-iron anchor found by Captain George Adams and his crew while they were dragging 4 miles off Chatham; they presented it to the town in 1960. The square at the head of MacMillan Wharf was dedicated to the memory of World War I veteran Manuel N. Lopes. The greeting on another postcard featuring Mr. Snader states that Provincetown is "The only town in the U.S. that has carried on the Colonial Tradition of a Town Crier."

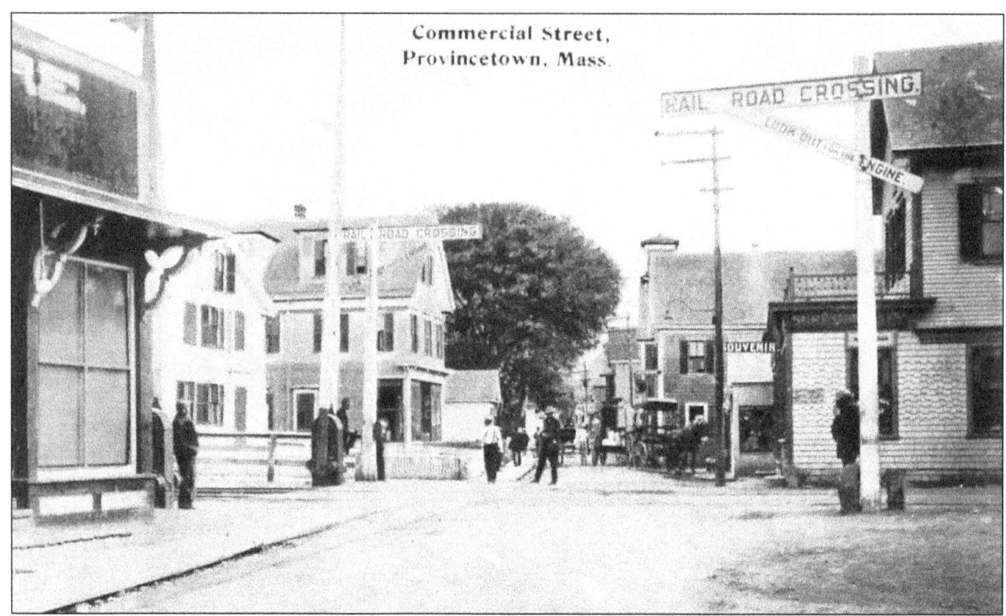

Commercial Street looking east (early-twentieth-century postcard published by UNCO). The large house on the left behind the railroad crossing sign was the home and store of Aylmer F. Small, who sold textiles and gentlemen's apparel. John W. Myrick had a barbershop in the small structure to the right. The old post office was located at the head of Railroad Wharf on the right side of the street behind the other railroad sign. The souvenir trade sign next door may belong to Irving Rosenthal's photography shop; the enterprising photographer advertised his store as being a "Headquarters for Sea Shells and Curiosities of the Deep."

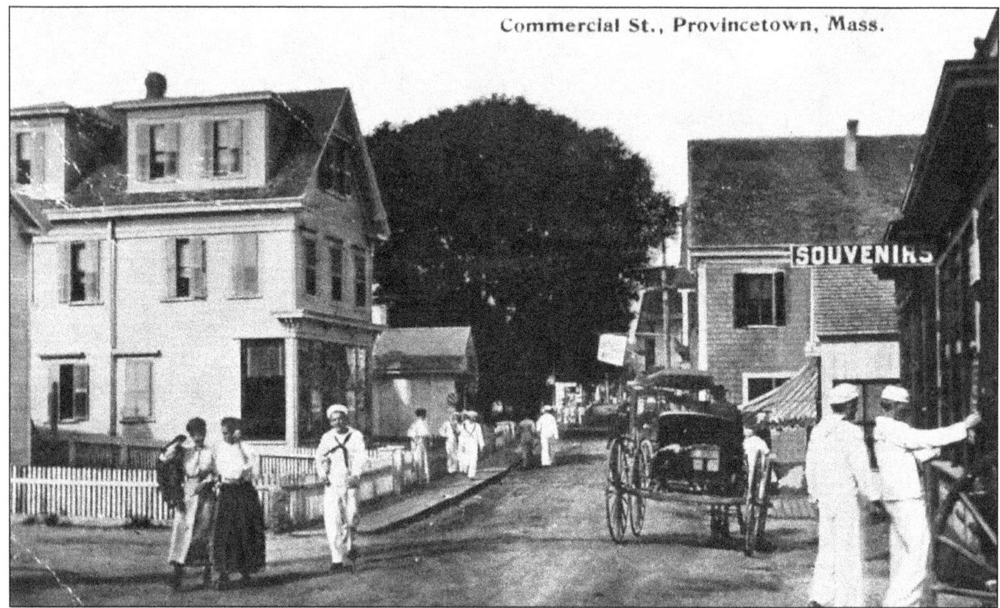

Commercial Street at Railroad Square looking east (c. 1915 postcard published by Tichnor Bros., Inc.). Mary Heaton Vorse has written that in 1941, "The streets were lined with sailors drifting up and down, looking for anything to do, hoping to find a girl, puzzled with Provincetown." A similar predicament awaited sailors who were in town during World War I.

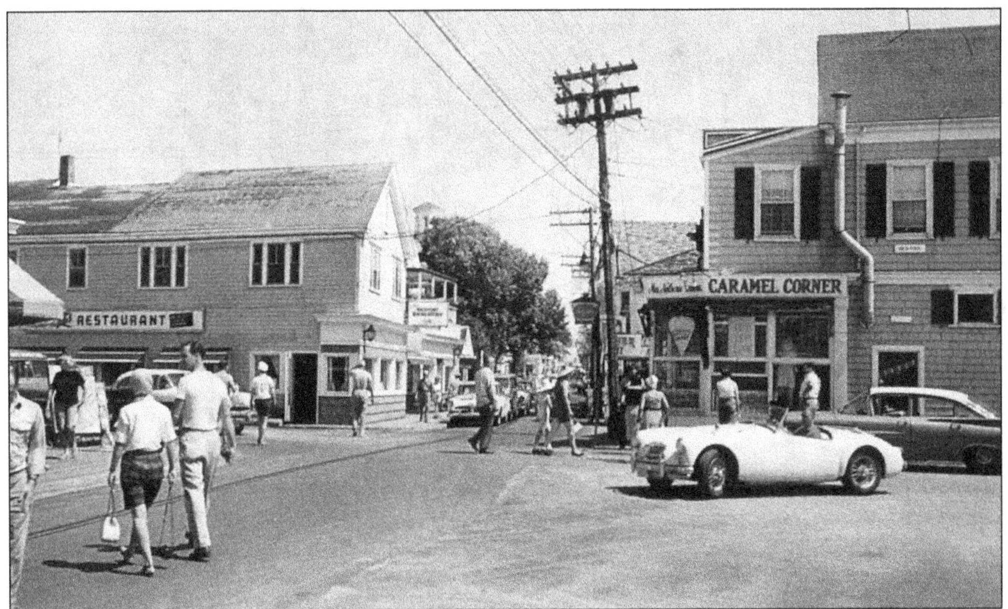

Commercial Street at the junction of Standish Street (c. 1962 postcard published by Mayflower Sales). Tourists jaywalk continuously at this spot of great pedestrian and vehicular activity referred to by locals as "the center of town." The Governor Bradford Restaurant has been located for decades in the *c.* 1870s building on the left corner of the two streets, and the structure on the opposite corner was built *c.* 1858 for the Equitable Life Insurance Company.

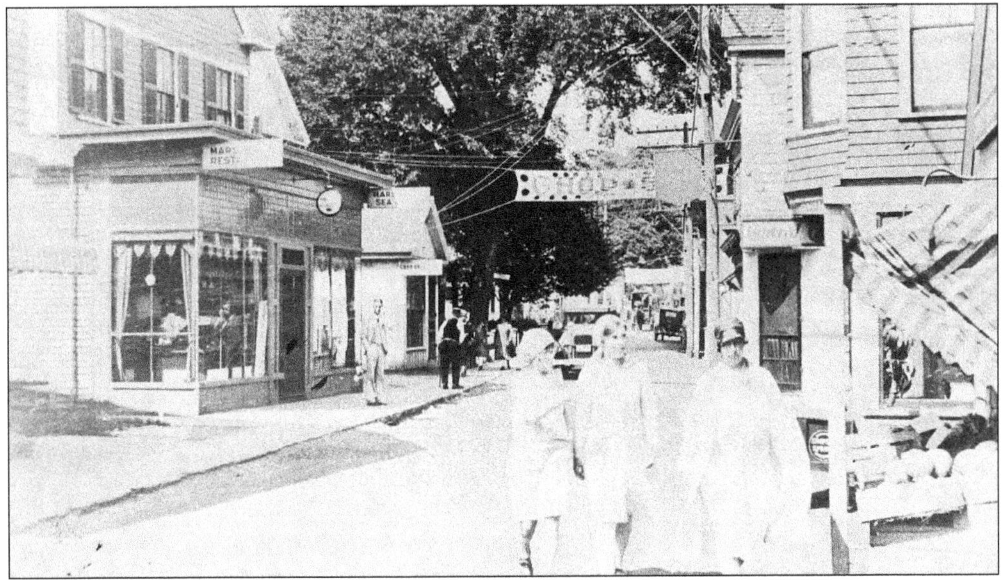

Commercial Street looking east from Standish Street (c. 1925 photograph). A mother and her daughters may have just finished lunch at Marshall's Restaurant and Sea Grill on the left, or at Wong's Chinese & American Restaurant on the second floor of a building at the right. Resident author Mary Heaton Vorse wrote that Provincetown was a "hot" town in the 1920s: several speakeasies were in operation and the Coast Guard tried in vain to stop the daily landing of booze along the outer harbor. Promiscuity followed the arrival of the second generation of laissez faire artists and authors at this time. (Courtesy Seamen's Bank.)

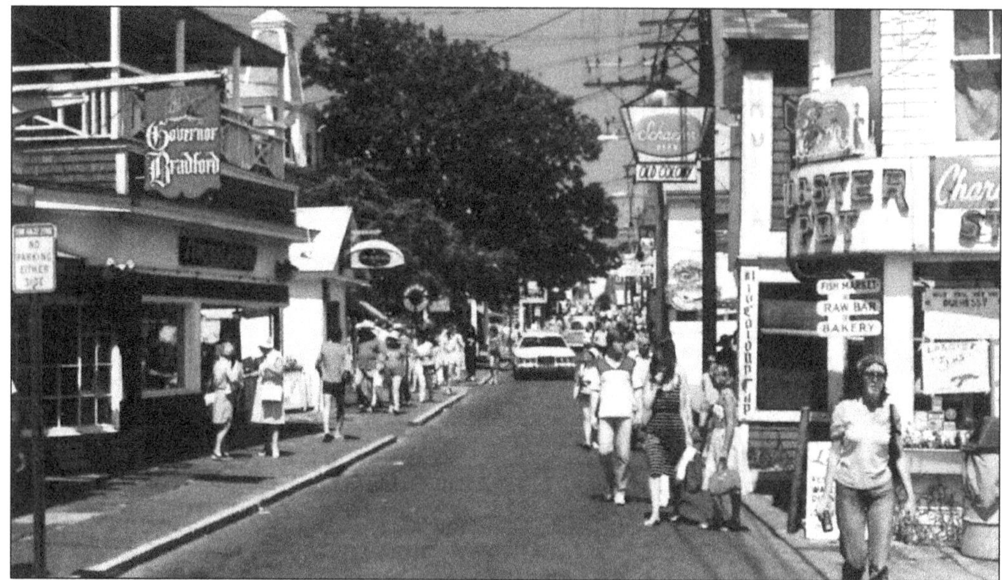

Commercial Street looking east near Standish Street (c. 1970 postcard published by Bromley & Co.). Plate-glass windows in the Governor Bradford Restaurant enabled passersby to view customers in the Compact Room. The remodeled house was at one time Silva's Ice Cream Parlor and then the First National Store. An intriguing handmade sign in the window of the Lobster Pot Restaurant asks, "Have you met the Duchess?" That *c.* 1880 fish house was converted into Mrs. Allen's Tea Room, and then became the elongated restaurant operated by Mr. and Mrs. Ralph Medeiros with the eye-catching bright red neon sign.

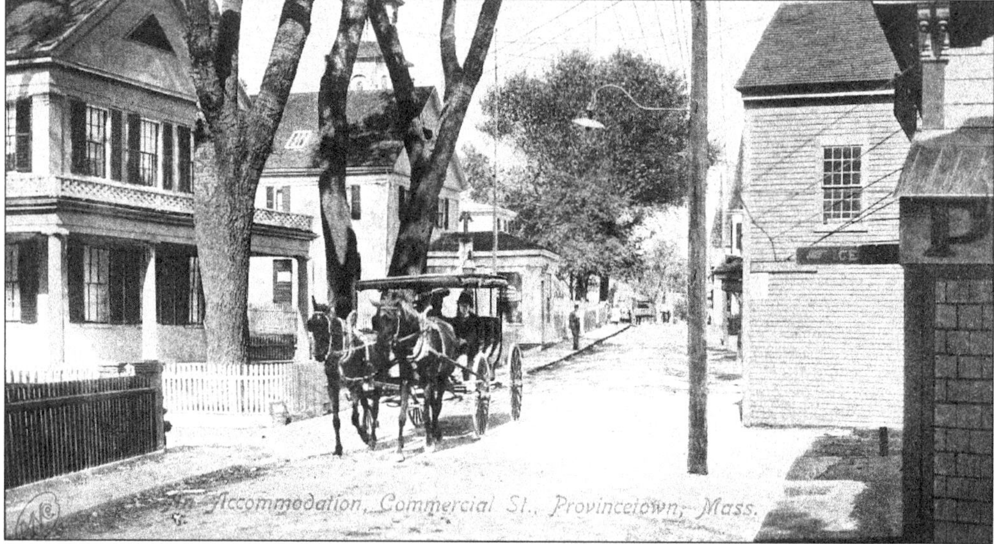

Accommodation near the corner of Freeman Street looking east (c. 1900 postcard published by The Metropolitan News Co.). In 1869 a newspaper reporter wrote, "Commercial Street is so narrow and there is so much teaming upon it that it is quite surprising that no more accidents occur [other than one involving a little boy run over by a dray]. Although an expensive operation the widening of this thoroughfare would be one of the greatest benefits that could be conferred upon the town." The reporter's suggestion was not heeded, but the town did install oil-burning street lamps in 1884.

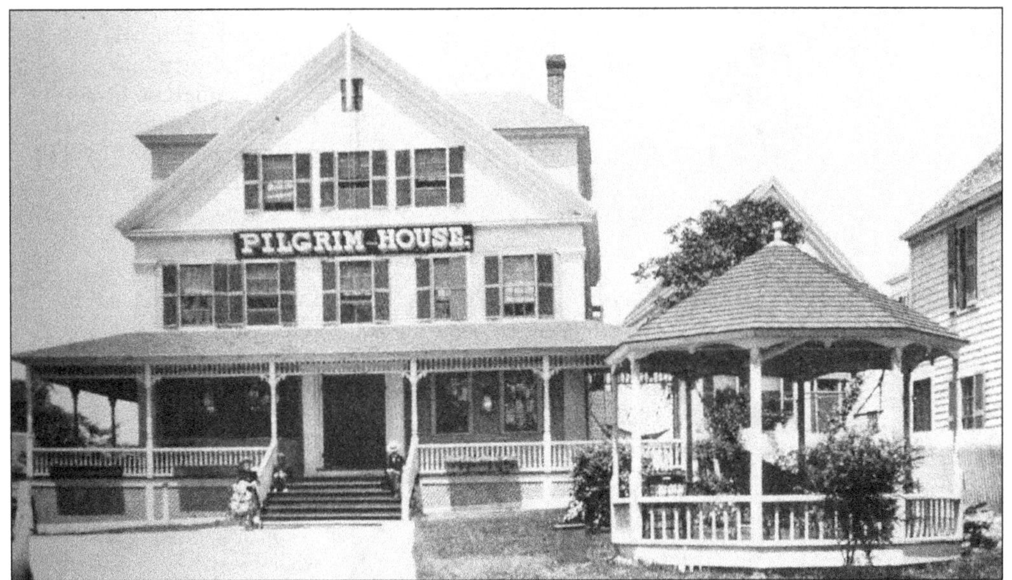

The Pilgrim House, 313 Commercial Street (1898 photograph by The Perry Pictures Co.). A shingled octagonal gazebo on the front lawn and a wraparound porch had settees and chairs for the thirty or so guests of the Pilgrim House. The original structure was completed around 1781, and when this photograph was taken, the oldest hotel in Provincetown (c. 1810) still contained features of the Greek Revival style as well as a large sign. The hotel was initially owned by Benjamin and James Gifford (father and son). Samuel "Uncle Sam" Sands Smith leased the hotel in 1873.

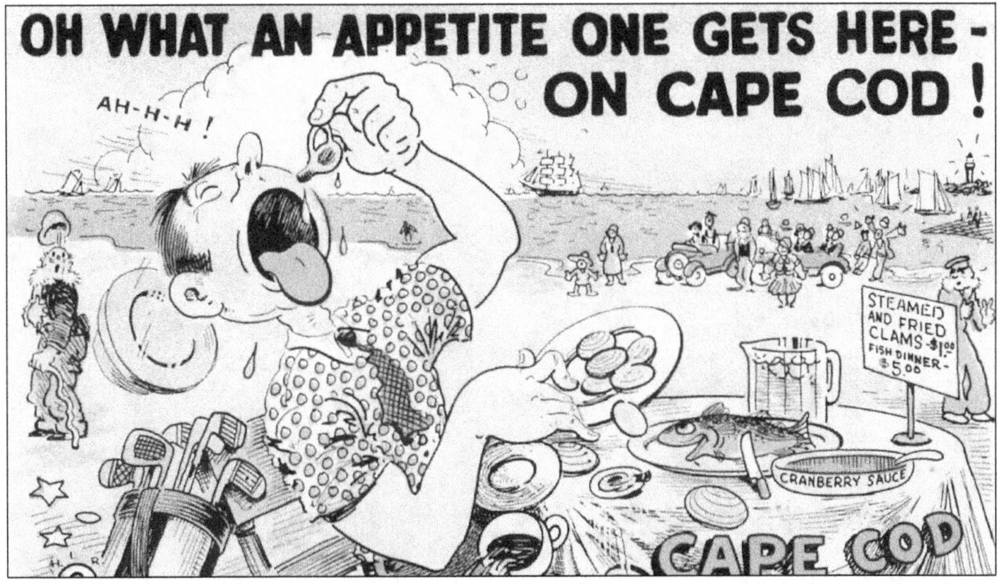

Culinary cartoon (c. 1920s postcard published by Cape Cod Post Card Co.). More relaxed and memorable meals than this one have been enjoyed by townsfolk and tourists at the Bonnie Doone, Ciro & Sal's, The Landmark Inn, The Mews, The Moors, Napi's, Pepe's, Plain and Fancy, Poor Richard's Buttery, The Red Inn, Vorelli's, and Tip for Tops'n on Bradford Street. The latter establishment—where "the Tip of the Cape is Tops in Service"—has been run by three generations of the Carreiro family.

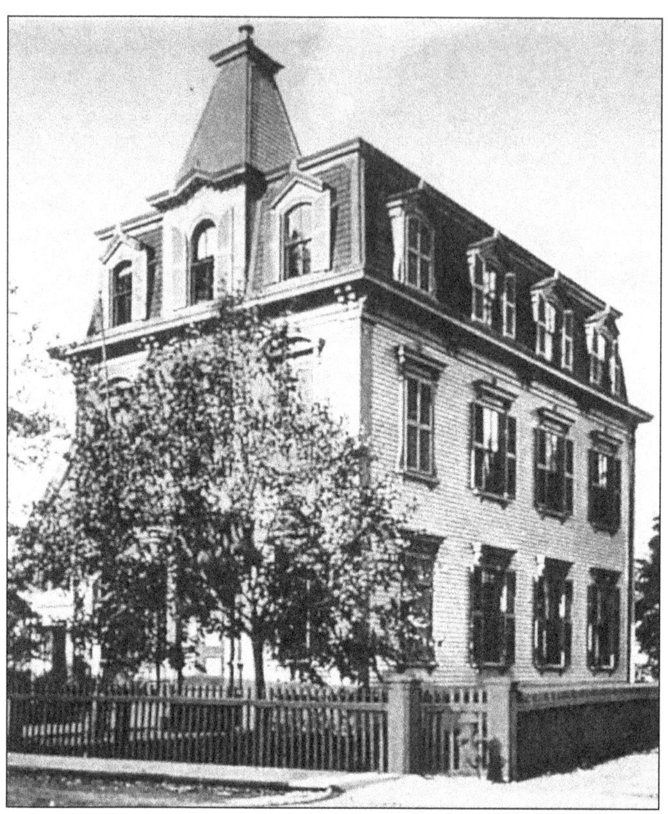

The Provincetown Public Library, 330 Commercial Street (early-twentieth-century postcard published by *The Advocate*). The munificence of Nathan Freeman, "an old and respected citizen of the town," provided inhabitants with a public library for their edification and enjoyment. Similar in appearance and date (1873) to the Lancy House at 230 Commercial Street (1874), the high-Victorian building's interior was set up according to Mr. Freeman's wishes—the library would occupy the first floor, the Young Men's Christian Association the second floor, and the third floor would be rented to defray operating costs. (Courtesy McGhee Collection.)

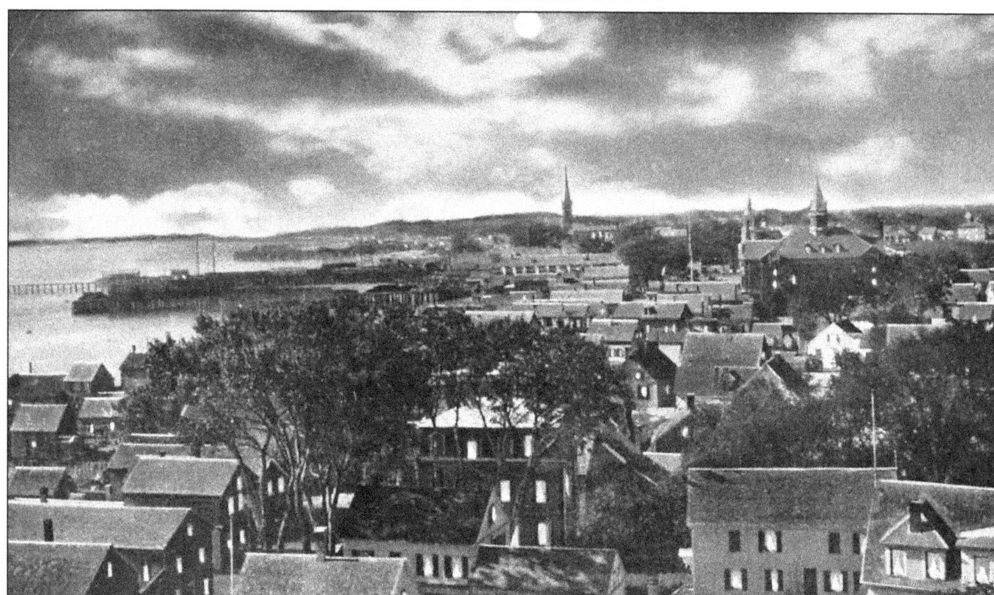

Sunset (c. 1909 postcard published by Robbins Bros., Boston, MA). This artistically enhanced view looking west was probably taken from the tower of the Center M.E. Church. In the mid-nineteenth century, when the bay was filled with many fishing vessels, the editor of *The Provincetown Advocate* wrote, "The harbor looked splendid Sunday night, so thickly studded with vessels' lights. No city is as brilliant at night as this display."

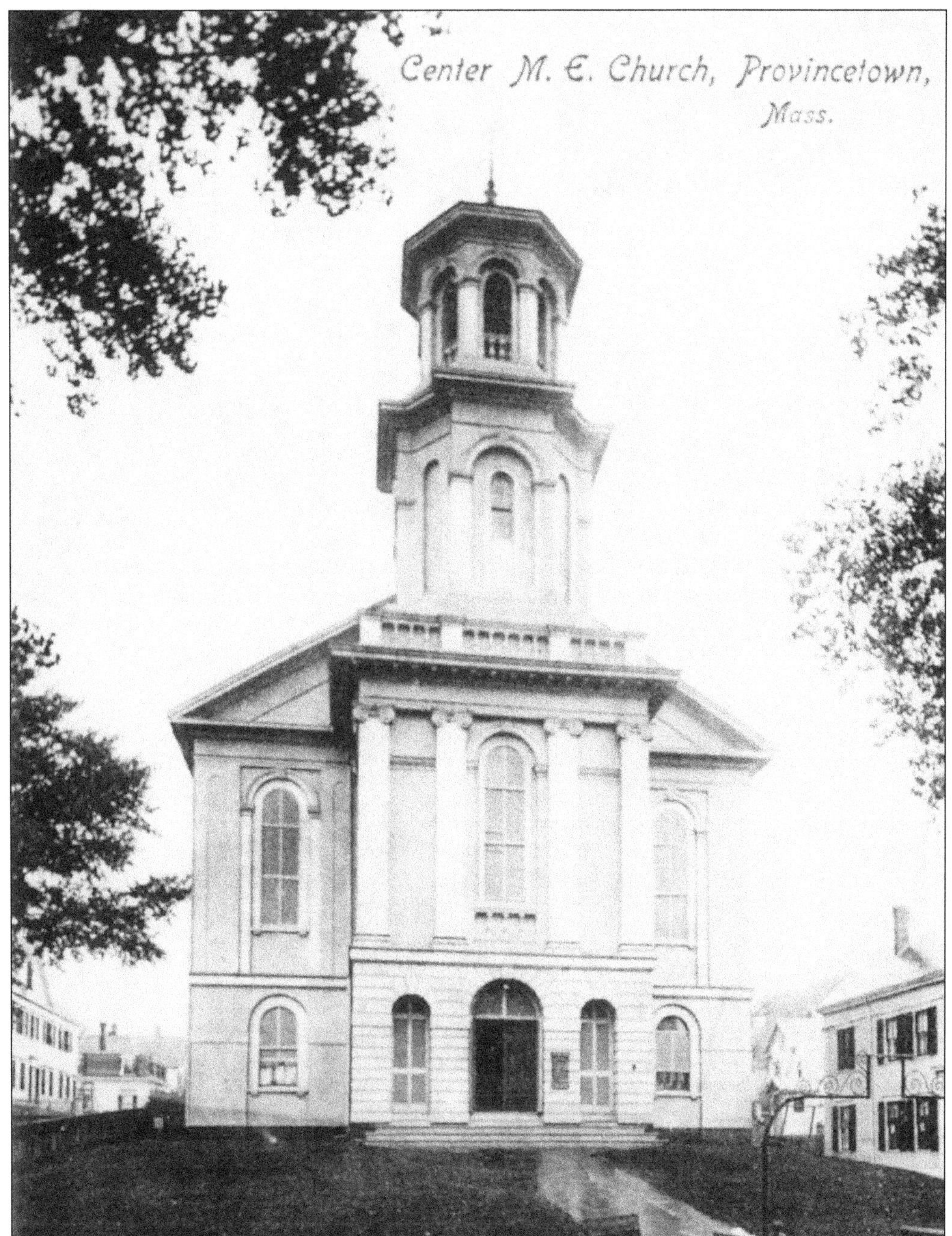

Center M.E. Church, 356 Commercial Street (early-twentieth-century postcard published by *The Advocate*). A Victorian cast-iron fence and wrought-iron entrance gate originally graced the fourth Methodist church in town. Arches dominate the facade of the former Methodist Episcopal church, which was built in 1860 for $22,000. The two-tiered octagonal tower had a spire of 162 feet, but it was partially removed and renovated after the disastrous Portland Gale of 1898. In 1958, the deconsecrated church became a fine arts museum established by millionaire Walter Chrysler Jr. The town purchased the building in 1975, and it is now known as the Provincetown Heritage Museum.

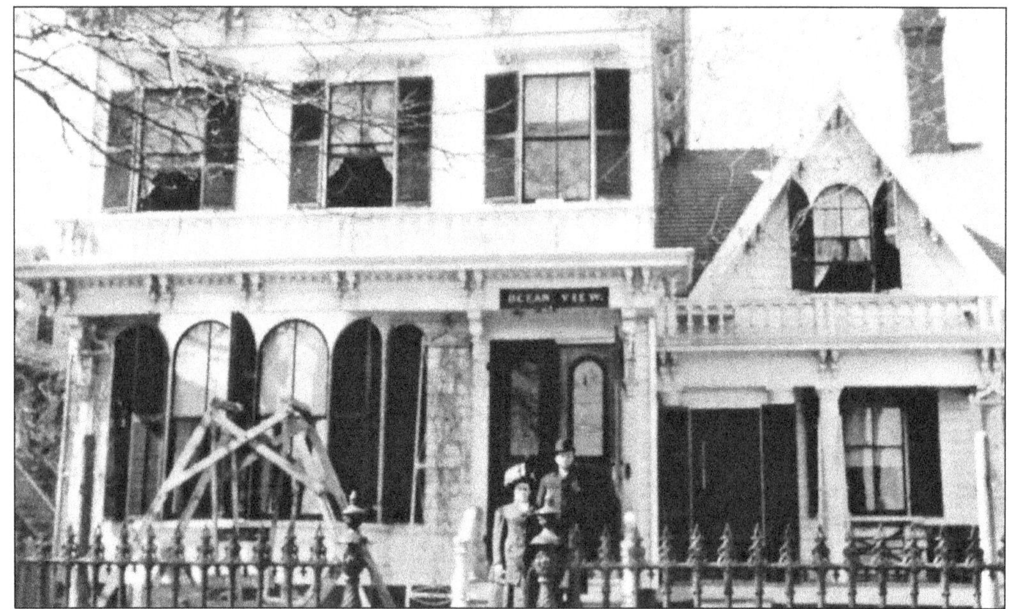

The Ocean View Guest House, 378 Commercial Street (c. 1930s photograph). The Italianate bracketed style was in vogue in 1850 when this house was built for Stephen Cook, the ship owner who became president of the Seamen's Savings Bank in 1876. Ironically, Cook's home became the Ocean View Guest House in the late 1920s (as president of the bank Cook encouraged the development of Provincetown as a summer resort, due to the dwindling fishing industry). The popular guest house was later renamed Somerset House for the British frigate *Somerset* that sank off the coast of Provincetown in 1778. (Courtesy Ken Conrad.)

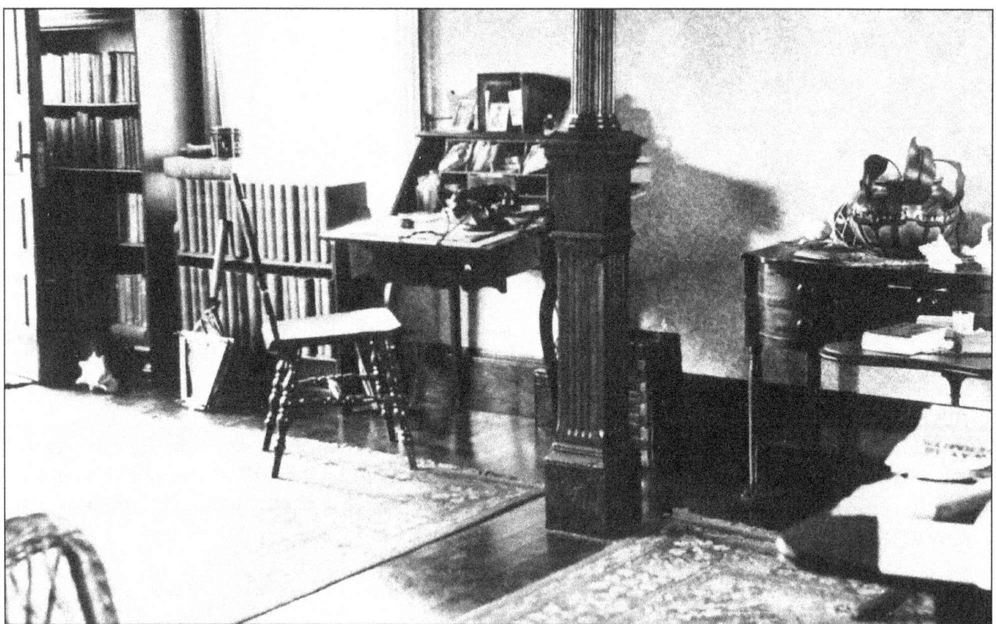

The parlor in the Ocean View Guest House, 378 Commercial Street (c. 1935 photograph). The somewhat cluttered room gave the guest house a homey appearance. (Courtesy Conrad Collection.)

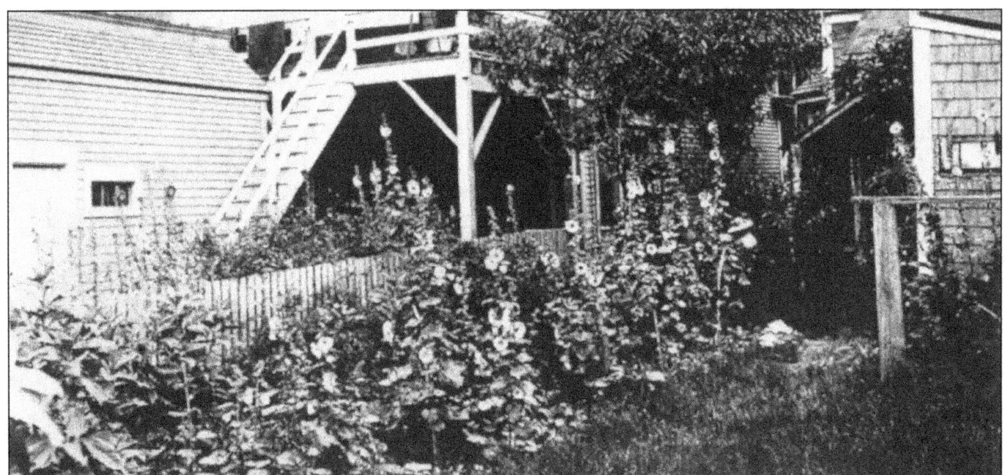

A Provincetown Back Yard (c. 1920 photograph). Clergyman Wallace Nutting (1861–1941) of Framingham, MA, who was also an author, photographer, and Colonial Revival furniture manufacturer, included this image of Provincetown in the "Cape Cod" section of his pictorial history *Massachusetts Beautiful*, published in 1923.

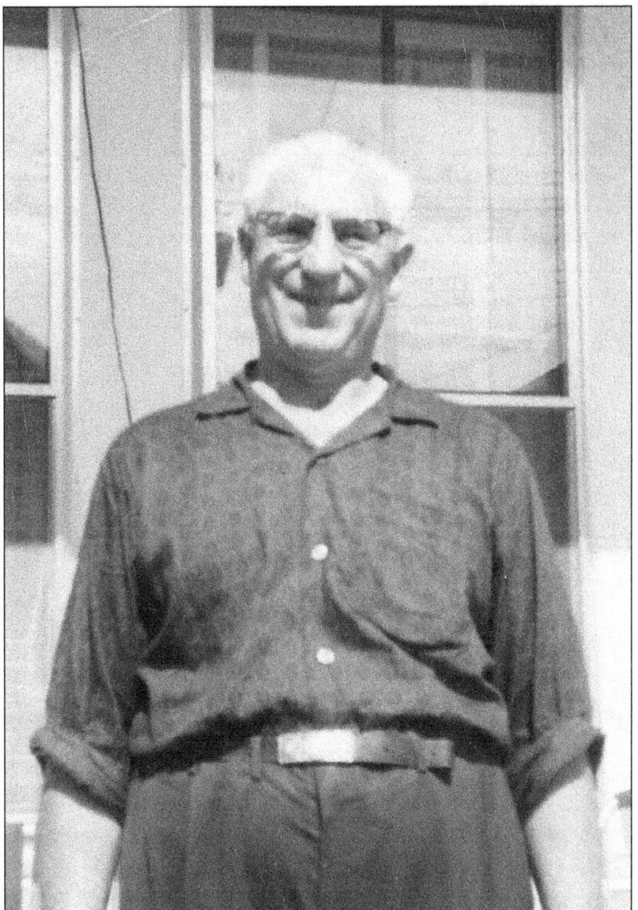

Paulino Urtiaga, proprietorof Casa Gernika, 378 Commercial Street (1962 photograph). A native of the Basque provinces in northern Spain, Mr. Urtiaga was a bartender in New York City when he met his wife Florence. The couple moved to Provincetown in the early 1940s and he and a friend acquired the Ocean View Guest House, which he then renamed Casa Gernika; it was known as a no-frills rooming house without any amenities. (Courtesy Conrad Collection.)

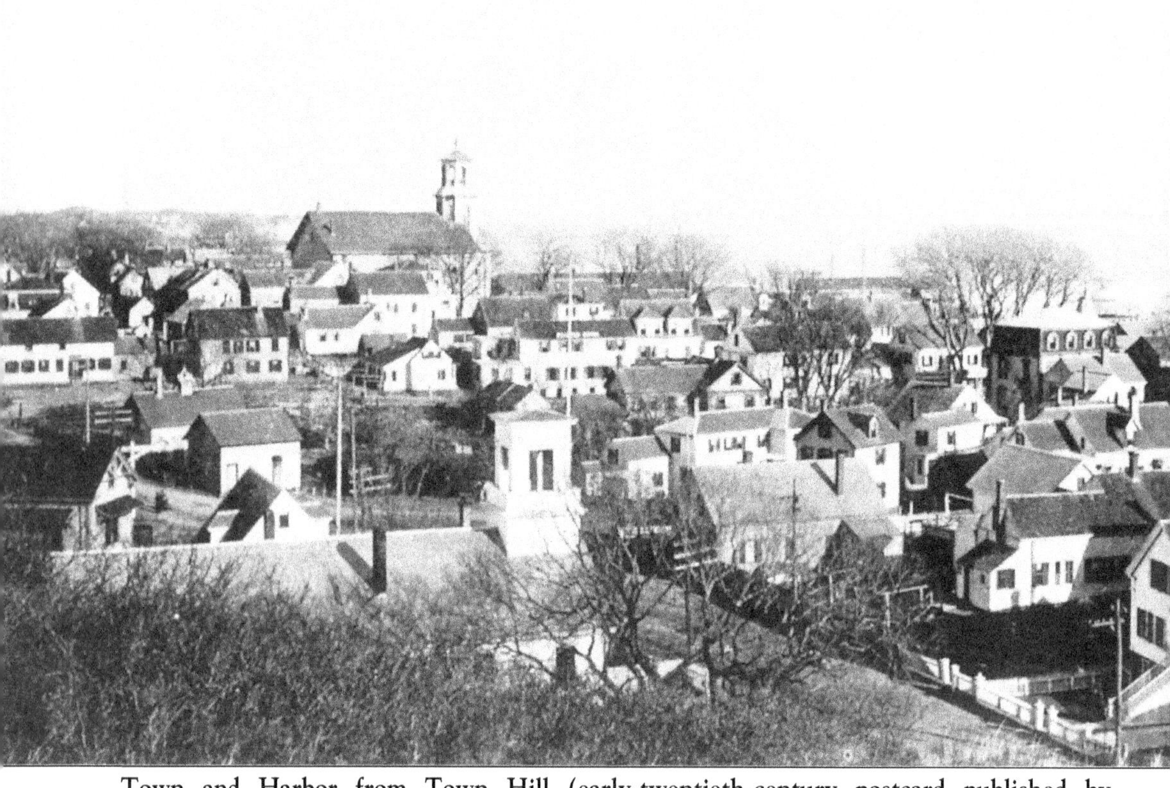

Town and Harbor from Town Hill (early-twentieth-century postcard published by I.L. Rosenthal, Germany). This black-and-white photocard presents a panoramic view of the town looking toward the East End. Modest houses, almost all with clapboard siding and painted white, nestle together with prominent public buildings along the town's two major

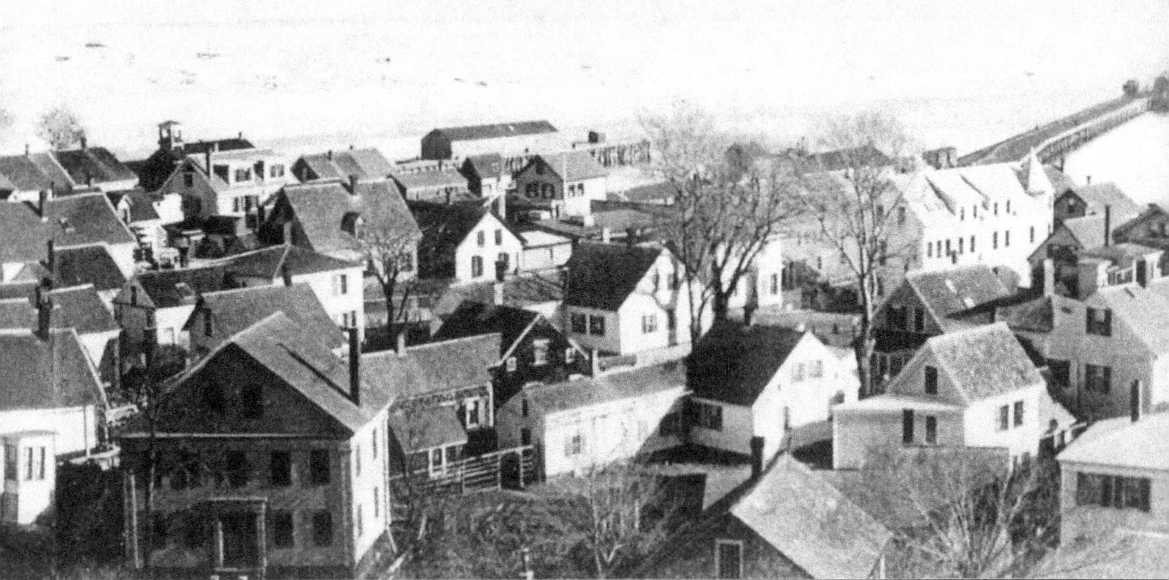

thoroughfares. In the second volume of *The History of Cape Cod* (1862), Frederick Freeman wrote, "The dwelling-houses are generally of neat and comfortable aspect; some are even more than this." Of the "four edifices for public worship," the historian stated that they "adorn the town, and unfold their doors for spiritual edifying."

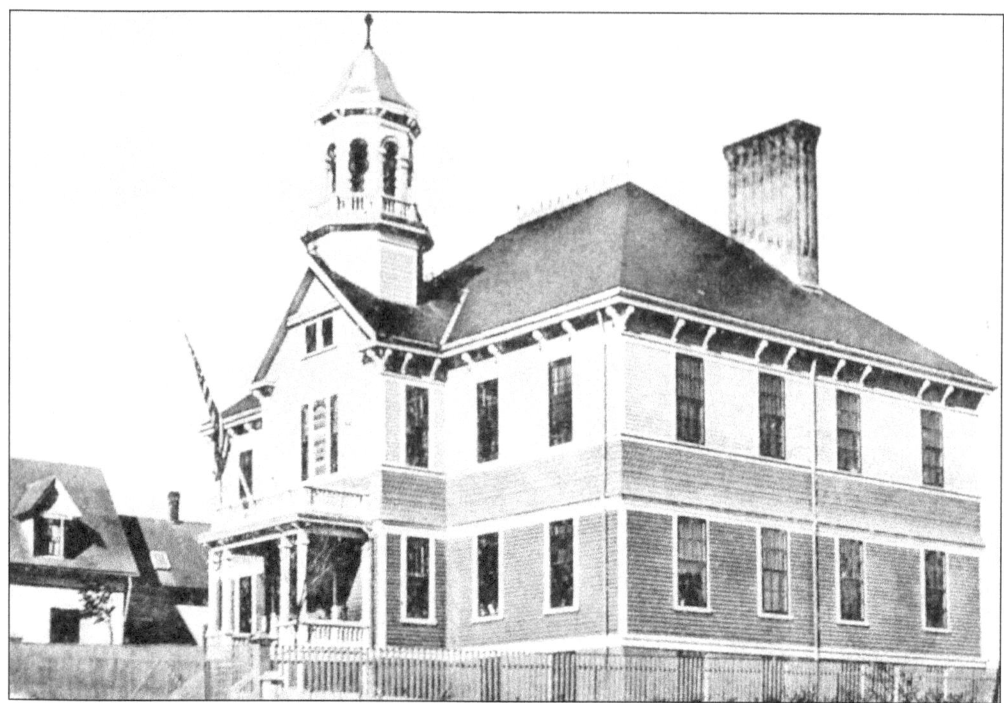

Governor Bradford School House, 44 Bradford Street (c. 1895 postcard published by *The Advocate*). Eighteenth-century architectural features such as a hipped roof, a projecting two-story portico with paired columns supporting a balustrade, and an octagonal, domed cupola were combined with Italianate brackets, imbrication, and a Queen Anne-style brick chimney to give the wood-framed schoolhouse a visually rich appearance. Erected in 1892 at a cost of about $17,000, it was destroyed by fire less than fifty years later in 1935. The wide entrance hall led from the vestibule through the center of the building to a larger hall at the rear. (Courtesy Seamen's Bank.)

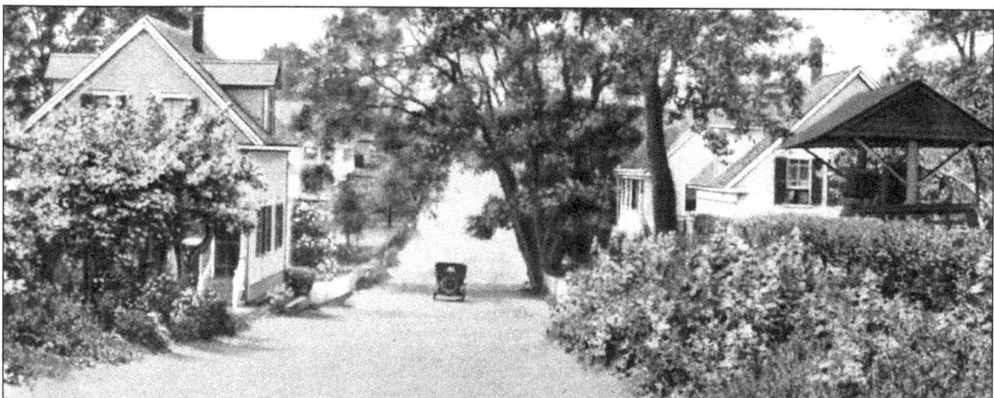

Bradford Street looking west from the corner of Court Street (early-twentieth-century postcard published by C.T. American Art Colored, Chicago). Remaining more residential than Commercial Street, Bradford Street was named for William Bradford, patriarchal leader and many-times governor of the Pilgrim Colony. Also called Parallel and Back Street, it was laid out c. 1873 at a cost of $29,000; three of the seven hills in town had to be lowered and a meadow and salt creek had to be filled before the road could be laid. Forty-three perpendicular streets, lanes, and courts are between the two main thoroughfares in the three areas of town.

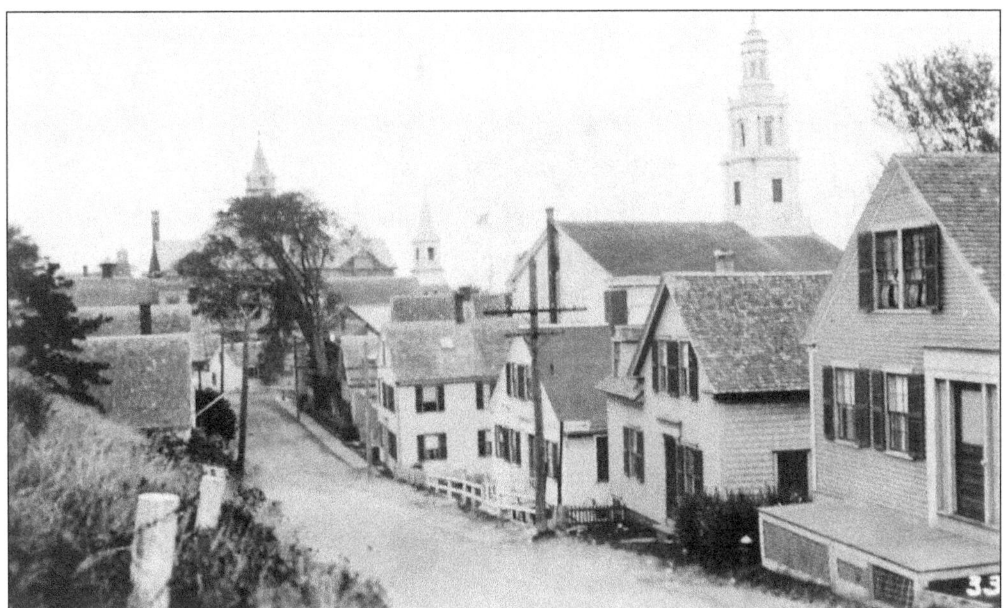

Bradford Street looking east (early-twentieth-century photocard; publisher unknown). Gable-end-to-the-street houses, and others with their main entrance on the side, were constructed on Bradford Street as soon as it was surfaced and opened to traffic. The street sign behind the utility pole at the right points to the Atlantic House, located on Masonic Place down the convenient alleyway steps. Some businesses on Bradford Street in the late 1930s included Connell's Garage, Fisherman's Market, Tony Roderick's taxi service, and the Tennis Club of Provincetown.

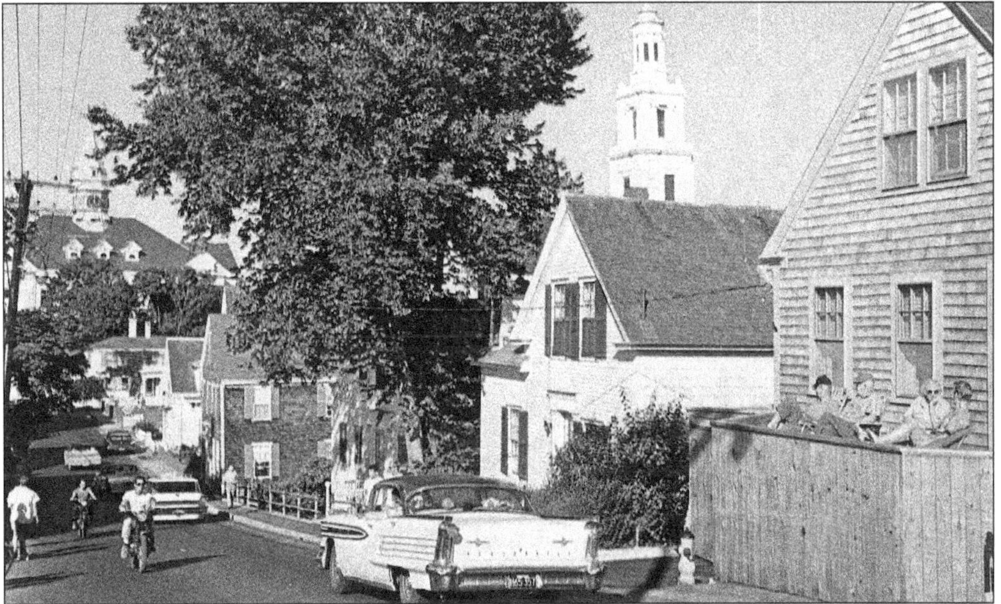

Bradford Street looking east (c. 1960 postcard published by Mayflower Sales Co.). A 1958 two-door Oldsmobile sedan with modified rear fins heads toward the town hall past two middle-aged couples relaxing on a small front porch. The town's centrally located municipal parking lot, the Grace Hall Lot, is located at the crest of the hill opposite the "Olds."

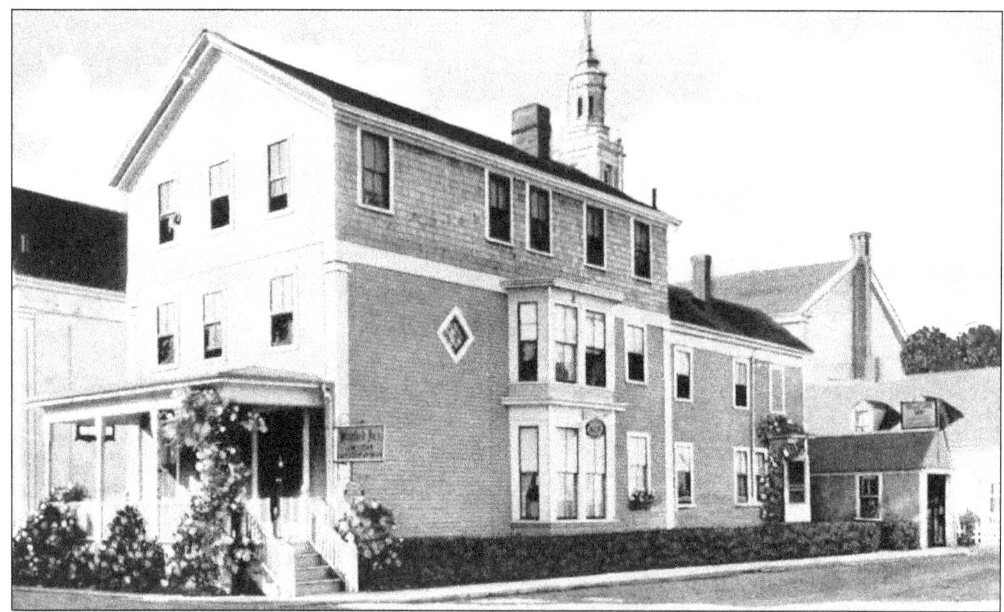

Bradford Inn, corner of Bradford and Gosnold Streets (c. 1920s postcard published by the Cape Cod Post Card Co.). Climbing roses and hydrangeas welcomed guests to this inn, as did owners Manuel "Pat" Patrick and his wife, Hilda Winslow Patrick, during the summer months. The shingled third floor, lacking its corner boards, was an obvious renovation to the original clapboard-sided house. The spire and rear chimney of the Universalist church dominate the background.

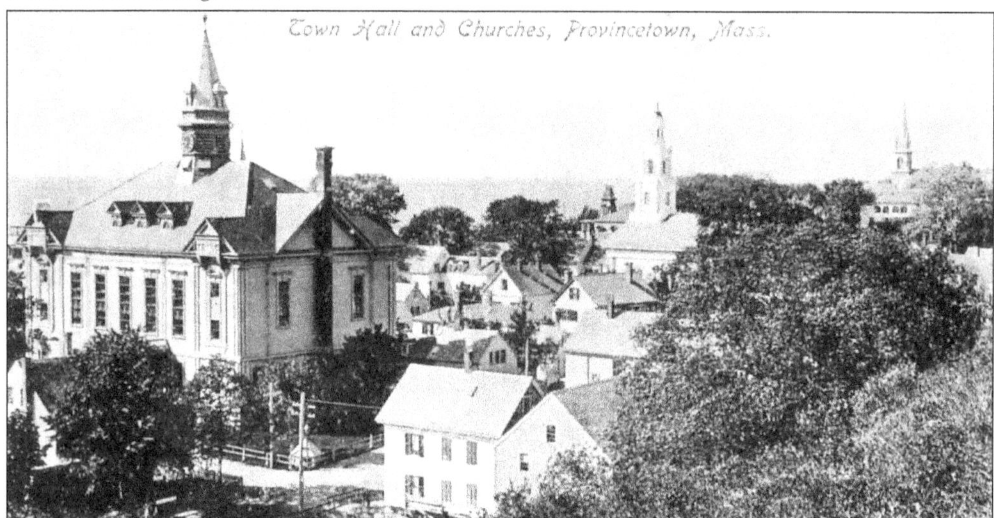

Town Hall and Churches (c. 1915 postcard published by *The Advocate*). The high-Victorian copper-sheathed clock tower of the town hall is one of three distinctive architectural landmarks in this view of the intersection of Bradford and Ryder Streets from High Pole Hill. During the early twentieth century weekly dances were held in the basement of the town hall where locals and tourists danced with each other; older Portuguese residents enjoyed dancing their native Camarritas. By 1896 there were about two thousand Portuguese in town, most involved in the fishing industry; they came mainly from the Azores, with an influx noted between 1911 and 1920. Earlier, Bravas came from the Cape Verde Islands.

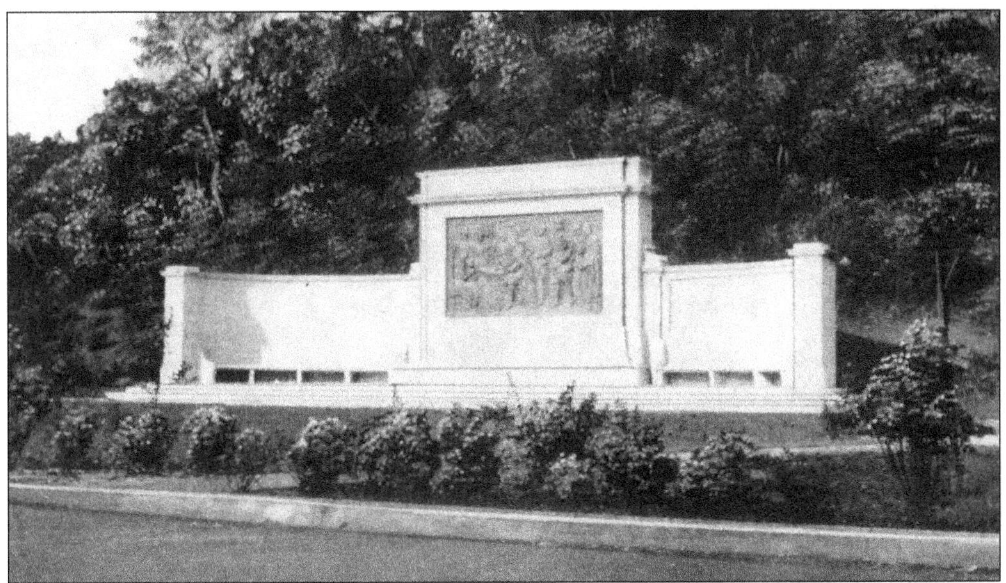

Memorial bas-relief of "Signing the Compact" (c. 1921 postcard published by H.A. Dickerman & Son). The park at the base of Monument Hill (High Pole Hill) on Bradford Street, known as the Town Green, was created in 1920—the same year Ryder Street was widened. The Pilgrim Tercentenary Commission of Provincetown had the 70-by-20-foot granite memorial with the 16-by-9-foot bronze bas-relief tablet erected at a cost of $40,000. The postcard's caption noted that "The structure is of finished Rockport granite, and of the finest workmanship, and is a worthy tribute to the memory of the founders of our country, to whose memory it is erected."

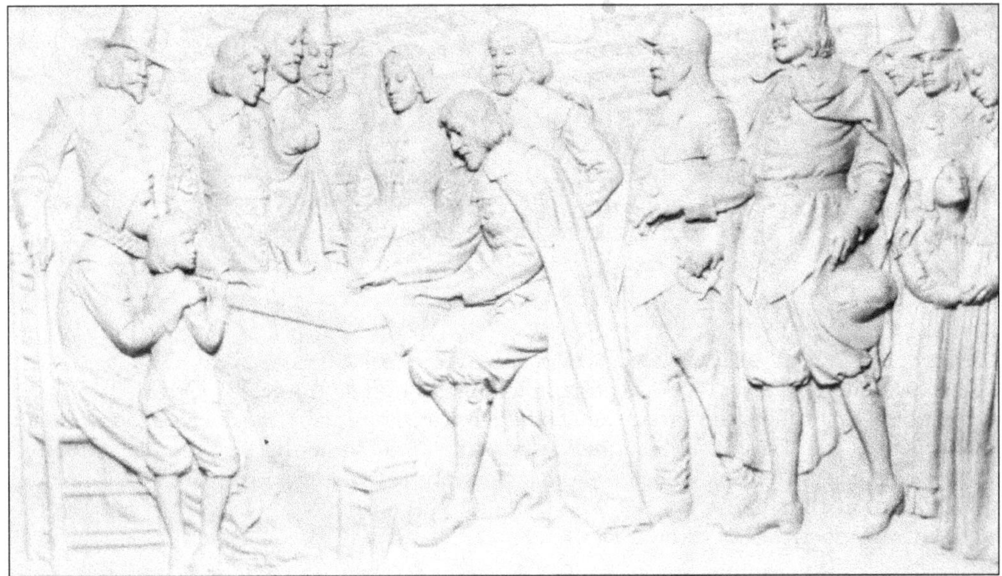

The memorial bas-relief of "Signing the Compact" (c. 1921 photocard; publisher unknown). Boston artist Cyrus E. Dallin (1861-1944) designed the bas-relief of the momentous occasion on board the *Mayflower* in Provincetown Harbor when the unique document was signed by the Pilgrim Fathers. The bronze tablet, which has become a visual icon in early American history, was cast by the Gorham Corporation of Providence, RI.

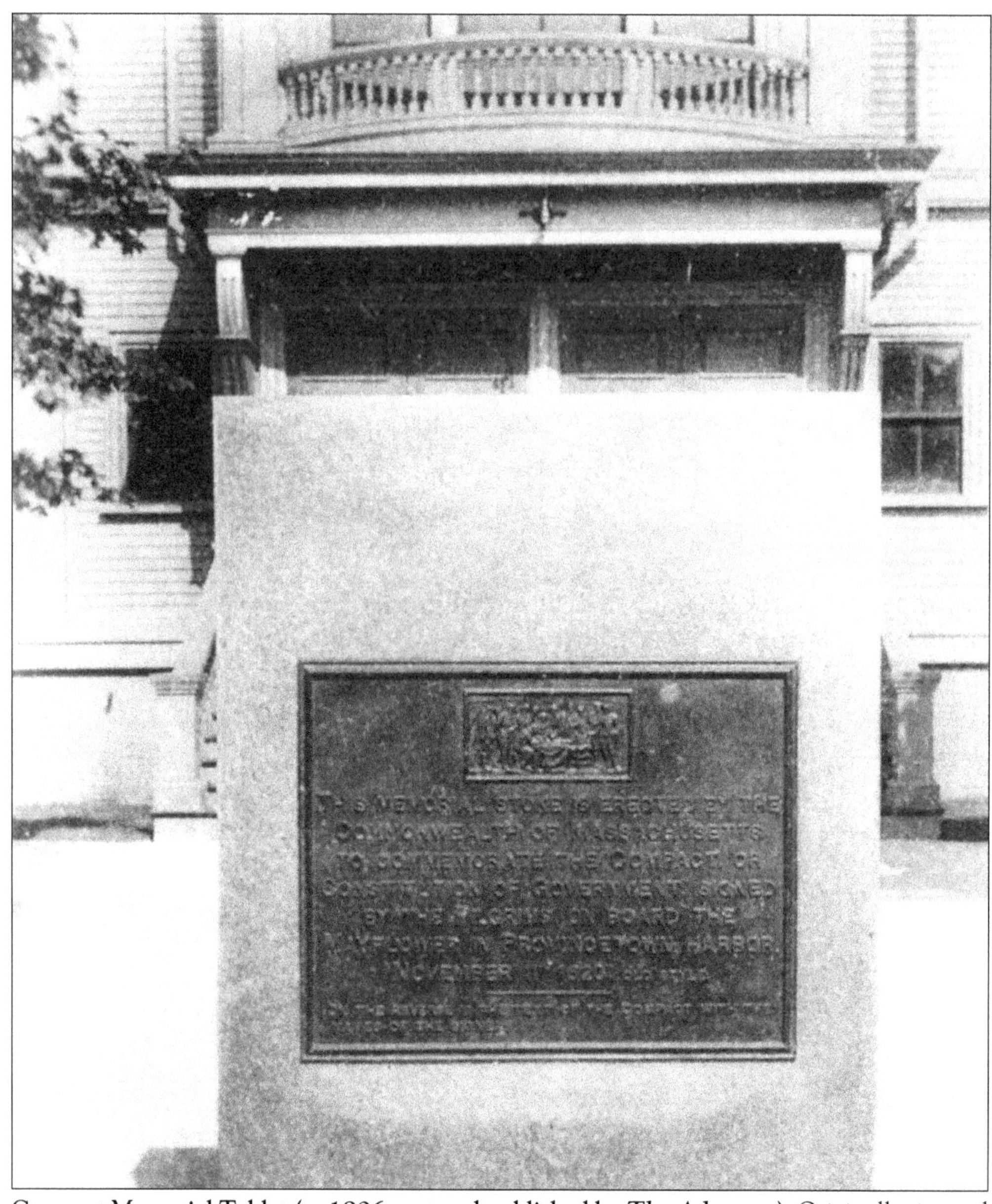

Compact Memorial Tablet (c. 1906 postcard published by *The Advocate*). Originally situated in front of the town hall, this bronze tablet affixed to a granite slab was relocated to its present location, the Town Green, around 1920. A tall, slate, tombstone-shaped memorial is located on the right side of the park dedicated "in memory of the five *Mayflower* passengers who died at sea and while the ship lay in Cape Cod Harbor." This memorial was erected in 1920 by the Massachusetts Society of Mayflower Descendents.

RIGHT: Compact Memorial Tablet (c. 1906 postcard published by *The Advocate*). A list of the forty-one, exclusively male signers of the Mayflower Compact appears under the text of the document. The names of the first six Pilgrims and that of Captain Miles Standish are familiar to many American schoolchildren.

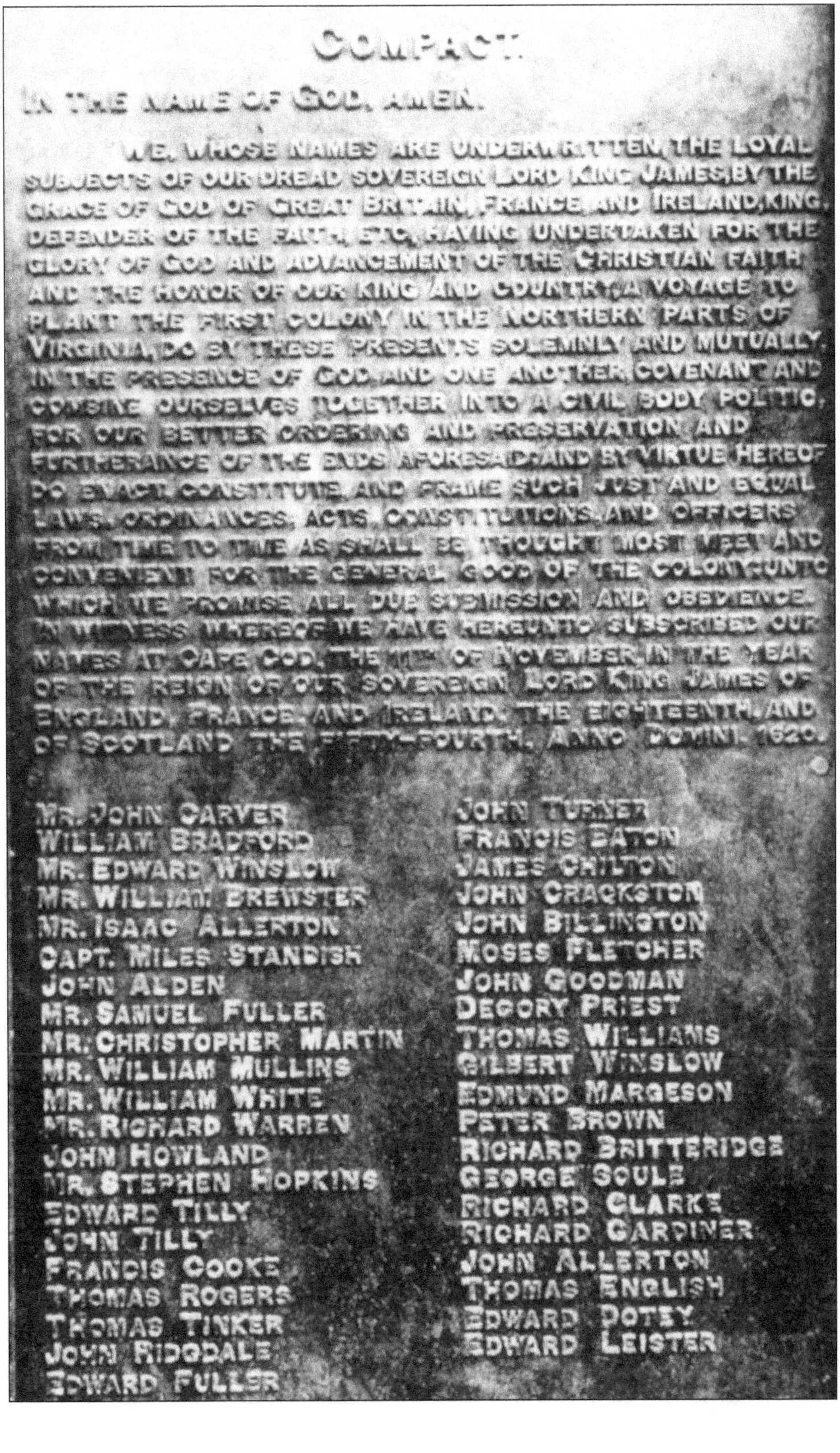

COMPACT

IN THE NAME OF GOD, AMEN.

WE, WHOSE NAMES ARE UNDERWRITTEN, THE LOYAL SUBJECTS OF OUR DREAD SOVEREIGN LORD KING JAMES, BY THE GRACE OF GOD OF GREAT BRITAIN, FRANCE, AND IRELAND, KING, DEFENDER OF THE FAITH, ETC, HAVING UNDERTAKEN FOR THE GLORY OF GOD AND ADVANCEMENT OF THE CHRISTIAN FAITH AND THE HONOR OF OUR KING AND COUNTRY, A VOYAGE TO PLANT THE FIRST COLONY IN THE NORTHERN PARTS OF VIRGINIA, DO BY THESE PRESENTS SOLEMNLY AND MUTUALLY, IN THE PRESENCE OF GOD AND ONE ANOTHER, COVENANT AND COMBINE OURSELVES TOGETHER INTO A CIVIL BODY POLITIC, FOR OUR BETTER ORDERING AND PRESERVATION AND FURTHERANCE OF THE ENDS AFORESAID; AND BY VIRTUE HEREOF DO ENACT, CONSTITUTE, AND FRAME SUCH JUST AND EQUAL LAWS, ORDINANCES, ACTS, CONSTITUTIONS, AND OFFICERS FROM TIME TO TIME AS SHALL BE THOUGHT MOST MEET AND CONVENIENT FOR THE GENERAL GOOD OF THE COLONY; UNTO WHICH WE PROMISE ALL DUE SUBMISSION AND OBEDIENCE. IN WITNESS WHEREOF WE HAVE HEREUNTO SUBSCRIBED OUR NAMES AT CAPE COD, THE 11TH OF NOVEMBER, IN THE YEAR OF THE REIGN OF OUR SOVEREIGN LORD KING JAMES OF ENGLAND, FRANCE, AND IRELAND, THE EIGHTEENTH, AND OF SCOTLAND THE FIFTY-FOURTH, ANNO DOMINI 1620.

MR. JOHN CARVER
WILLIAM BRADFORD
MR. EDWARD WINSLOW
MR. WILLIAM BREWSTER
MR. ISAAC ALLERTON
CAPT. MILES STANDISH
JOHN ALDEN
MR. SAMUEL FULLER
MR. CHRISTOPHER MARTIN
MR. WILLIAM MULLINS
MR. WILLIAM WHITE
MR. RICHARD WARREN
JOHN HOWLAND
MR. STEPHEN HOPKINS
EDWARD TILLY
JOHN TILLY
FRANCIS COOKE
THOMAS ROGERS
THOMAS TINKER
JOHN RIDGDALE
EDWARD FULLER

JOHN TURNER
FRANCIS EATON
JAMES CHILTON
JOHN CRACKSTON
JOHN BILLINGTON
MOSES FLETCHER
JOHN GOODMAN
DEGORY PRIEST
THOMAS WILLIAMS
GILBERT WINSLOW
EDMUND MARGESON
PETER BROWN
RICHARD BRITTERIDGE
GEORGE SOULE
RICHARD CLARKE
RICHARD GARDINER
JOHN ALLERTON
THOMAS ENGLISH
EDWARD DOTEY
EDWARD LEISTER

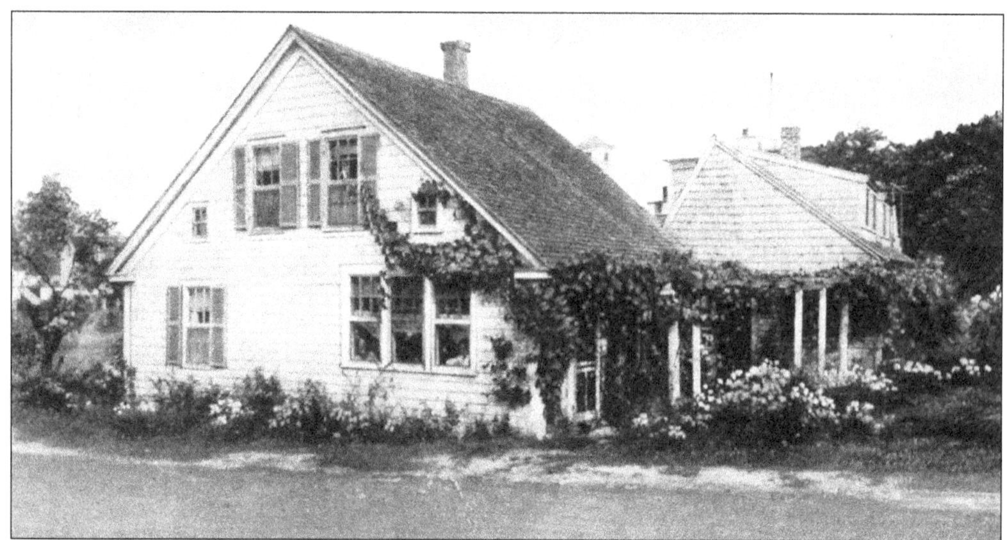

Cesco's Italian Restaurant, 211 Bradford Street (c. 1930 postcard published by H.A. Dickerman & Son). Diners peer from the three-part window of the picturesque restaurant with its arbored walkway located near the corner of Howland Street. Francesco "Chesco" Ronga's "gay, volatile, and changeable" Neapolitan temperament was combined with a tendency to sing robust Italian operatic arias, but what made the "Cape Spaghetti Expert" famous were the herbs and sixteen other ingredients he flavored his pasta dishes with between 1916 and 1934.

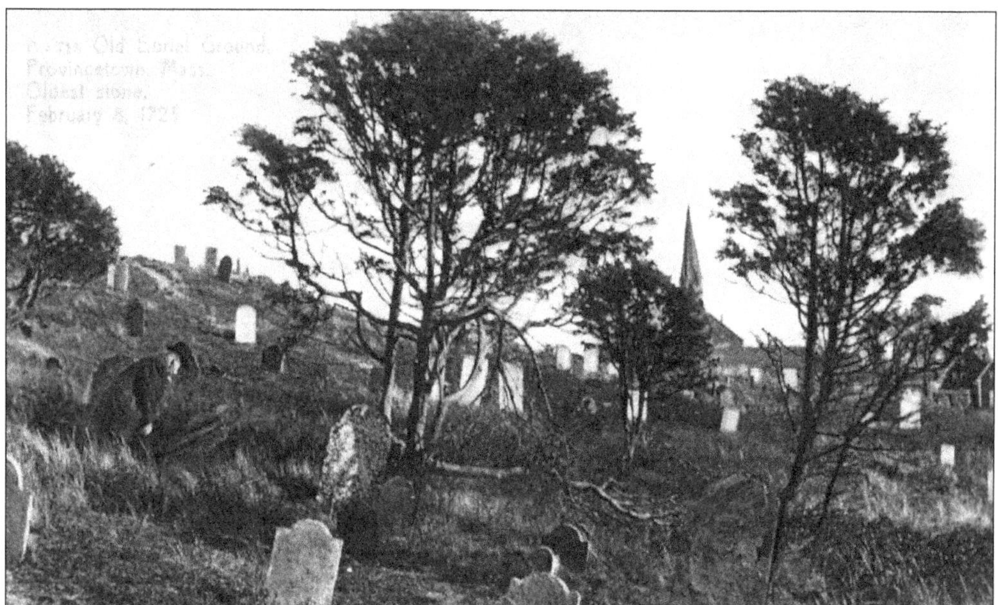

Old Burial Ground (c. 1900 postcard published by *The Advocate*). An elderly gentleman is shown inspecting the ancient gravestones in the town's oldest cemetery, located on the slope of a hill between Winthrop and Court Streets; the Centenary M.E. Church on the corner of Winthrop Street can be seen in the background. Near the entrance to the cemetery is the oldest, lichen-covered stone, which commemorates Desire Cowing, who departed this life in 1723–24. The first jail in Provincetown, "reflecting no discredit on the highly moral community," was built in 1845 on nearby Winthrop Place.

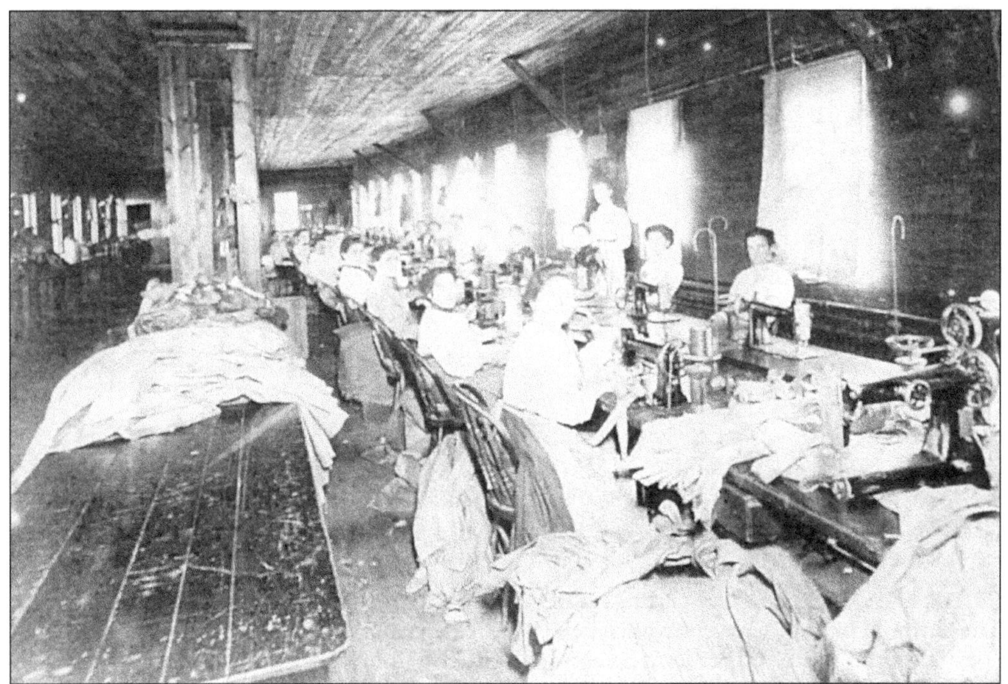

The Puritan Shirt Factory, opposite 21 Court Street (1890 photograph). This atypical town business provided employment for young single women and the wives of fishermen. The seamstresses pause in the making of the heavy men's shirts for their photograph to be taken in front of the draped, but sun-filled, windows. Arnold Dwyer once owned the land on which the wooden factory was situated. (Private Collection.)

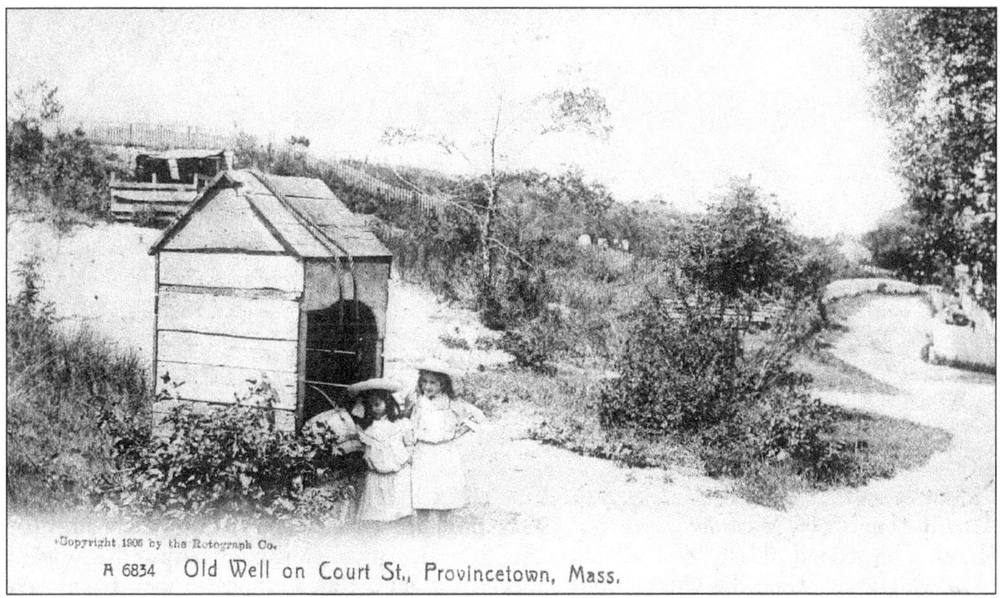

Old Well on Court Street (1905 postcard published by the Rotograph Co., New York). Edwardian-dressed sisters pause for a drink of cool water from the wellhead on rural Court Street. Town ponds at that time included Great Pond, Shank Painter Pond, Pasture Pond, Clapps Pond, Grassy Pond, and Duck Pond.

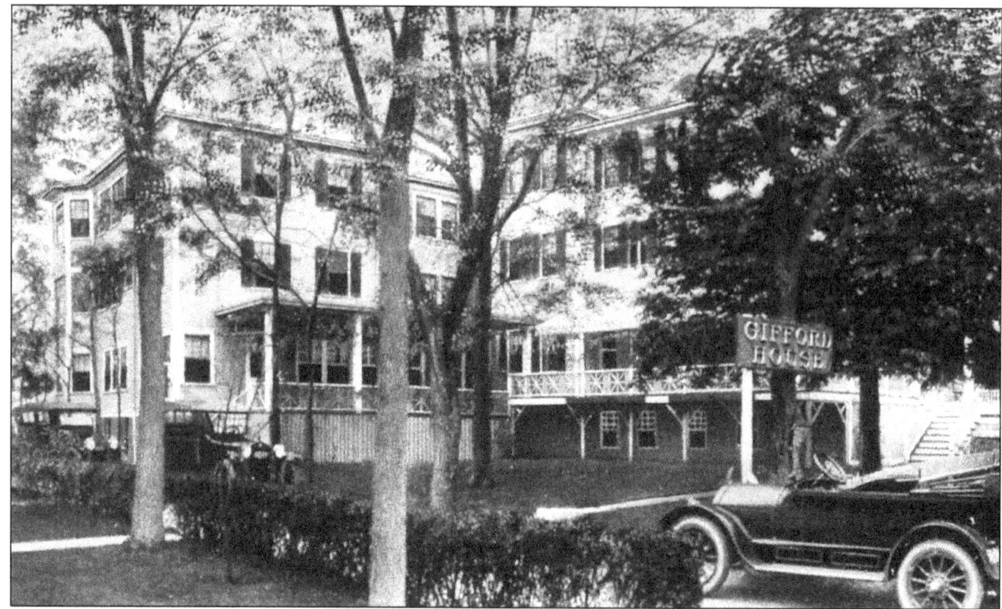

The Gifford House, 9 Carver Street (c. 1919 postcard published by H.A. Dickerman & Son). Located at the corner of Bradford Street, the "only true hotel in Provincetown" was built in 1858. It was owned and operated by Moses Gifford, an early president of the First National Bank, and was known as Gifford's Summer Hotel in the 1890s. By 1931 all rooms in the hotel had a connecting bath, with hot and cold running water.

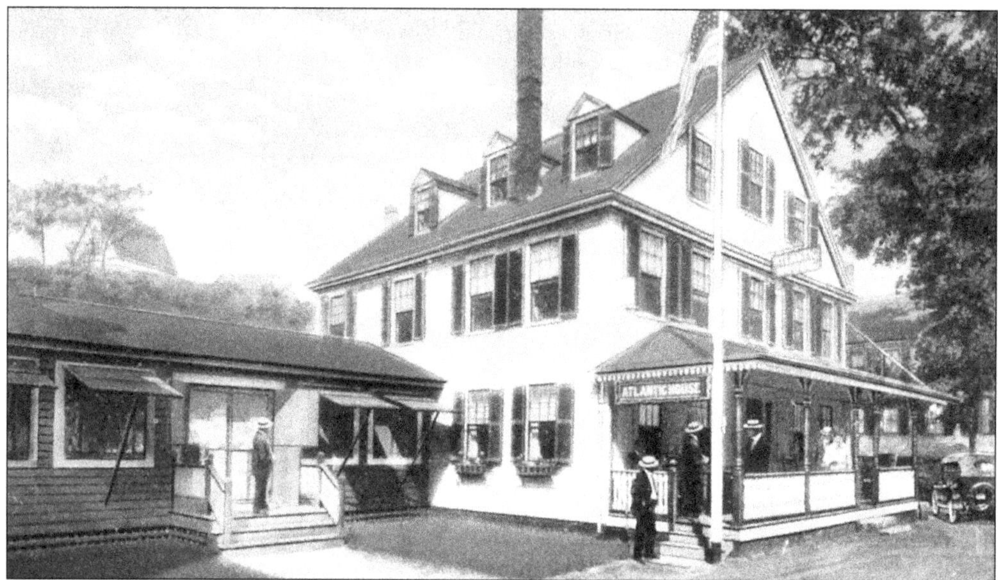

Atlantic House, 6 Masonic Place (c. 1930s postcard published by The Advocate Gift Shop). The second oldest hotel in town, the Atlantic House, was built during the War of 1812. Originally called the Union House, it served as an early courthouse; rooms have been rented since 1888. The hotel was the last stop for Lysander Paine's Provincetown-to-Orleans stagecoach line, which made a U-turn there and then proceeded toward Bradford Street (where the steps are located) and on to Orleans. The one-story addition was probably built around the time the postcard was issued. A "Guests Heated" sign in the hotel prompted many a chuckle.

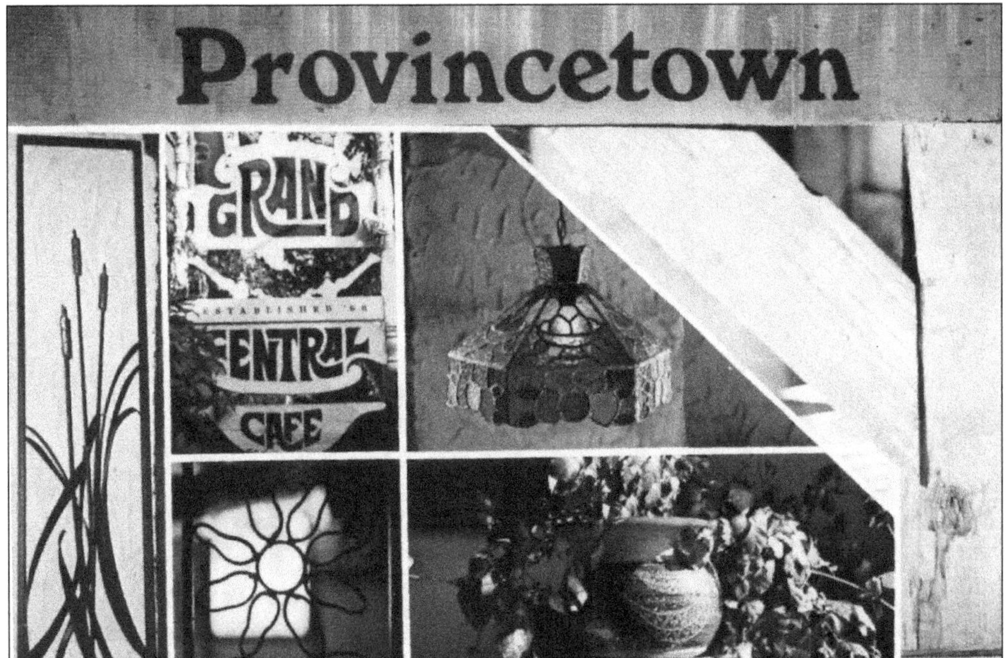

Local handicrafts on display at the Grand Central Café, 5 Masonic Place (c. 1970 postcard published by J. Lazarus). These handmade objects of clay, wrought iron, and glass were "on display at the Grand Central Café . . . a celebrated example of Provincetown's intimate restaurants which combine quaint charm with exceptional food & drink."

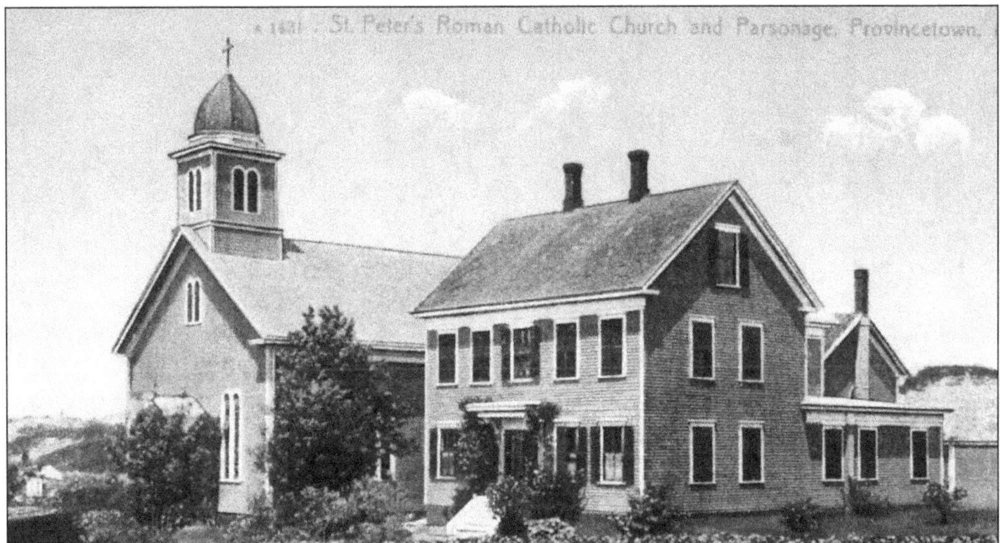

St. Peter the Apostle Church and Parsonage, 11 Prince Street (early-twentieth-century postcard published by *The Advocate*). The first Irish Catholic marriage occurred in town in 1852, about a decade before Portuguese natives arrived. Both ethnic groups desired a Catholic house of worship, thus providing the impetus for the construction of this church, built by Freeman Smith of Harwich for $8,000. Raised on the site of the "Old White Oak," the third Congregational church in Provincetown, the new Catholic church was dedicated on October 11, 1874.

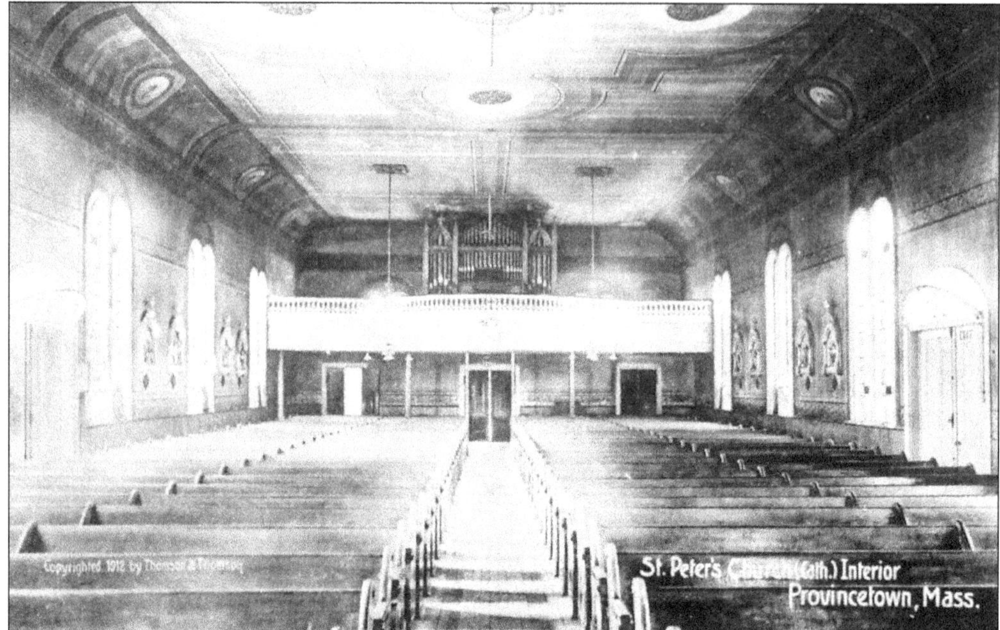

Interior of St. Peter the Apostle Church, 11 Prince Street (1912 postcard published by *The Advocate*). Parishioners could admire the painted cove ceiling and walls frescoed by the Smalls of Chatham; this decoration was considered "highly creditable to them." In 1890 it was noted that, "A fine organ, presided over by a Provincetown lady, with a choir of excellent singers, render the celebration of High Mass, according to the Catholic ritual, in a very solemn and effective manner." The capacity of the church is "six hundred souls."

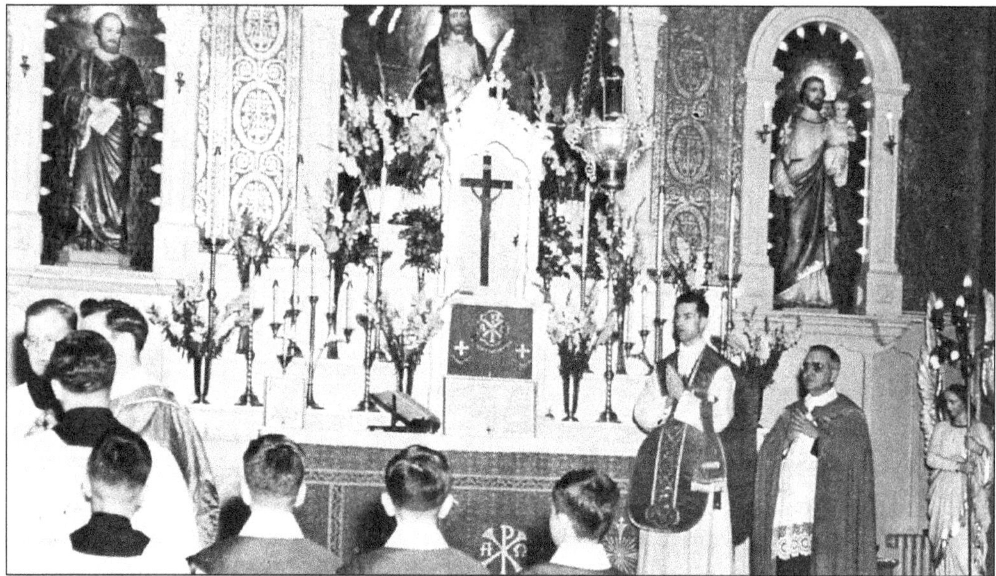

St. Peter the Apostle's church altar (1949 photograph). Father Leo Ferreira's first mass was celebrated on February 20, 1949, during the 75th diamond anniversary of the church. The congregation's first pastor, the Reverend Father John J. McGuire, was instrumental in forming the St. Peter's Aid Society in March of 1875, to be of mutual financial benefit to the parishioners. (Courtesy St. Peter the Apostle Church archives.)

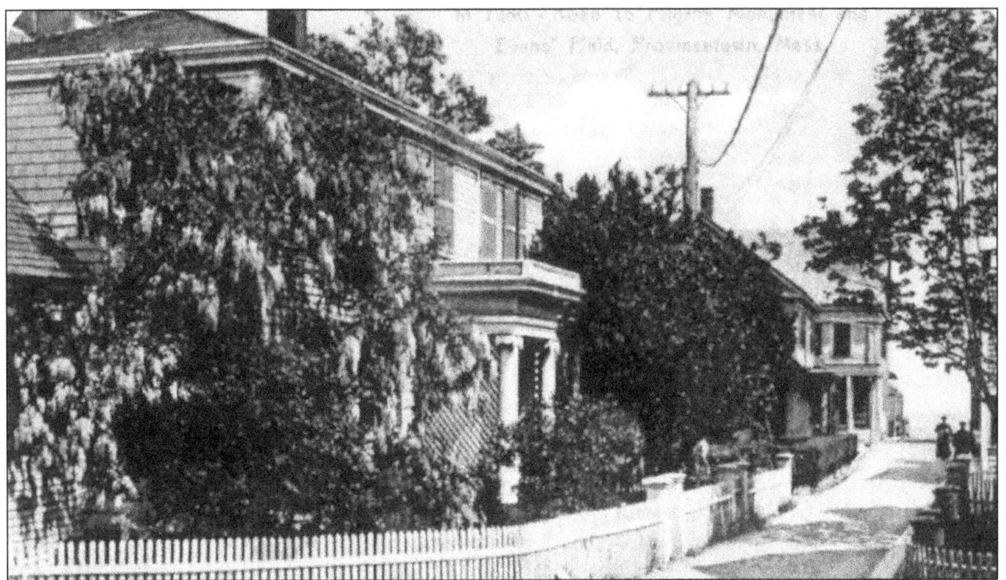

(Not) Road to Pilgrim Monument and Evans Field (c. 1910 postcard published by F.H. Dearborn, Provincetown). In this view of the Federal-period sea captain's home, the photographer was looking toward the harbor from the corner of Bradford and Gosnold Streets, not in the other direction! Members of the Bowley and Small families occupied the c. 1800–30 house with its paired Ionic capitals and purple wisteria in full bloom climbing to the roofline. The hipped-roof house is similar in date and style to another sea captain's home at 396 Commercial Street.

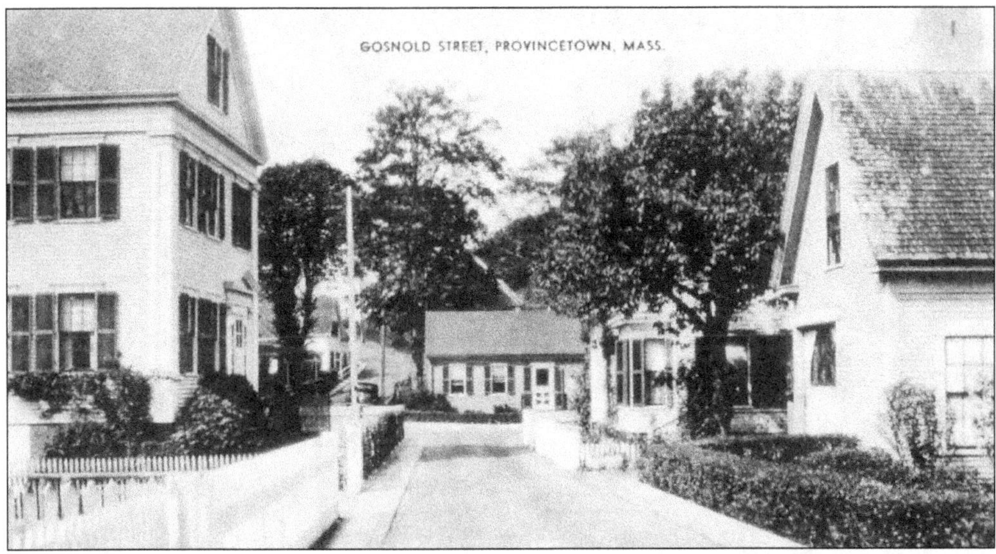

Gosnold Street looking toward Bradford Street (c. 1940s postcard published by The Town Crier Shop). British explorer Bartholomew Gosnold surveyed the Cape in the *Sparrow Hawk* and wrote in 1602, "We had again sight of the land . . . being as we thought an island, by reason of a large sound that appeared westward between it and the main . . . we did perceive a large opening, we called it Shoal Hope. Near this cape we came to anchor . . . where we took great store of codfish, for which we altered the name and called it Cape Cod." (Courtesy Stephen J. Schier.)

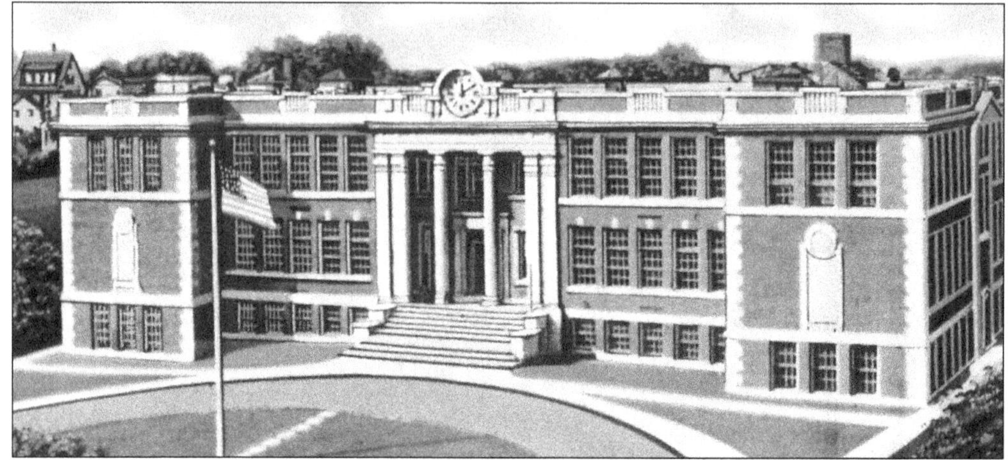

Provincetown High School, 12 Winslow Street (c. 1935 postcard published by The Mayflower Sales Co.). The current Colonial Revival brick educational institution (depicted here by an artist) was built in 1931 on the left side of High Pole Hill adjacent to the first town hall. The original high school in town, located on the upper floor of the first town hall, was replaced in 1880, when a new high and grammar school was constructed. When this building burned on March 26, 1930, it was in turn replaced by the above building.

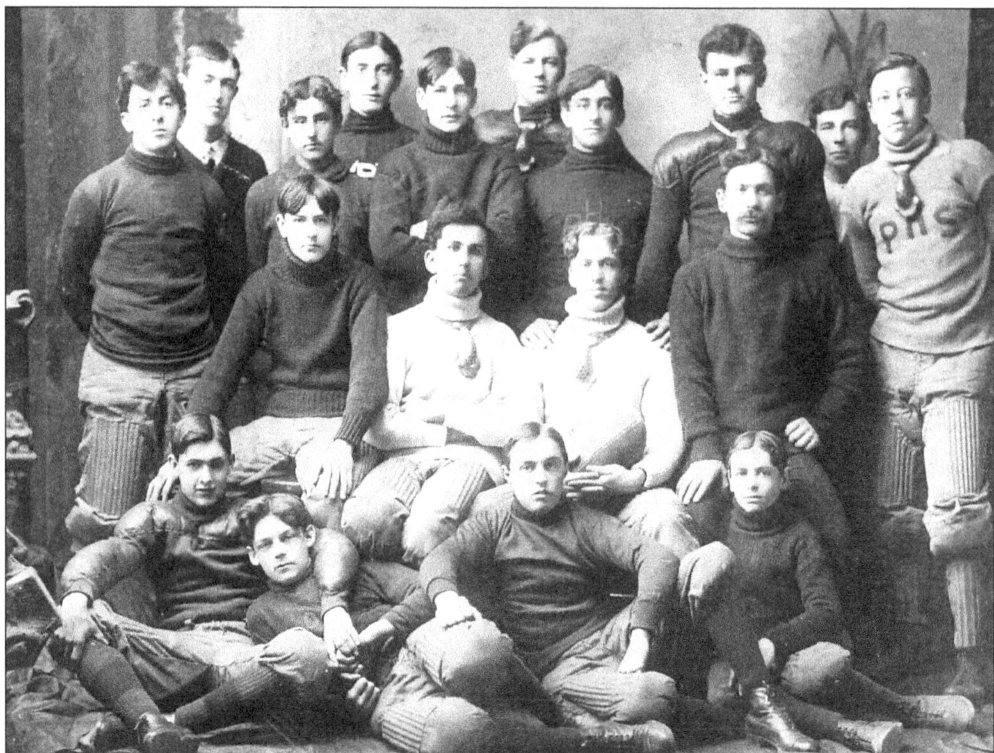

The Provincetown High School football team (c. 1900 photograph). Four members of the unfortunately unidentified football team sport pronounced perforated nose guards. Football was omitted from the school's athletic program for three years because the equipment was ruined when the high school was destroyed by fire in 1930. (Courtesy of the Cape Cod Pilgrim Memorial Association.)

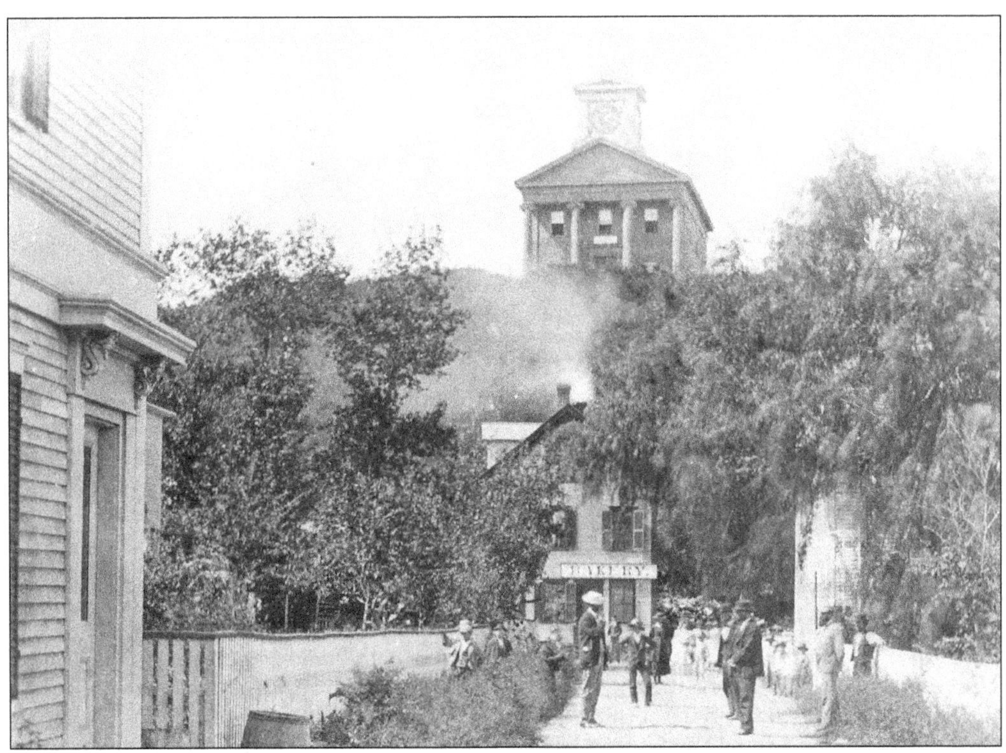

Old Town Hall from Ryder Street (c. 1875 stereopticon view taken by George H. Nickerson). High Pole Hill, which had served as a landmark for those at sea, was acquired from seven owners and partially leveled for the construction of Provincetown's first town hall in 1853. The Greek Revival-style public building incorporated a clock in its tower, and was built for a sum of almost $15,000. It served the town for less than twenty-four years, as it was consumed by fire on February 16, 1877. In this early view townsfolk stroll along Ryder Street, perhaps after having made a purchase at the bakery on Bradford Street.

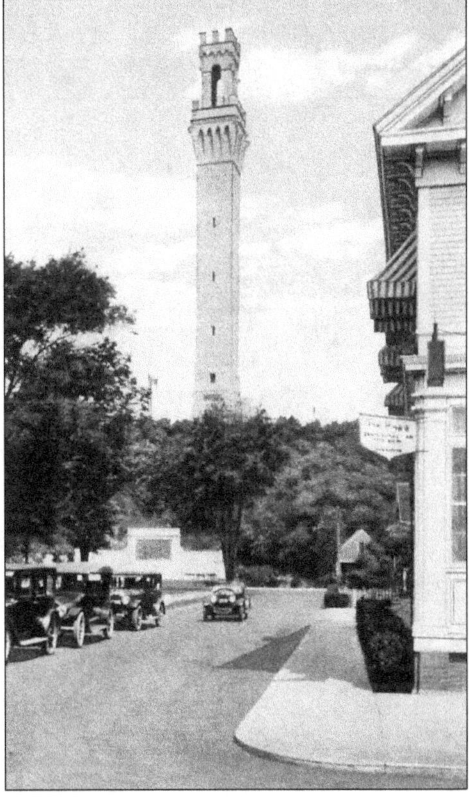

Ryder Street looking toward Bradford Street (c. 1929 postcard published by E.D. White Co.). Five houses on Ryder Street were razed in 1920 to widen this street at the right of the town hall. A fudge and candy store has been located on the first floor of the building at the right for decades; it was formerly the second location of the Seamen's Savings Bank. The impressive granite and bronze bas-relief "Signing of the Compact" monument can be seen on the Town Green at the base of High Pole Hill.

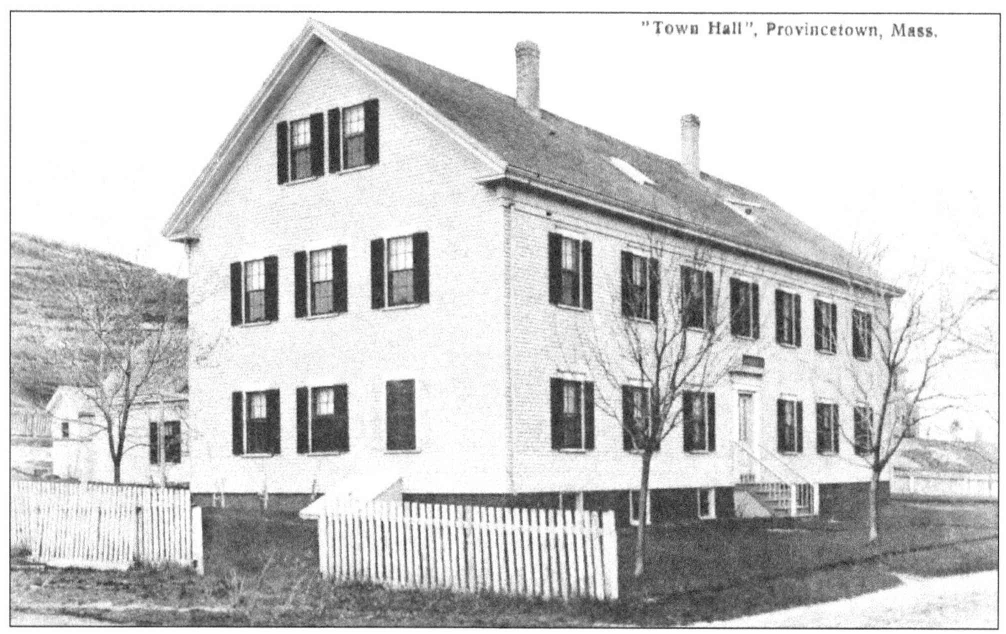

(Not the) "Town Hall," 26 Alden Street (early-twentieth-century postcard published by *The Advocate*). This long, c. 1870 building has been known as the town asylum, the almshouse, and the town farm. After serving as the Cape End Manor for almost forty years, it was converted to town offices and named the Grace Gouveia Building to honor the beloved Provincetown schoolteacher. High Pole Hill, where the first town hall was situated, is to the left and may have caused the misidentification of this building.

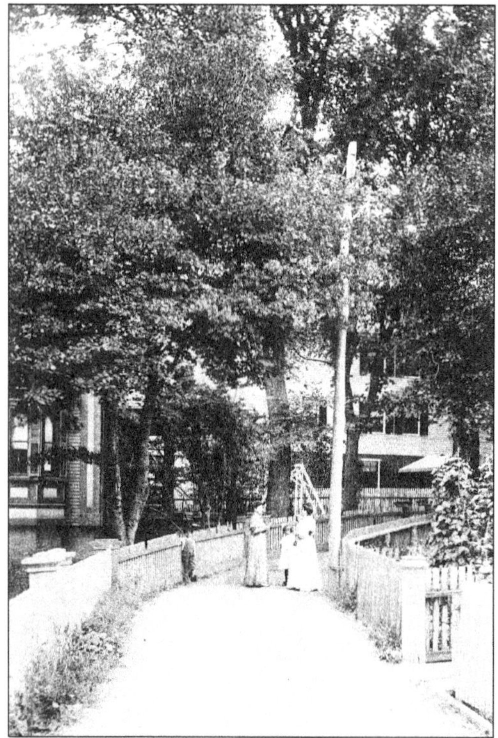

Freeman Street (c. 1910 postcard published by *The Advocate*). Gracious ladies exchange greetings on the curved dirt road between Standish and Center Streets. The street and the public library on the corner of Commercial Street were named to honor the town's philanthropic citizen, Nathan Freeman.

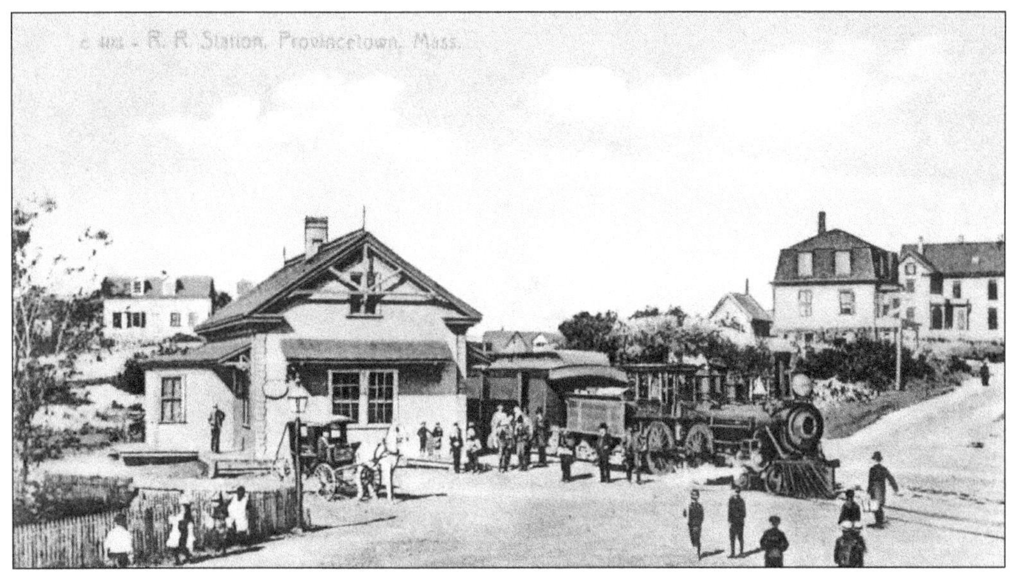

Railroad Station, Bradford and Standish Streets (early-twentieth-century postcard published by *The Advocate*). The single-story and gable-roofed train station was built in 1873 to the right of High Pole Hill. A two-room structure, it contained a baggage room, ticket office, pot-bellied stove, and other amenities. The railroad was an extension from Wellfleet, and the tracks crossed Bradford and Center Streets and extended to Steamboat Wharf, thereafter also referred to as Railroad Wharf. Raymond Ellington was a depot master in town for the Old Colony Railroad, which later became the New York, New Haven & Hartford Railroad. The Cape Codder, a Pullman special from major cities, began service in 1930, but by the early 1940s passenger service was, unfortunately, discontinued. (Courtesy the Cartophilians.)

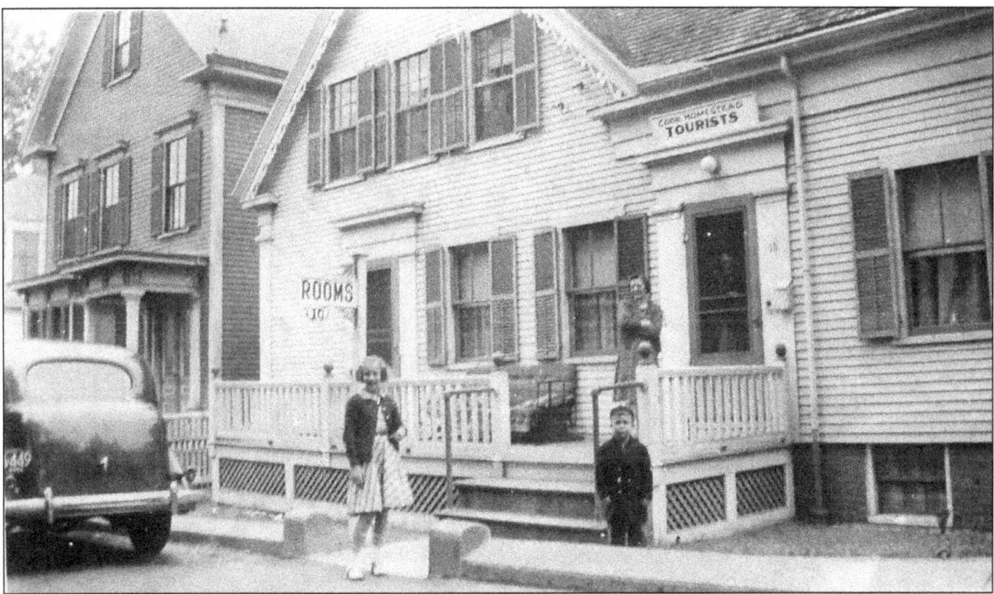

The Cook Homestead for tourists, 10 Johnson Street (c. 1940 photograph). Adelaide Kenney and her family ran this guest house with its decorative barge-board cornice, located between Center and Arch Streets. One of the town's fire engine houses is located on the same side of the street. (Courtesy Skip and Arpina Stanton.)

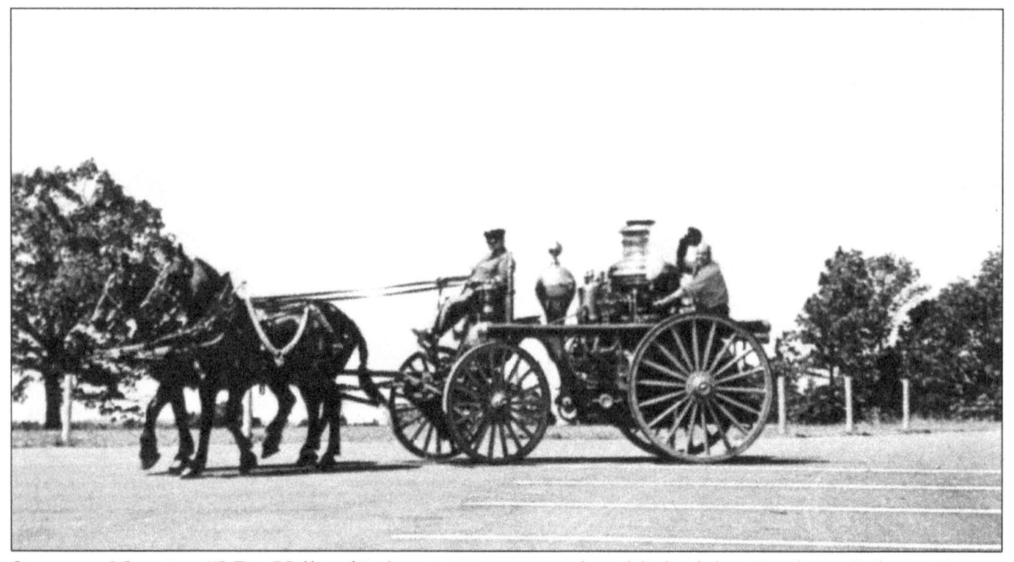

Steamer No. 3—"J.D. Hilliard" (c. 1969 postcard published by Yankee Colour Corp., Southboro, MA). A volunteer bucket brigade was organized in Provincetown in 1829 and the first hand-engine, the Washington, was ordered from a Boston manufacturer in 1836; it was stationed in one of the five pumper houses built between 1870 and 1885. The J.D. Hilliard was a steam fire engine and it was built by the Amoskeag Locomotive Works in Manchester, NH. In 1890 the five-member crew consisted of a foreman, an assistant, a clerk, the engine man, and an assistant engine man.

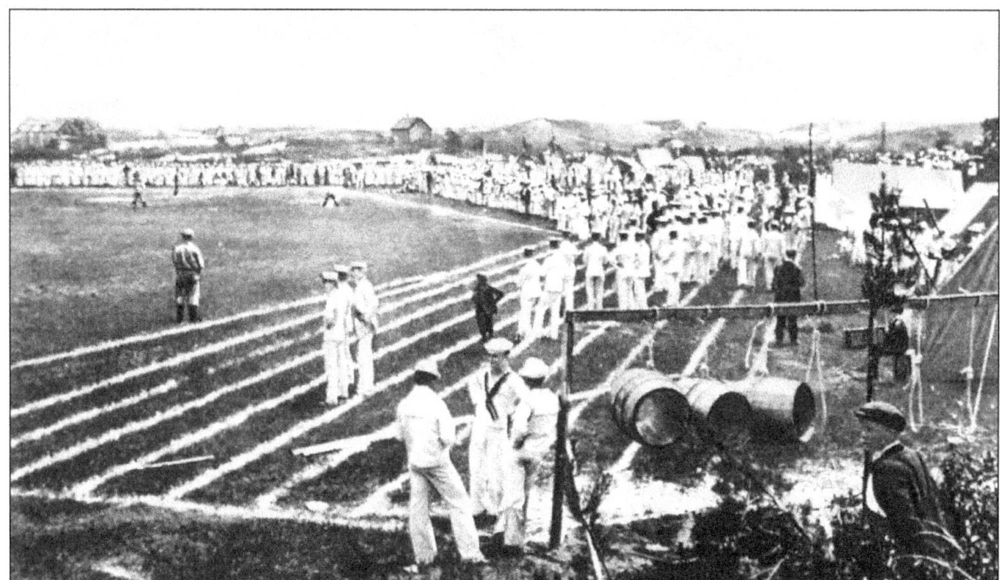

Evans Field, the athletic grounds of the Atlantic Fleet (1905 postcard published by *The Advocate*). An exercise arena for seamen of the twenty-ship Atlantic Fleet was provided by their own strength when in two days they converted a cranberry bog into a quarter-mile running track centering a baseball diamond. Tents and pennants from the various battleships gave a festive look to the area named in honor of Rear Admiral Robley D. Evans, commander of the Atlantic Squadron. On this July Fourth a tug-of-war match took place between teams from the *Alabama* and the *Illinois*.

Four

The Pilgrim Memorial Monument and Museum

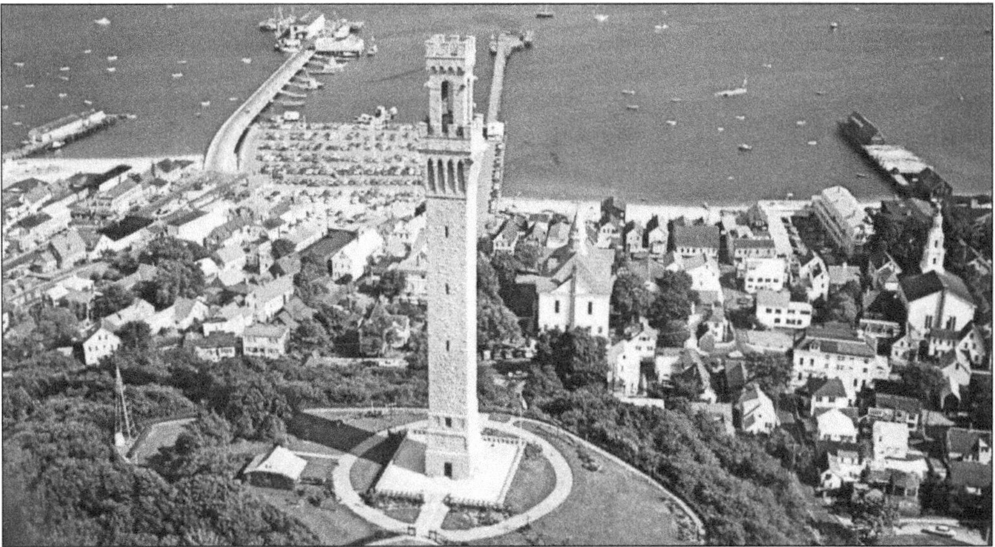

Aerial view of Provincetown with the Pilgrim Memorial Monument (c. 1971 postcard published by Colourpicture, Boston, MA). When one thinks of old-time Yankee thrift and conservatism, it is ironic and interesting to note that the highest all-granite structure in the United States is located in Provincetown, and that it was approved in its grandiose form by local committee members of the Cape Cod Pilgrim Memorial Association (founded and incorporated on February 29, 1892). Cape Cod historian Frederick Freeman wrote that as early as 1857, "The citizens have often expressed surprise at the policy and propriety of overlooking their own town as the most suitable point for the erection of a monument in memorial of the Pilgrim Fathers . . . and that 'the Pilgrim Monument should here be reared.' " And reared it was about fifty years later—initial funding was begun in 1892 with the collection of $1,200. Construction began on August 20, 1907, and completion and dedication occurred on August 5, 1910. This most prominent historic landmark in America is situated on a 7-acre site on High Pole Hill, and it is visible from 40 miles at sea. Realizing that a lighthouse or other indigenous form of architecture would not make enough of a visual impact, the committee decided on an Italian Renaissance design copied from the tower of the Torre Del Mangia in Siena, Italy. The majestic result is 252 feet, 7.5 inches in height, and the top is 353 feet above sea level.

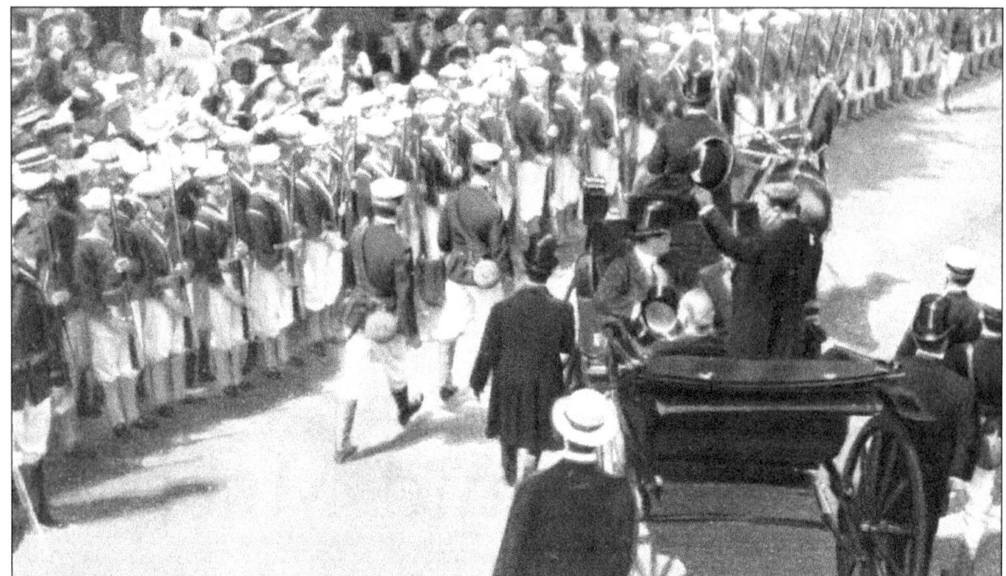

President Roosevelt en route for Town Hill (1907 postcard published by *The Advocate*). Sailors from seven battleships stand at attention on both sides of Commercial Street as Theodore Roosevelt (1858–1919) stands with two other dignitaries and waves his top hat to cheering townspeople and tourists alike, who shouted "Roosevelt, Welcome! Hurrah—here he comes!" Josiah L. Young, the chauffeur for the day, recalled many years later that it was the "worst day's work I ever had . . . driving Teddy Roosevelt on Aug. 20, 1907, when he came here to lay the cornerstone of the Pilgrim Monument. What a responsibility."

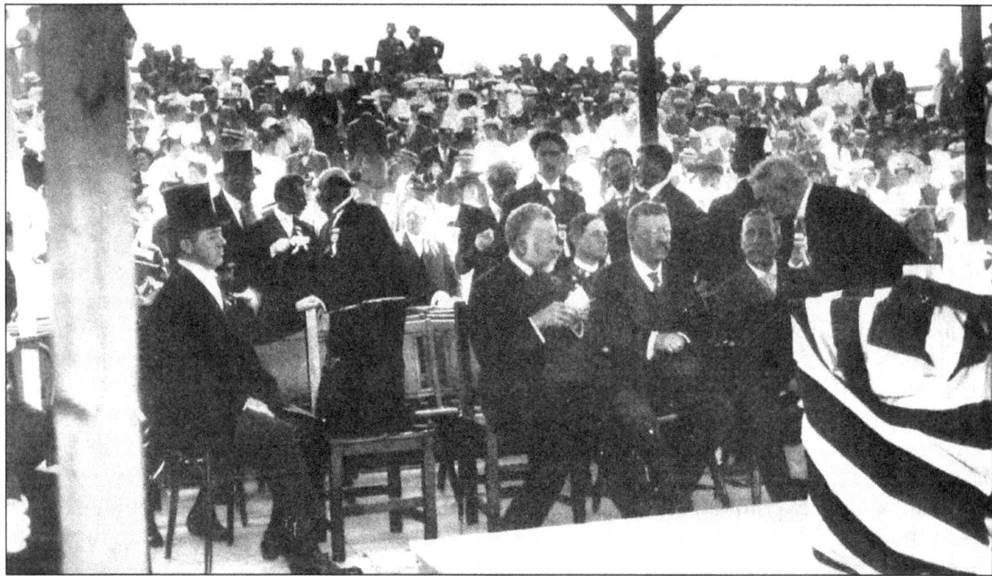

The laying of the Corner Stone (1907 photograph). Dignitaries who were on hand for the momentous occasion and who gave addresses included Governor Curtis Guild Jr. (to President Roosevelt's right) and Senator Henry Cabot Lodge (looking toward J. Henry Sears, the gentleman bending toward the "bully pulpit" president). Mr. Sears, a resident of Brewster, was elected president of the Cape Cod Pilgrim Memorial Association in 1905, and he lobbied Congress for three years to appropriate funds to build the monument.

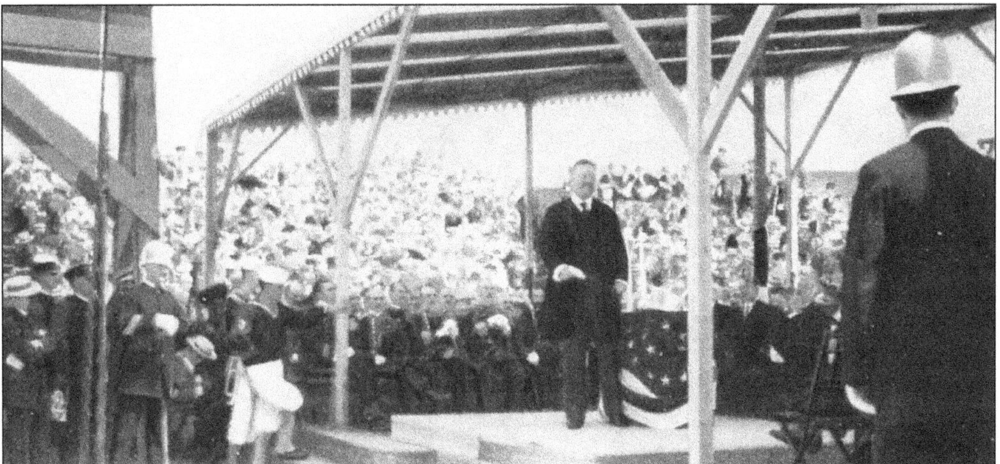

President Roosevelt delivering Address at laying of Corner Stone (1907 postcard published by *The Advocate*). A canopy over the platform covers the flag-draped cornerstone as the 26th President delivers his oration. In his lengthy speech, the President remarked, "You, sons of the Puritans, and we, who are descended from races whom the Puritans would have deemed alien—we are all Americans together. We all feel the same pride in the genesis, in the history, of our people; and therefore this shrine of Puritanism is one at which we all gather to pay homage, no matter from what country our ancestors sprang."

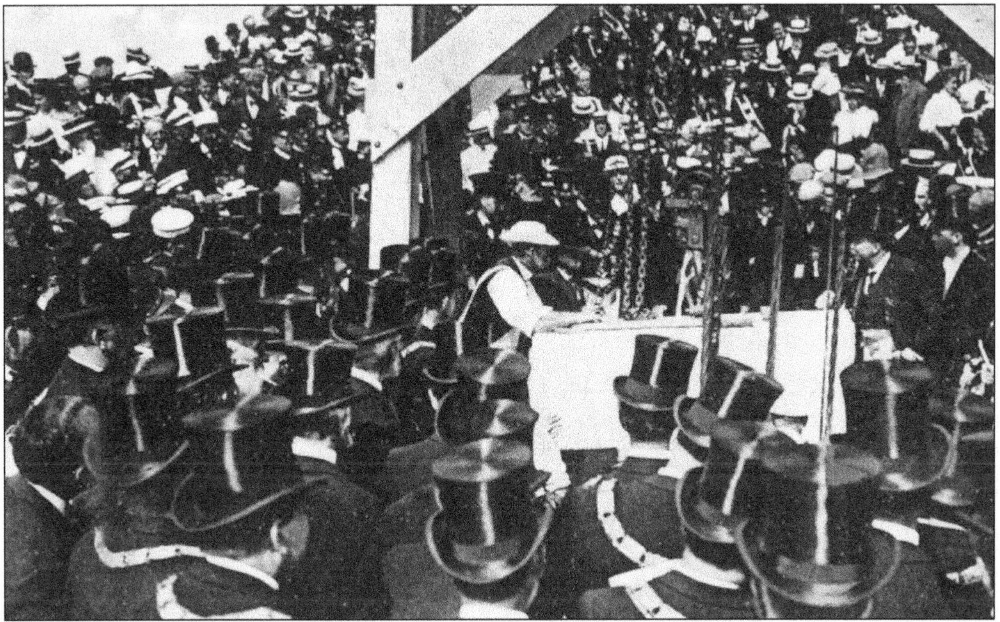

President Roosevelt laying the Corner Stone of the Pilgrim Monument (1907 postcard published by *The Advocate*). Masons from around the state crowd around as President Roosevelt, a Mason himself (following the Grand Master in order), uses the silver trowel to spread cement on the cornerstone made of North Carolina granite. After other Masons followed suit, the 4,800-pound block was lowered in three stages, each with Grand Honors. Upon anointing the stone with corn (the symbol of nourishment), wine (representing refreshment and concord), and oil (the symbol of union, harmony, and love in the land), the Grand Master then presented the Square, Level, Plumb, and Plan to the architect.

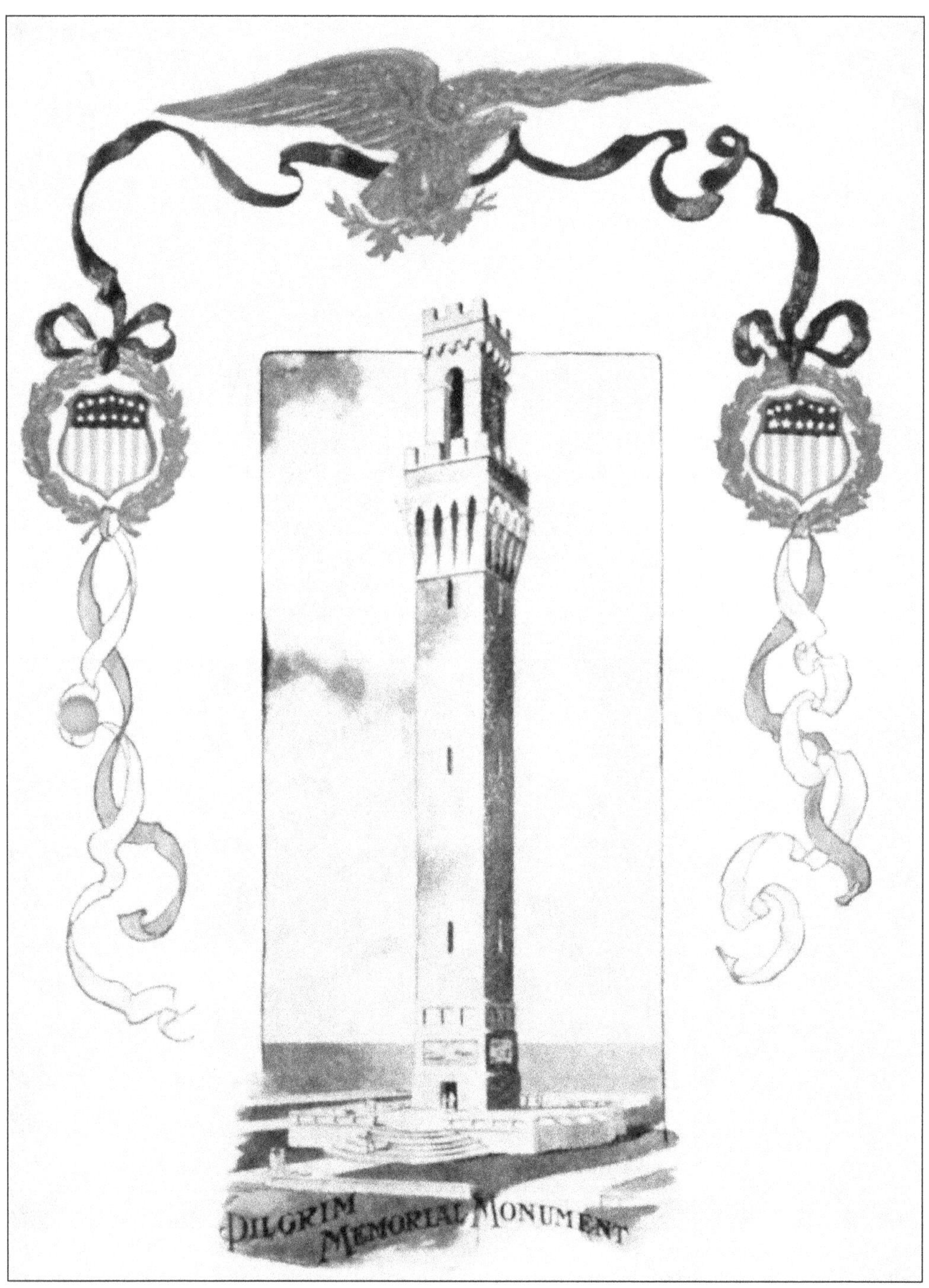

A Grand Ball souvenir program (August 20, 1907). The monument's design appears on the front cover of the small program along with an embossed and gilded American eagle with pendant laurel wreaths containing red, white, and blue shields. The gala event took place at the town hall on the Tuesday evening of the cornerstone-laying ceremony with music provided by the Salem (MA) Cadet Band Orchestra. Listed inside the program in the order of dances are fourteen waltzes (several repeats), a "Schottische," and a galop. (Courtesy Hall Collection.)

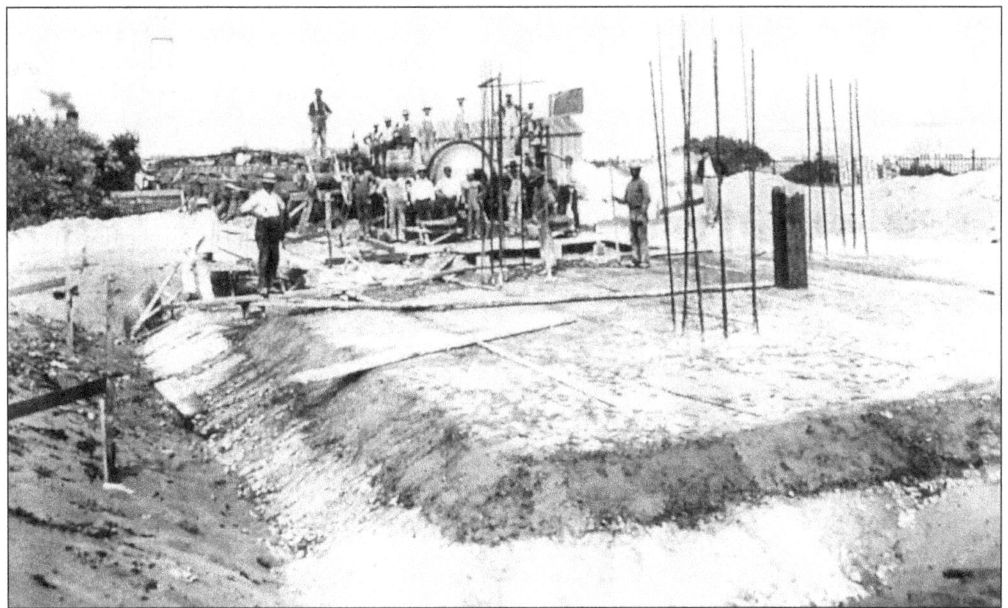

The Pilgrim Memorial Monument's foundation (1907 photograph). Work on the concrete foundation was begun by the Aberthaw Construction Company of Boston on June 20, and it was completed on the eighth day of August. The solid concrete foundation is 60 feet square at the base and 8 feet below the surface. Each of the four corners has six rods of twisted steel buried far below the ground, and similar twisted rods appear 18 inches apart on the sides. (Private Collection.)

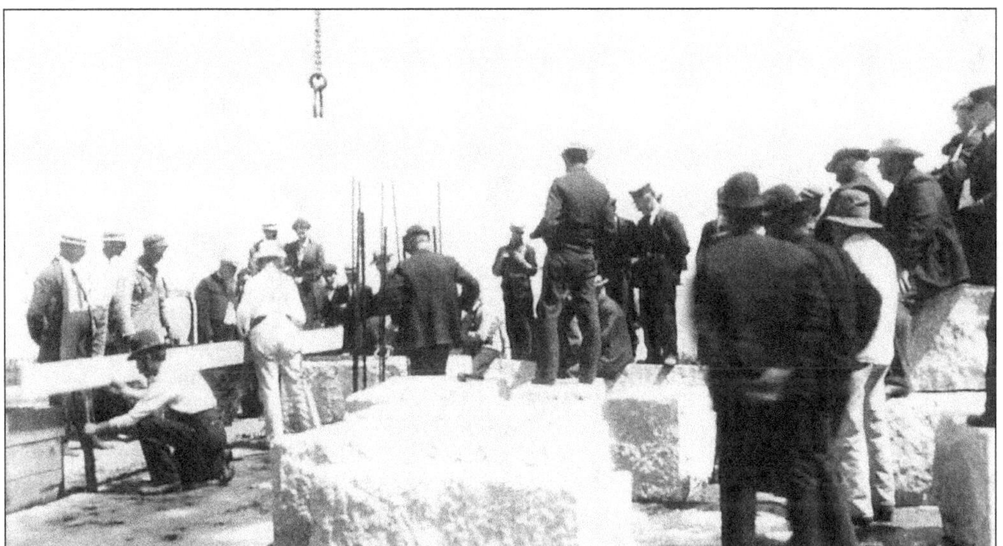

Laying the first stone of the structure after the cornerstone (1908 photograph). Town officials and committee members of the Cape Cod Pilgrim Memorial Association were on hand for the actual start of the monument's construction on June 18, 1908. Will A. Clark served as inspector of the project and he made daily reports to Boston-based Colonel Edward Burr of the United States Engineer Corps, who was appointed superintendent of construction. The heavy granite blocks were moved by derricks and small open railway cars to the hill's summit, where they were measured and dressed by the stonecutters. (Private Collection.)

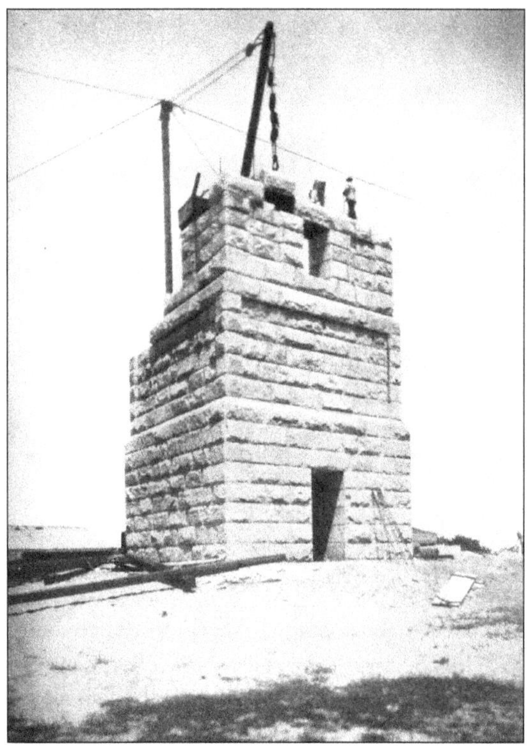

The construction progresses (1908 photograph). Two-and-one-half tiers of the monument with a door and a window appear in this view of the construction 40 feet above the base. One hundred thirty-three granite memorial stones were placed in random locations on the inside walls beginning at the 17th tier. The first to be set in position acknowledged *Mayflower* descendants who resided in Rhode Island and the Providence Plantations.

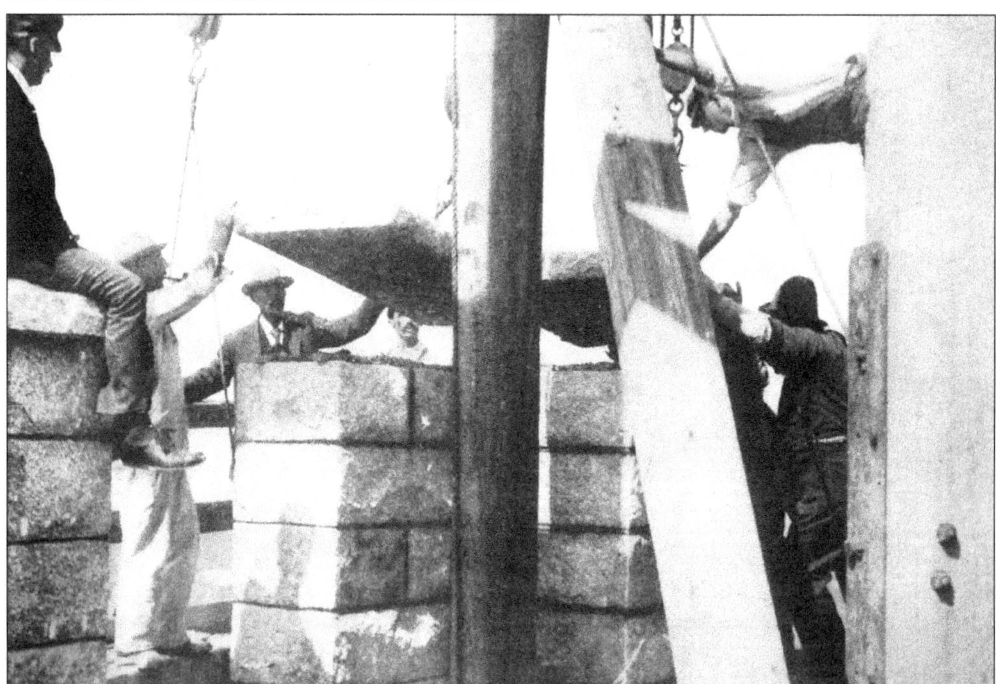

Laying the last stone (1910 photograph). A seated dignitary watches as construction workers place the final capstone on one of the monument's corners. The interior work, including the installation of the 116 stairs and 60 incline ramps near the top, was completed on March 29, 1910.

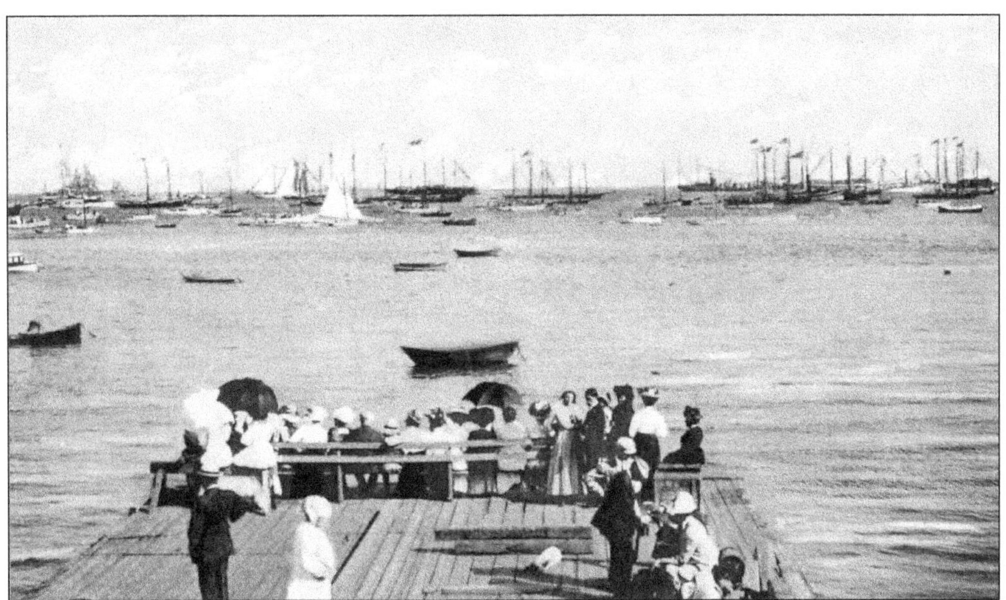

Provincetown Harbor at Dedication of Pilgrim Memorial Monument (1910 postcard published by *The Advocate*). A woman in a Pilgrim-inspired costume chats with friends while other people watch the vessels in the harbor—including eight battleships of the Atlantic Fleet—bedecked with colorful flags and pennants. Three years earlier, when President Roosevelt laid the trowel on the monument's cornerstone, all the battleships in the harbor fired a salute at the same time, causing many windows in town to shatter!

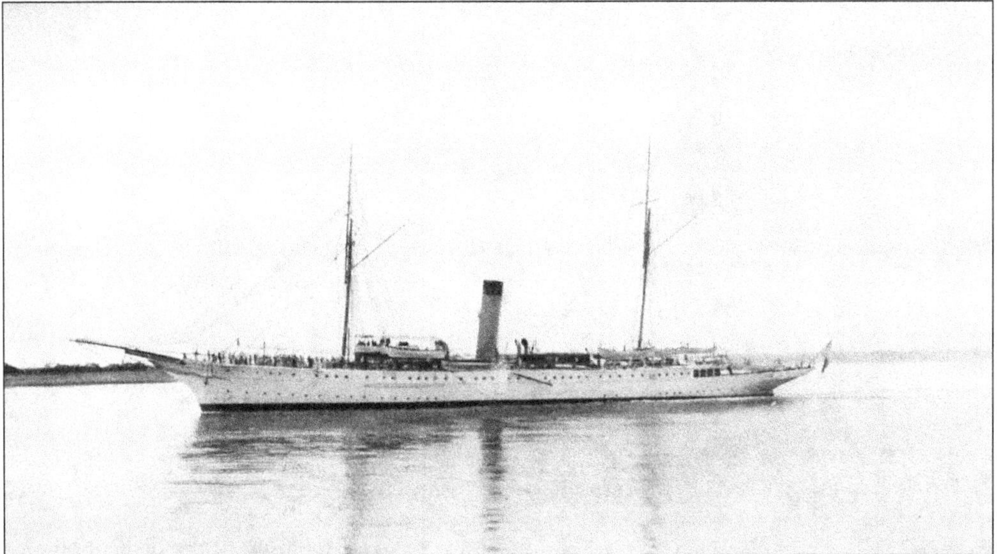

The U.S.S. *Mayflower* in Provincetown Harbor (1910 photograph). On the day of the monument's dedication, the presidential yacht anchored near the spot where the first *Mayflower* had dropped sails. President William Howard Taft (1857–1930) mentioned that the yacht "is somewhat different in size and comfort and . . . in luxury from that which brought the Pilgrims, but there are certain stories I should like to deny. We have no special bath tubs made for any executive of any particular size (Laughter). I don't know whether they had bath tubs on the *Mayflower*. Presumably it was pretty cold for a bath when they arrived in these waters."

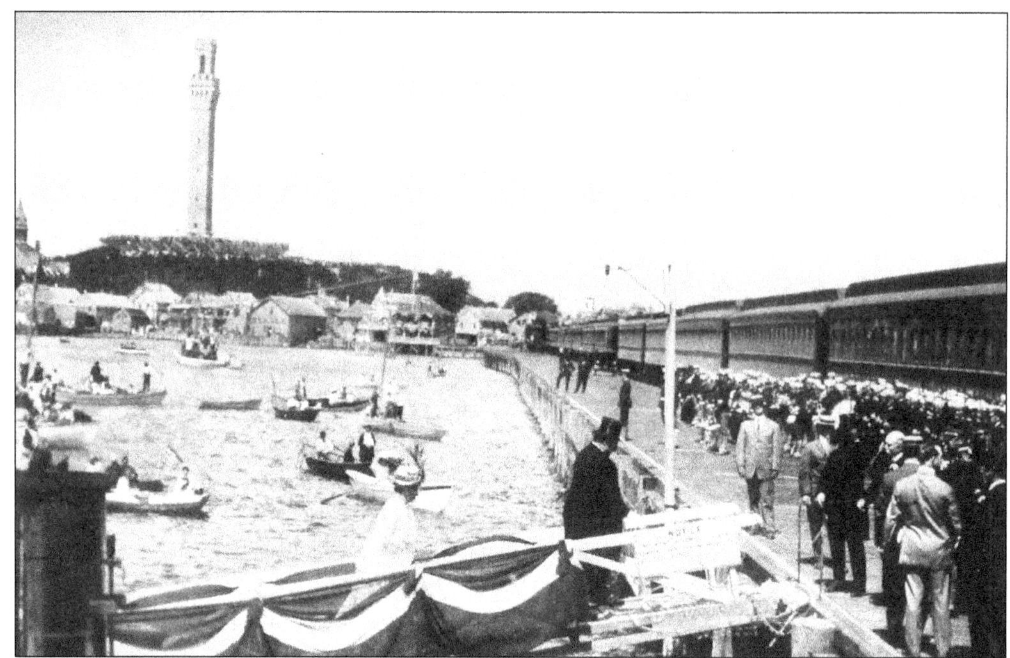

President and Mrs. Taft landing at Railroad Wharf (1910 photograph). The 27th President of the United States and his wife were greeted in Provincetown by Governor Eben S. Draper, President Sears, and Mr. Artemus P. Hannum, a board of selectmen member and chairman of arrangements for the local committee.

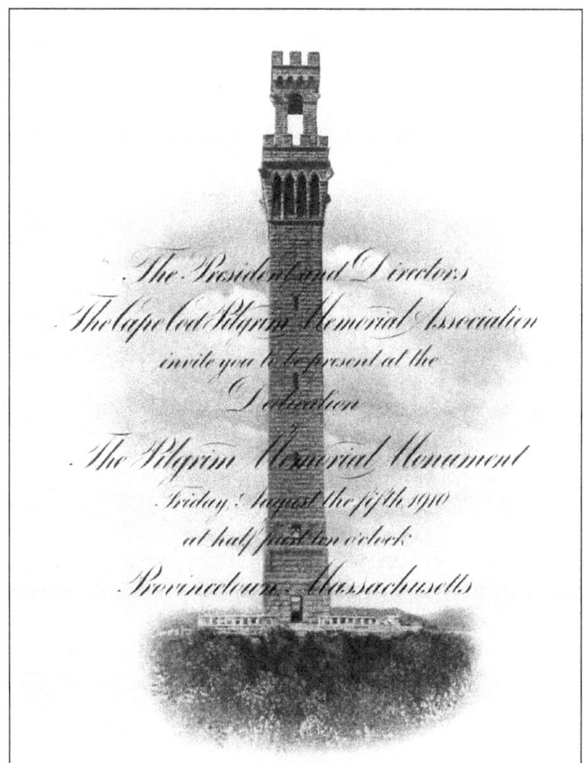

The President and Directors
The Cape Cod Pilgrim Memorial Association
invite you to be present at the
Dedication
of
The Pilgrim Memorial Monument
Friday, August the fifth, 1910
at half past ten o'clock
Provincetown, Massachusetts

An Invitation to the dedication of the Pilgrim Memorial Monument (1910). A flowing script was superimposed over the monument on the small, printed invitation that announced the start of the ceremony "at half past two o'clock." (Courtesy Hall Collection.)

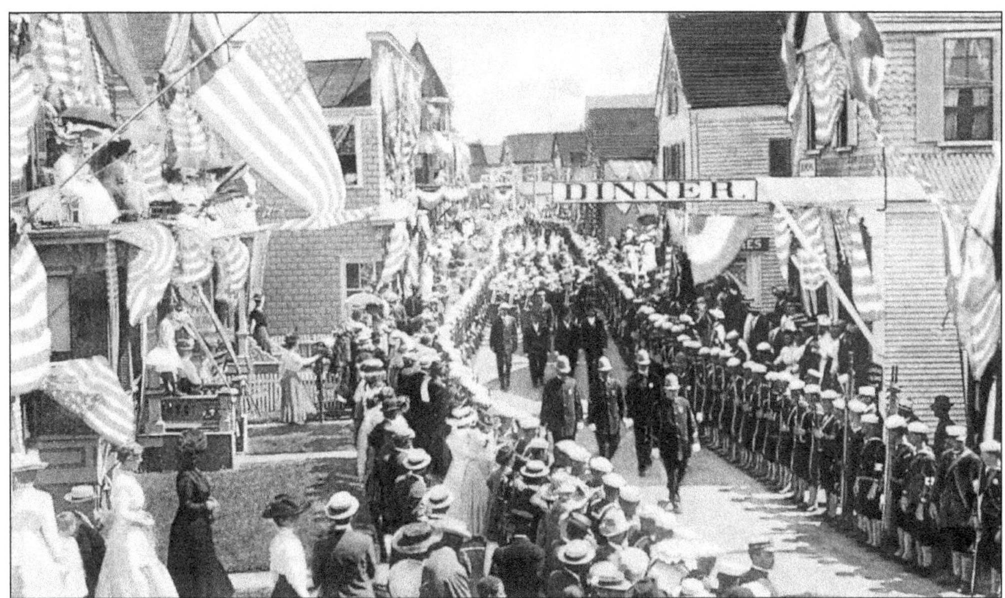

President Taft's arrival at Provincetown (1910 postcard published by *The Advocate*). Police officers lead the presidential parade along Commercial Street from Railroad Wharf toward High Pole Hill. People dressed in their best summer finery peer from bunting-draped windows, sit on porch roofs and stairs, and gather behind the line of sailors to get a glimpse of the dignitaries. President Ulysses S. Grant (1822–1885) had visited Provincetown by train in 1874, but not on such a grand historic occasion.

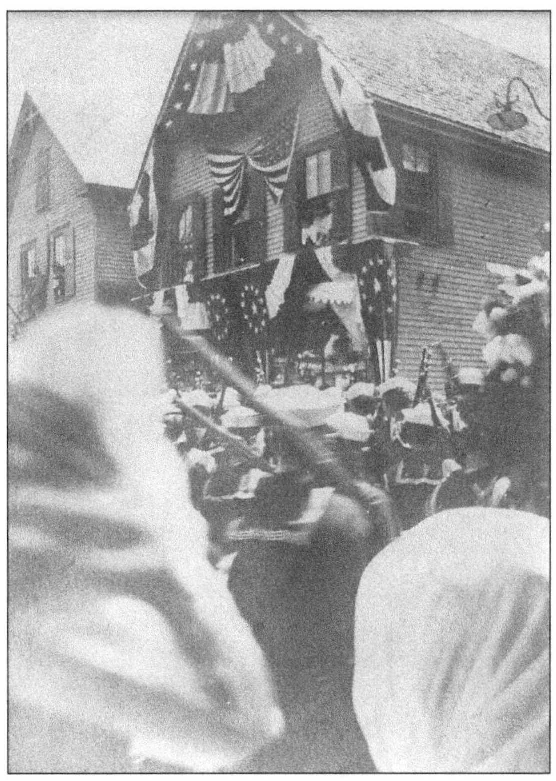

The parade for President Taft (1910 photograph). Mr. and Mrs. Harrison Wiley of Salem, MA, undoubtedly planned their summer vacation to coincide with the monument's dedication on August 5; they stayed with Addie's parents in South Wellfleet. Even though this historic photograph with sailors marching by on Commercial Street doesn't include the Taft entourage, it was fortunately placed in their photograph album. (Courtesy Thelma E. Wiley.)

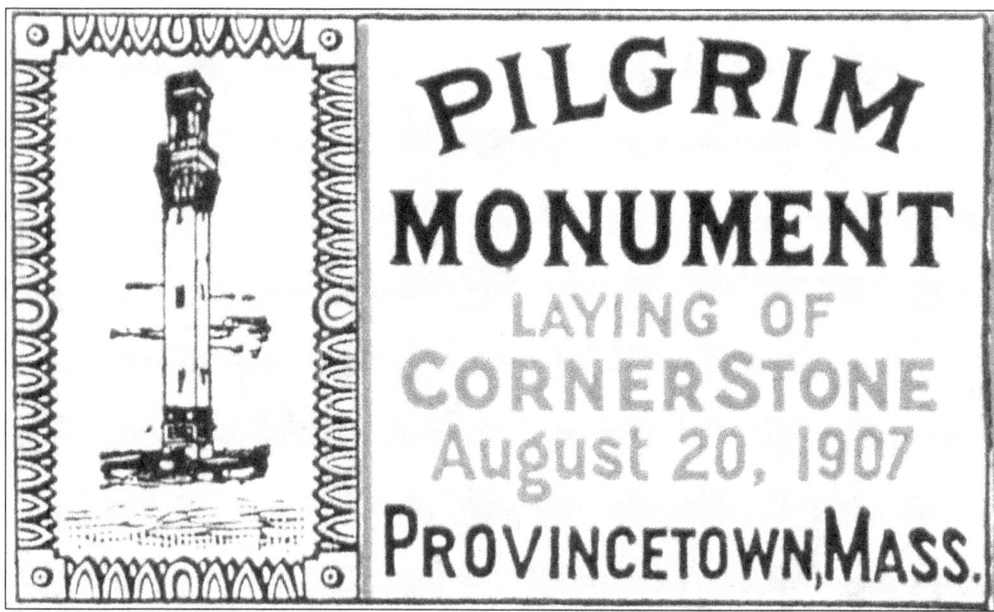

Commemorative stamp, August 20, 1907. Red and blue ink printed on a sand-colored background was the scheme chosen for this unusual piece of paper ephemera. (Courtesy McGhee Collection.)

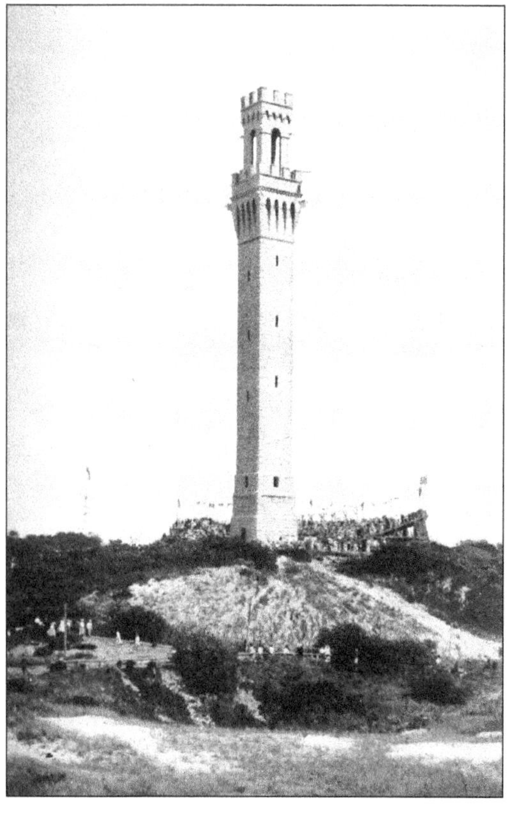

The Pilgrim Monument during the ceremonies of dedication (1910 photograph). The dedication platform was set up on the south side of the pristine monument, with seating for almost three thousand guests. Many probably inspected the transplanted Italian tower, which is 28-feet square at the top; the arched windows in the belfry are 29 feet, 10 inches high by 7 feet wide.

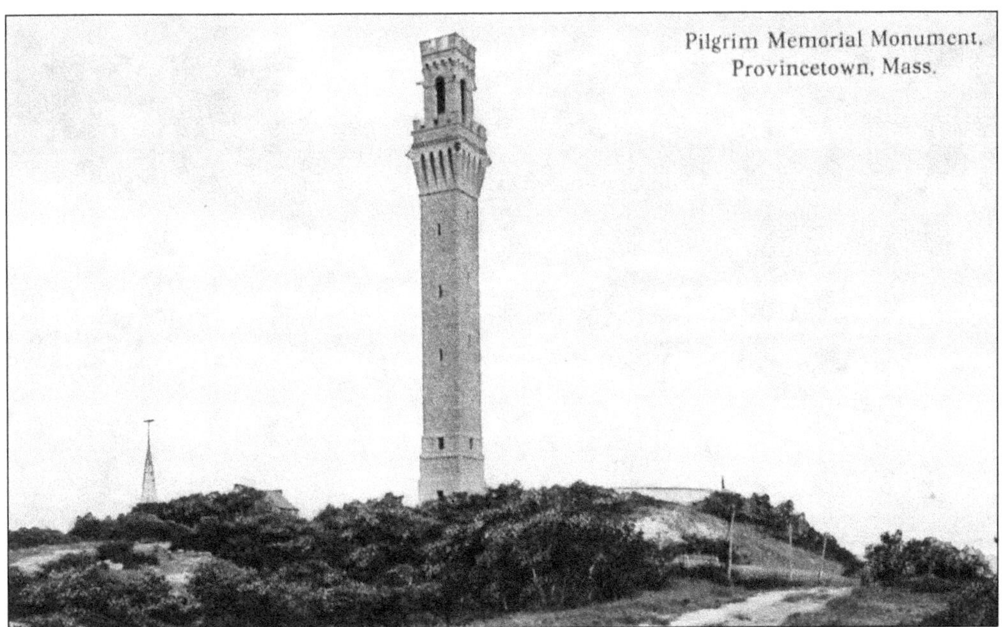

Pilgrim Memorial Monument (c. 1920 postcard published by C.T. Photochrom). Three tiers of hand-carved granite gargoyles grace the four corners of the lofty campanile-inspired tower. An earlier, more traditional monument was the marble tablet that was placed in front of the town hall on this hill on November 8, 1853, by the Cape Cod Association; it unfortunately was destroyed when the building was consumed by fire on February 16, 1877.

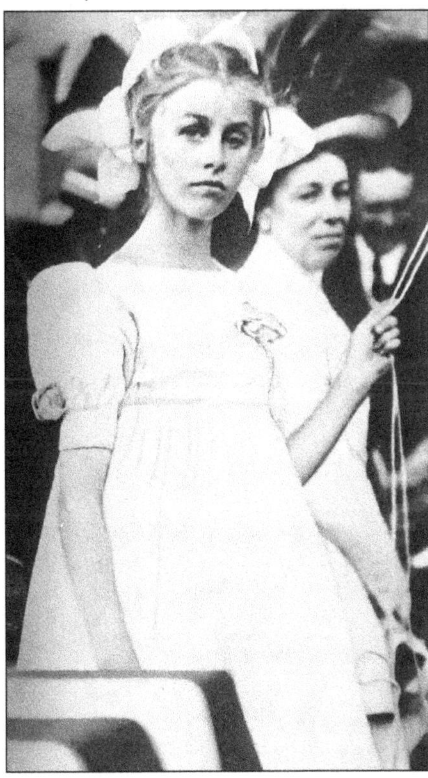

Unveiling the dedication tablet (1910 photograph). The First Lady looks over the shoulder of Barbara Hoyt of New York, "a young miss" and a direct descendant of Elder William Brewster, as she pulls the cords that part the flags covering a bronze tablet inserted above the south doorway of the monument. The five-paragraph inscription that memorializes the Pilgrims was composed by Charles W. Eliot, LL.D., the keynote orator of the dedication ceremony.

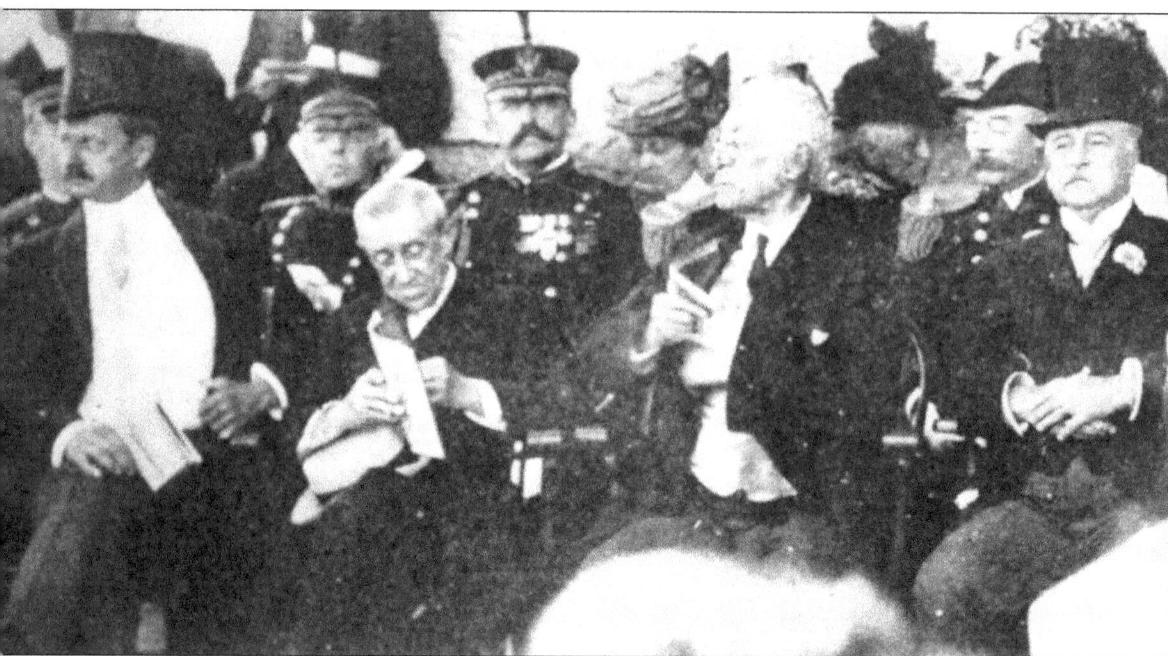

Distinguished orators at the dedication ceremony (1910 photograph). Mrs. Taft, wearing a feathered chapeau, is seated with seven gentlemen, six of whom would soon give speeches to honor the first landfall of the Pilgrims, the compact they originated, and the construction of the monument itself. Seated from left to right are George Von L. Meyer (secretary of the navy), the Reverend James De Normandie, Charles W. Eliot, LL.D. (president emeritus of Harvard University), Governor Eben S. Draper, J. Henry Sears (president of the Cape Cod Pilgrim Memorial Association), President William Howard Taft, and Massachusetts Senator Henry Cabot Lodge. Dr. Eliot remarked, "[We] salute tenderly and reverently the Pilgrims of the *Mayflower*, and recalling their fewness, and their sufferings, anxieties, and labors, felicitate them and ourselves on the wonderful issues in human joy, and freedom of their faith, endurance, and dauntless resolution." President Sears said, "The monument is built as firmly and as strong

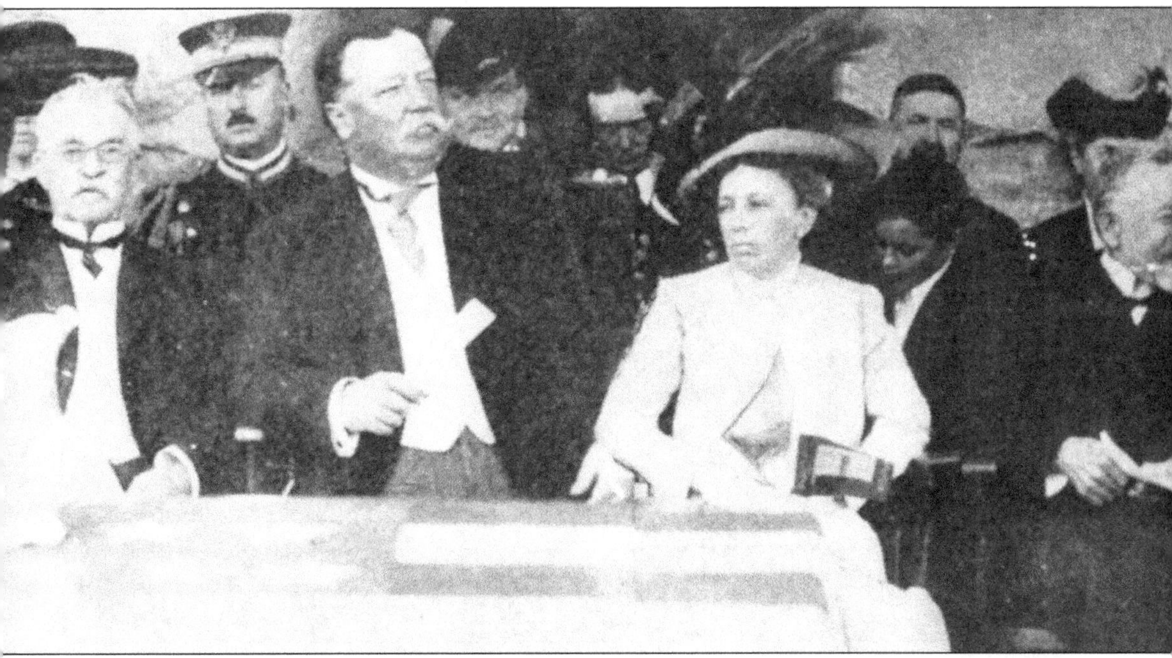

as is possible for human hands to build. . . . The work is now done, and here we, inthe presence of our distinguished guests, dedicate it to the American people. It will stand here for generations to recall to the nation the event which was the corner stone of the Republic." President Taft stated, "This magnificent monument, rearing its head high on the most conspicuous promontory of our coast, will fittingly remind the traveler by sea of the beginnings of New England, and note the fact that those whose spirit of liberty was to persist for centuries, even to the foundation and preservation of our great Republic, here first saw the land and here first put foot upon the shore." Senator Lodge remarked, "High ideals in the conduct of life are what survive, and that is why the Pilgrim narrative stands forth in the pages of every history as one of the great events of the time, not because they were among the founders of the Republic, but because they had great purposes and, by their conception of duty, influenced the fate of men."

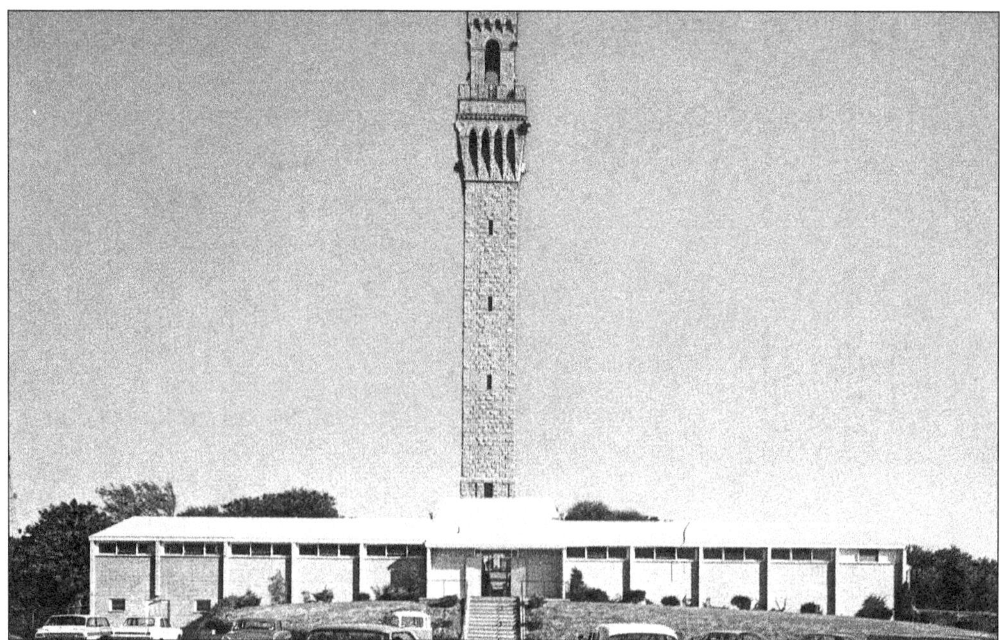

The Provincetown Museum and Pilgrim Memorial Monument (c. 1965 postcard published by Bromley & Co.). The museum, which is also operated by the Cape Cod Pilgrim Memorial Association, was built in 1961. Historical information is published by the association and it collects, preserves, exhibits, and interprets artifacts pertaining to Provincetown and outer Cape Cod.

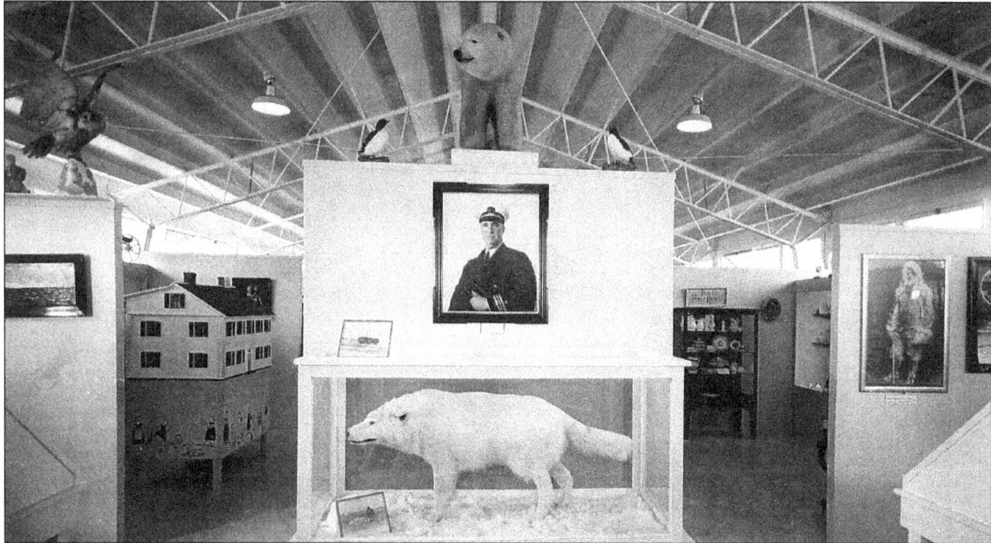

The MacMillan exhibit in the Provincetown Museum (c. 1965 photograph). An oil portrait of Admiral Donald Baxter MacMillan (1874–1970) is surrounded by stuffed Arctic mammals and birds, including a rare albino wolf, which were captured on one of his several expeditions to the frozen wasteland. A photograph of the young explorer who accompanied Robert Edwin Peary (1856–1927) on several expeditions to the North Pole can be seen at the right. MacMillan, Provincetown's most famous son, was the first man to use aircraft in exploration. (Courtesy Pilgrim Monument & Provincetown Museum.)

Five

The West End

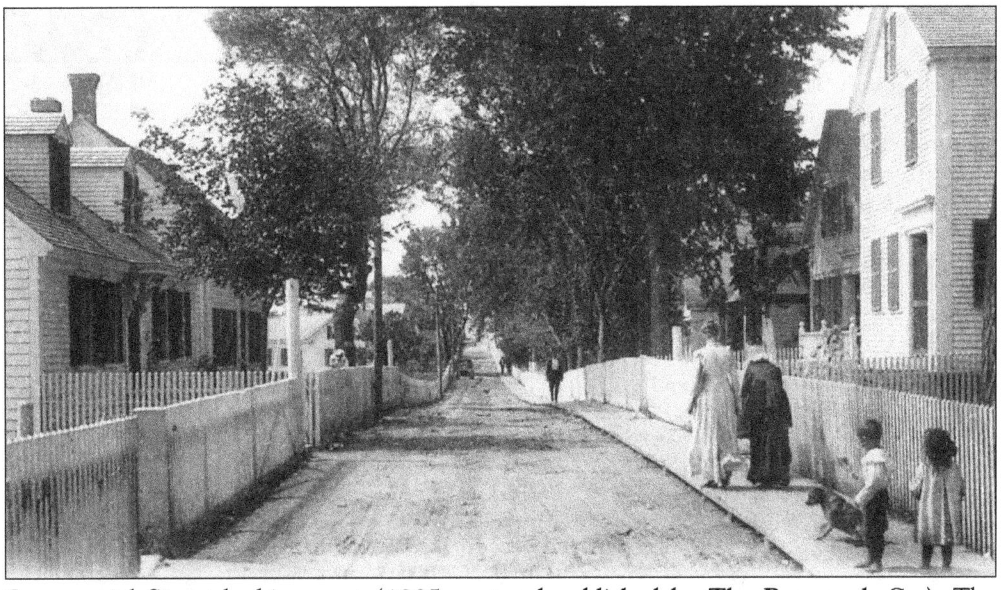

Commercial Street looking west (1905 postcard published by The Rotograph Co.). The historic and cultural West End of town is also considered by many to be the most quaint and quiet. The anchoring of the *Mayflower* in the harbor on November 11, 1620 (Old Style calendar), the drawing up and signing by the Pilgrims of the Mayflower Compact the same day, and the landing near the beginning of Commercial Street were three premier events in local and national history. Curved streets, roads, and lanes in the West End make walking enjoyable for architectural aficionados and gardening buffs. The earliest house in town, the *c.* 1746 Seth Nickerson House at 72 Commercial Street, and the nearby *c.* 1850 Octagon House—also known as the "Hatchway House"—contrast in style and repose with several houses "floated-over" from Long Point during the mid-nineteenth century. Cape Verdean and Azorean fishing families lived initially in the West End; they soon intermingled with the Yankee stock, or as Mary Heaton Vorse wrote, "The southern rose has been grafted on the sturdy stock of New England neatness and thrift." Artists, authors, playwrights, and actors lived, painted, wrote, and performed here, where many wharves once lined the panoramic harbor.

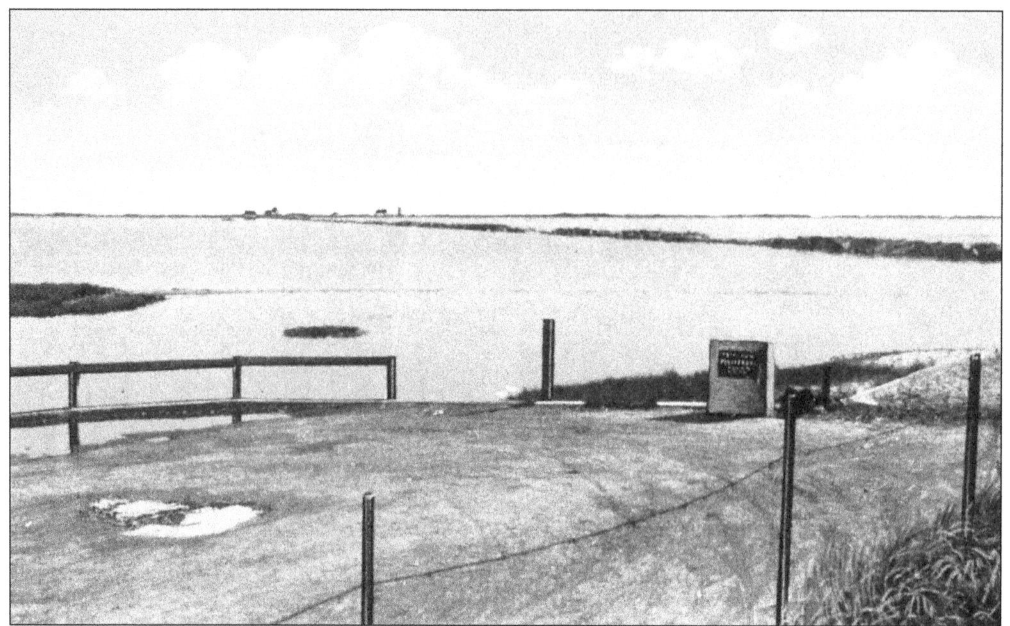

End of State Highway . . . The First Landing Place of the Pilgrims (c. 1920 postcard published by H.A. Dickerman & Son). The Research Club of Provincetown had this tablet-mounted granite memorial, known as the Pilgrim Plaque, erected in 1917. The redesign of this area with a rotary placed the memorial in a flat plaza with commemorative granite benches and walkway stones. In 1911 the government built the breakwater in the background, and Wood End Light is nearby on the opposite shore.

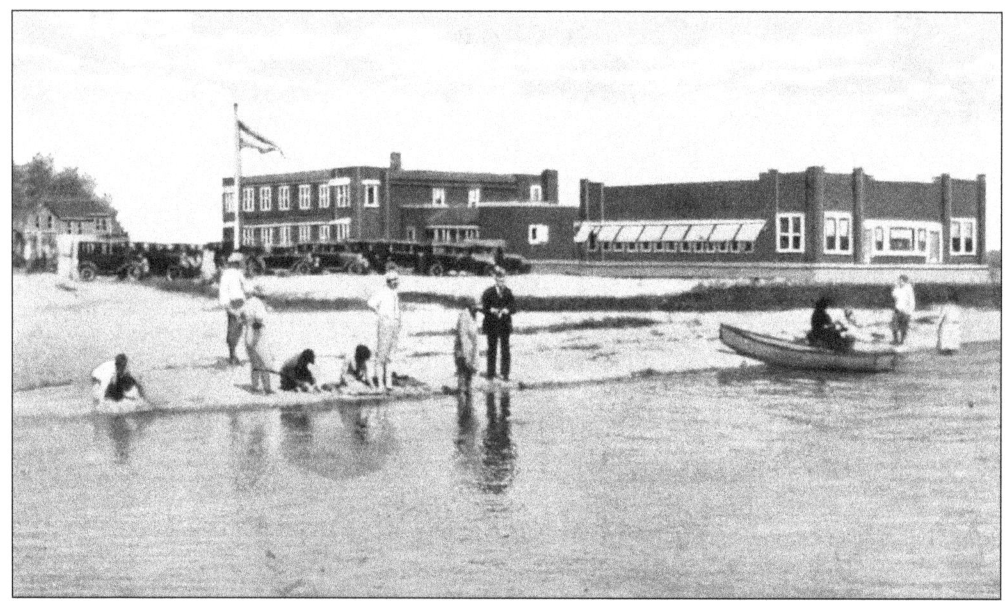

Provincetown Inn, 1 Commercial Street (c. 1925 postcard published by E.D. West Co.). The flat-topped inn's proximity to the "First Landing Place of the Pilgrims" must have been an inducement to tourists planning a vacation who had a sense of history. Wading and boating occupied youngsters who were probably oblivious to the spectacular views at the tip of Cape Cod.

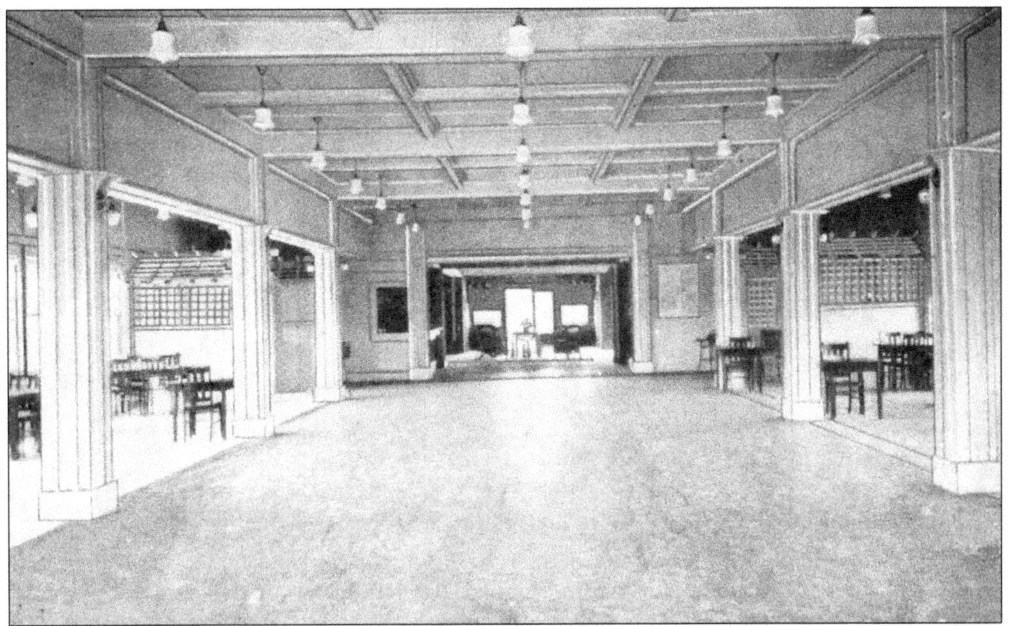

Interior of the Provincetown Inn, 1 Commercial Street (c. 1935 postcard published by The Provincetown Inn, Inc.). A coffered ceiling with pendant bell-shaped, electric lights illuminated what may have been the dance floor; golden oak tables and chairs were arranged in groups in the flanking alcoves. In 1966 Don Aikens painted polychrome murals in the inn based on old Provincetown postcards.

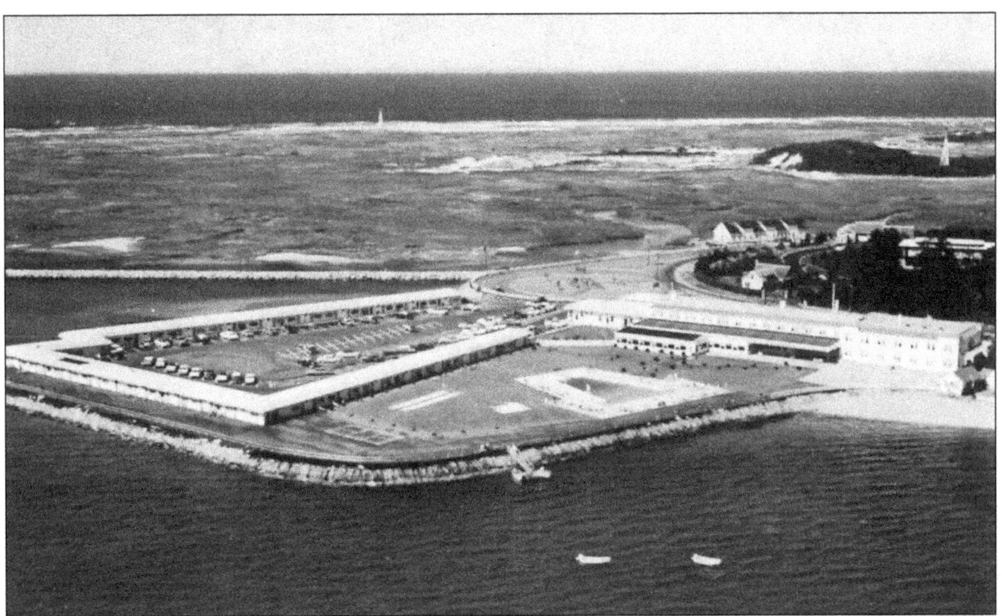

Provincetown Inn & Motel, 1 Commercial Street (c. 1975 postcard published by Mike Roberts, Berkeley, California). The caption states that the complex is "At the tip of Cape Cod, on the exact spot where the Pilgrims first landed on Nov. 11, 1620. The airview shows the Inn & Motel with the Pilgrim Hat-Pool centrally located."

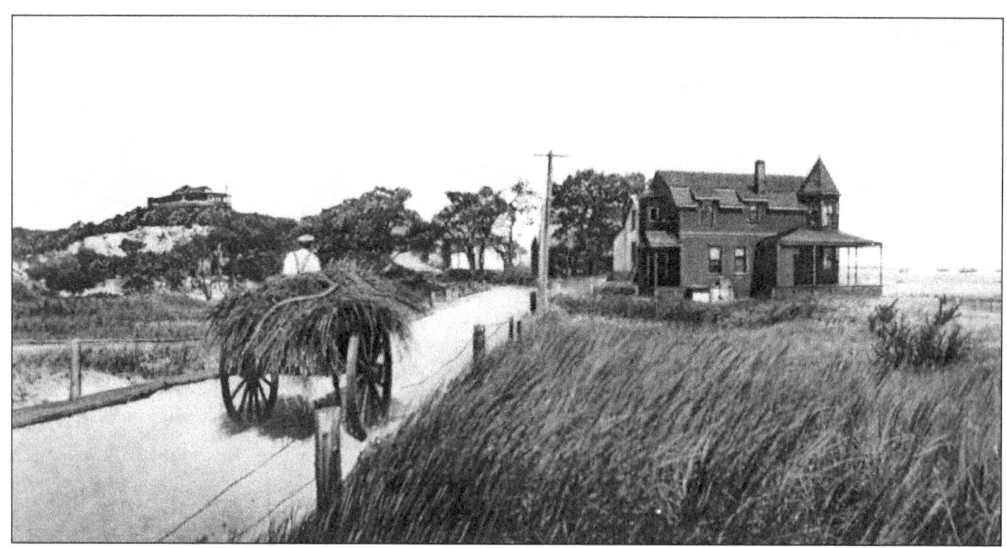

"Way Up Along," looking east on Commercial Street (early-twentieth-century postcard published by *The Advocate*). The building atop the dune in the distance is Higgins Bungalow, which later became Land's End Inn. Located previously on the select site was "Castle Dune," an unusual structure purchased by Dr. Carl Murchison, a Worcester, MA, professor, where he and his family resided for twenty years until it was destroyed by fire in 1956. They then engaged the services of Walter Gropius Associates to design the contemporary house that still occupies the site.

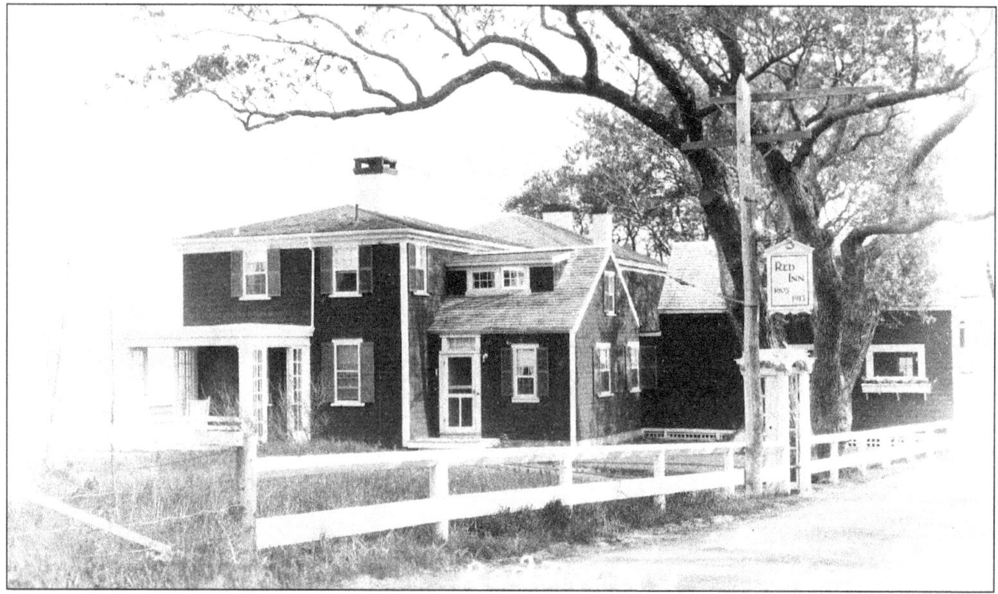

The Red Inn, 15 Commercial Street (c. 1920 photocard, publisher unknown). The original Federal-period hipped-roof house was built in 1805 by Captain Freeman Atkins for his bride, Maria Gross of Wellfleet. New York architect Henry Wilkinson renovated the structure about a hundred years later, and his sister Marion ran it as The Red Inn "on the European plan, offering rooms with bath, a garage, and chauffeurs' accommodations." The Wilkinsons' niece, Miss Charlotte Wilson, later operated the inn for over thirty years. Many illustrious persons have been guests or enjoyed afternoon tea here while overlooking the harbor.

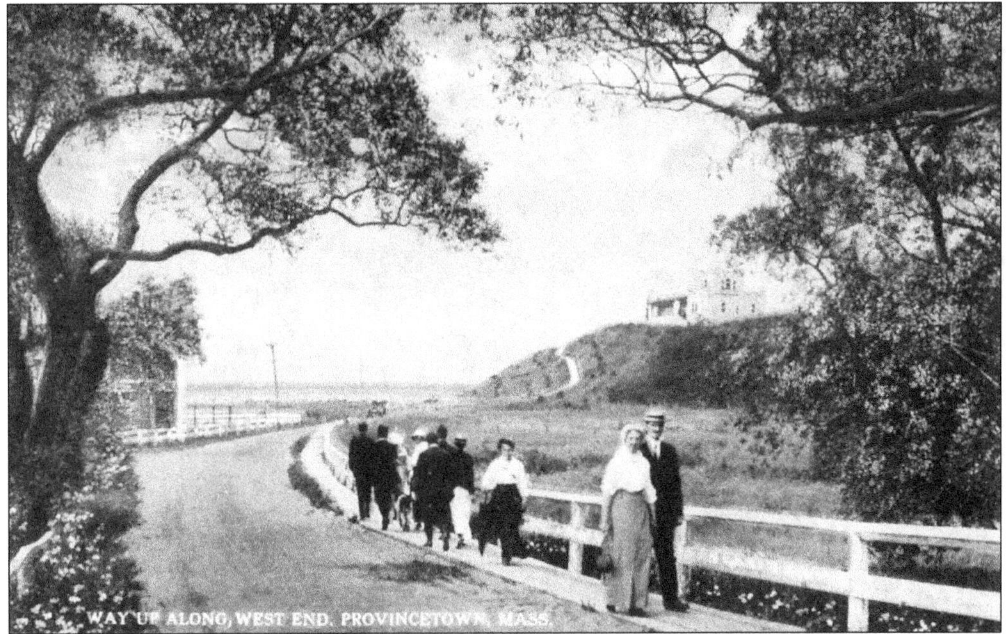

Way Up Along (c. 1915 postcard published by C.T. Photochrom). In contrast to "Down Along" in the East End, "Way Up Along" (as it was referred to by locals) was near the tip of the cape where the hills roll. This view of pedestrians almost opposite The Red Inn also depicts Castle Dune on the hill at the right; the atypical Provincetown structure was initially named "Hollingsworth."

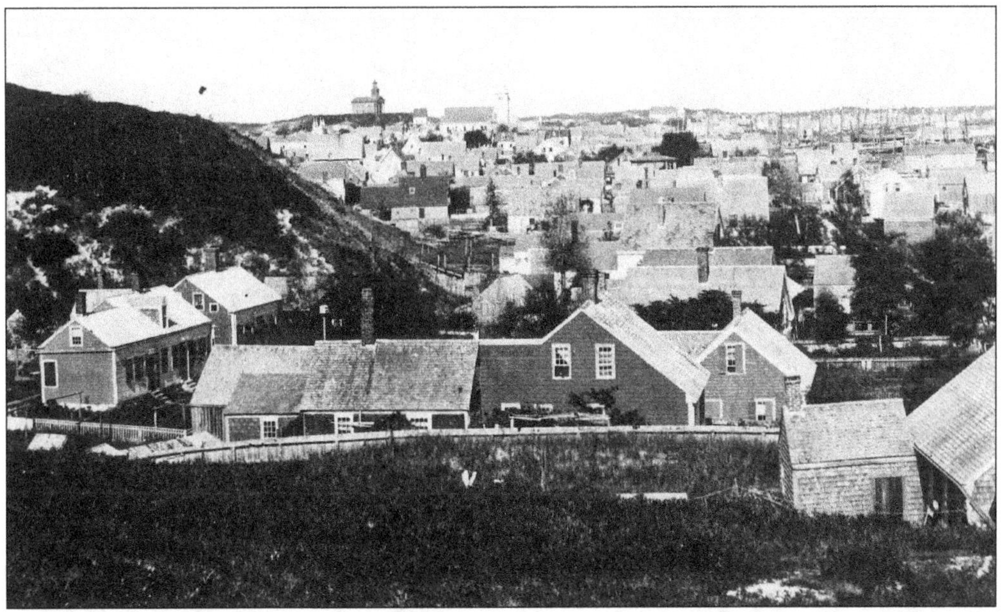

Provincetown from Gull Hill (c. 1885 stereopticon view by George H. Nickerson). The most prominent architectural landmark in the distance is the solitary town hall towering over churches and tall masts of vessels in the crowded harbor. The cottages in the foreground of Gull Hill appear to have either weathered or dark-painted shingles, in contrast to the traditional white-painted facades usually associated with Cape Cod houses.

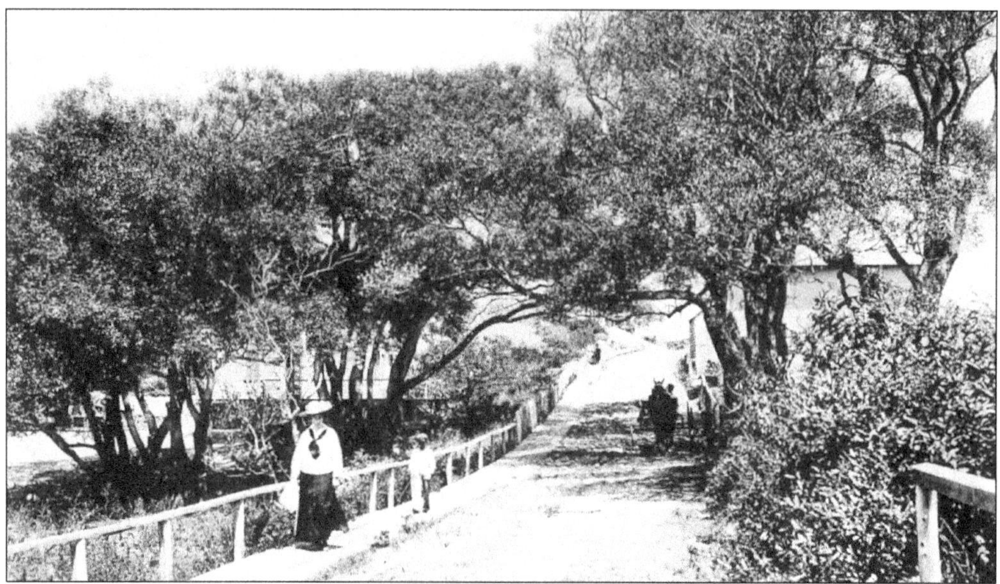

Way Up Along (c. 1915 postcard published by *The Advocate*). This view of Commercial Street looking east reveals the house at number 18 on the left behind the archway formed by tree branches. A young woman in the foreground is wearing a middy blouse and a black taffeta tie with matching black skirt, a popular seaside outfit for women between 1915 and 1920. A seated woman artist is at work on the plank sidewalk on Gull Hill.

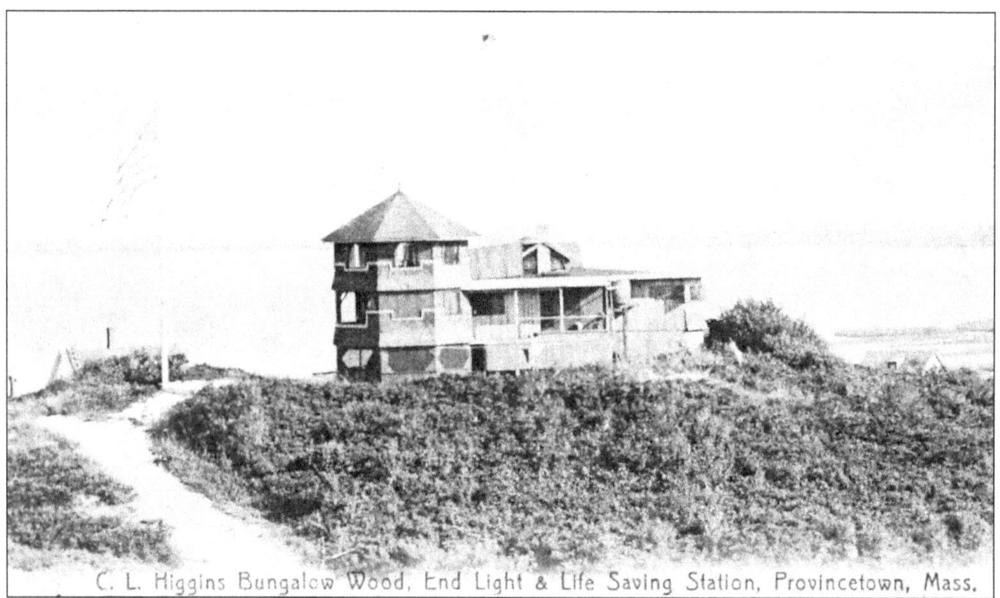

C.L. Higgins's Bungalow, 22 Commercial Street (c. 1905 postcard published by *The Advocate*). A two-story, octagonal, shingled library tower was the outstanding architectural feature of the bungalow Charles L. Higgins had built on Gull Hill. The retired Boston haberdasher and world traveler enjoyed the non-conformist home he had created during the last four years of his life.

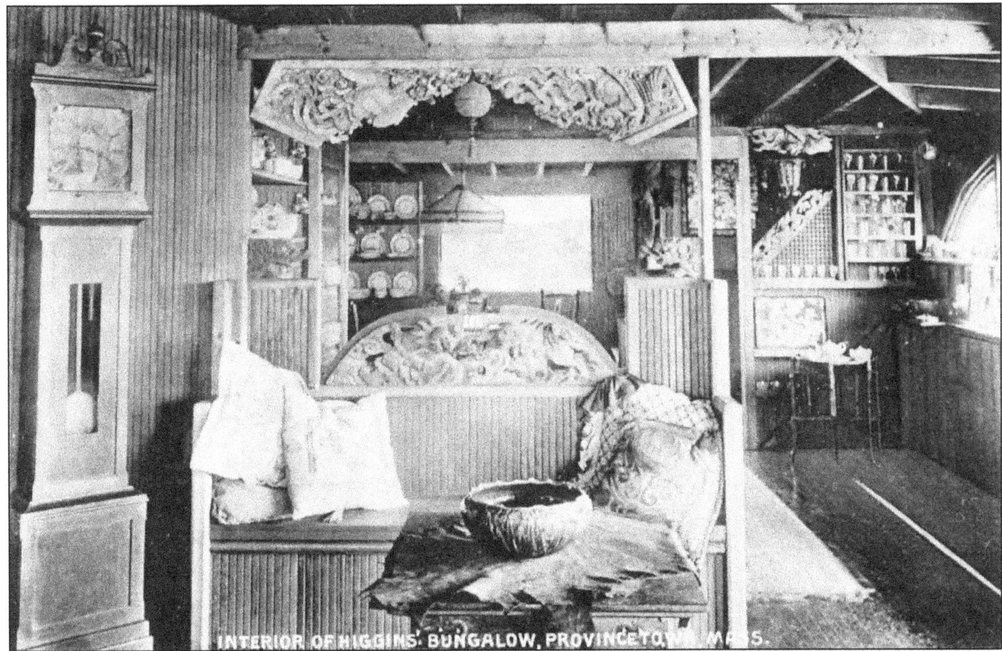

Interior of Higgins' Bungalow, 22 Commercial Street (c. 1913 postcard published by *The Advocate*). Japanese woodcarvings, probably painted in polychrome, and tastefully arranged furniture and decorative accessories such as the molded ceramic bowl on the hide-covered table and the large, patterned pillows, gave the teak-paneled Far Eastern ensemble a distinctive appearance. Indeed, as the postcard correspondent wrote, "This is the interior, its just like a palace, & the most romantic spot I ever struck."

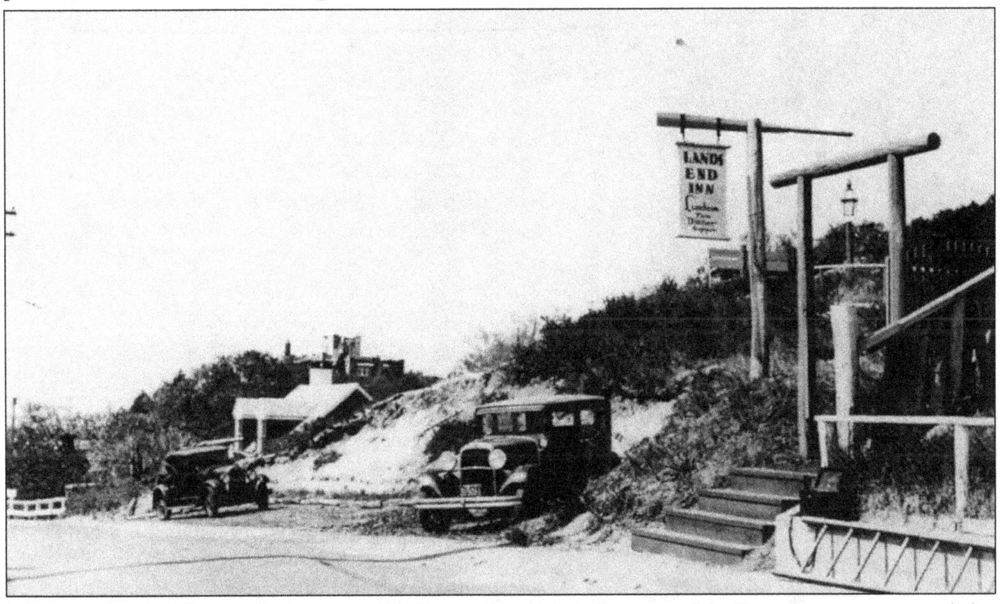

The Land's End Inn, 22 Commercial Street (c. 1932 photograph). Two vintage automobiles are parked near the entrance stairs to this fashionable guest house, acquired from the Higgins' estate in the 1920s. Luncheon, tea, dinner, and supper kept the staff busy. (Courtesy Provincetown Public Library.)

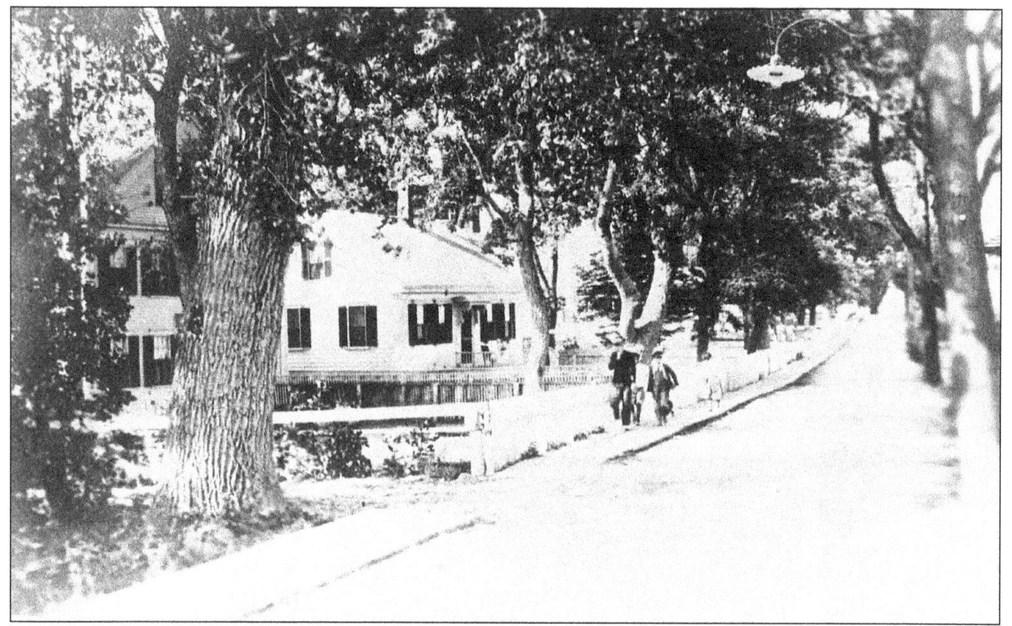

Commercial Street looking east (early-twentieth-century photograph). A family walks along the plank sidewalk past a full Cape Cod cottage (number 46) and passes in front of a Greek Revival-style house (number 44) on a sunny afternoon. Overhanging, fluted street lampshades were in use by this time. (Courtesy Seamen's Bank.)

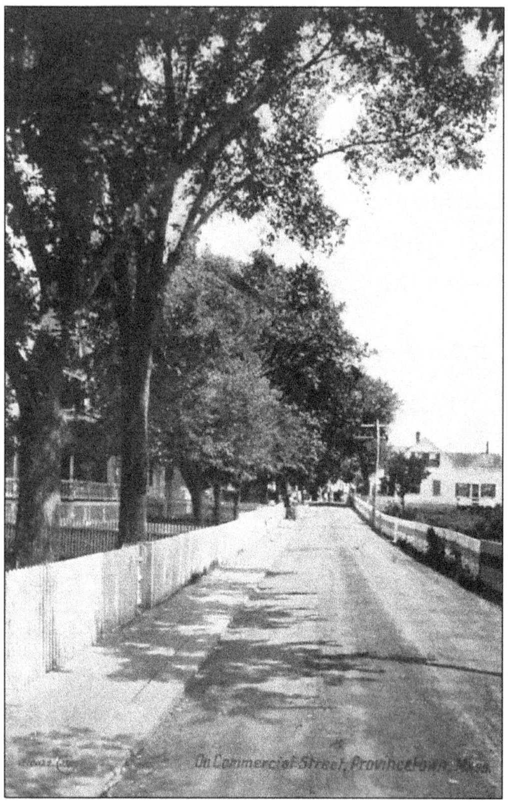

On Commercial Street looking east (c. 1915 postcard published by *The Advocate*). The house on the right (number 59) is the headquarters of the Center for Coastal Studies, a scientific organization that observes aquatic mammals and presents environmental programs for the public's edification.

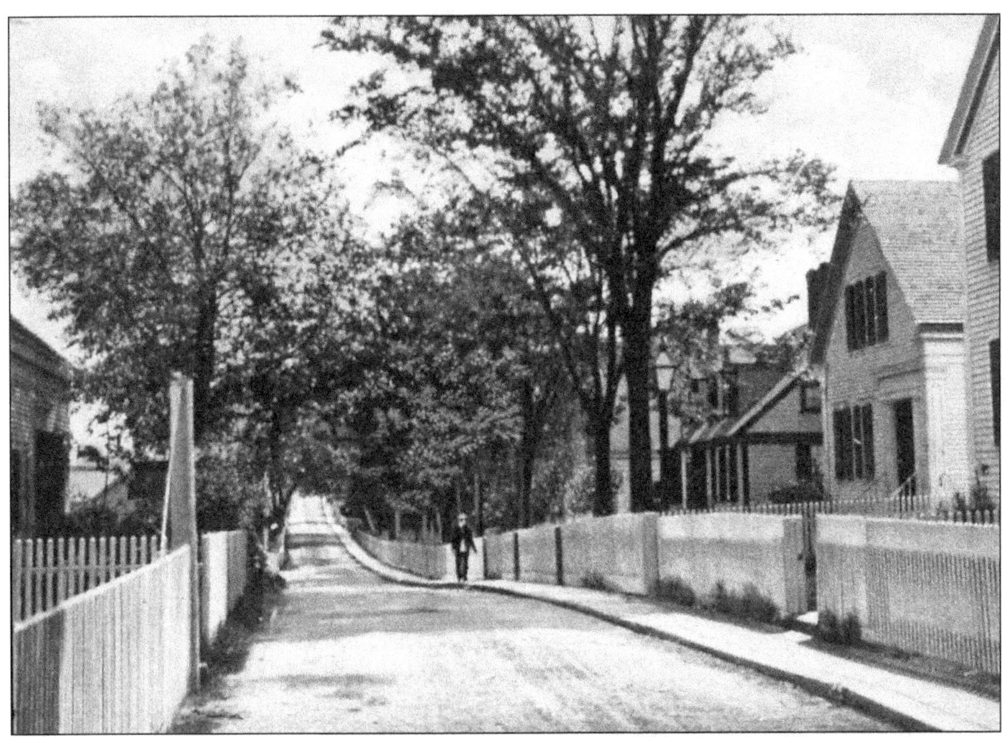

Commercial Street looking west (c. 1905 postcard published by H.C. Leighton, Portland, Maine). Narrow Commercial Street disappears into foliage as it progresses toward the tip of the cape. From right to left on the extreme right are the 1807 House (number 54), which was originally on the other side of the street and later served as a stop on the Underground Railroad; the Tod Lindenmuth House (number 56), where the well-known artist and his family lived from 1925 to 1940; and number 58, a house with a square, blue-and-white enameled plaque (made by local artist Claude Jensen) indicating that it was "floated over" from Long Point.

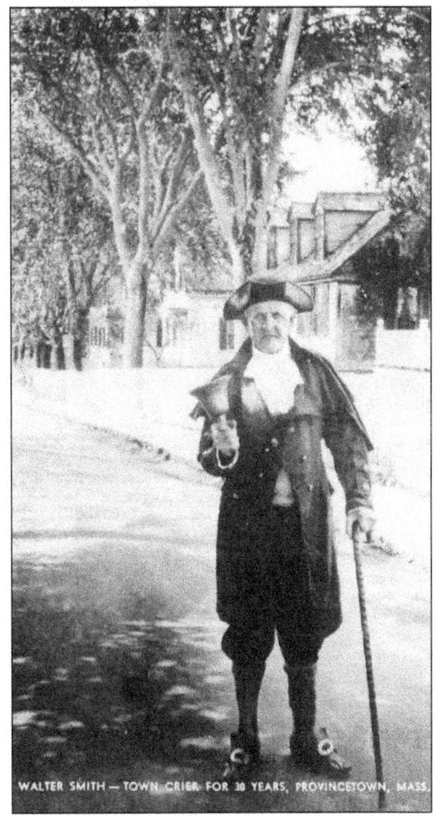

Walter Smith—Town Crier for 30 years (c. 1925 postcard published by The Town Crier Shop). Provincetown town criers announced auctions, entertainment events, personal affairs, public meetings, store sales, etc. on their morning and afternoon routes. In the center of town barkers proclaimed the daily specials of popular restaurants, many of which had their names on banners attached to both sides of Commercial Street. Walter "Hoppy" Smith is shown wearing Colonial garb near the 1807 House, but he also wore everyday clothing in his position as official town crier until he retired in 1930.

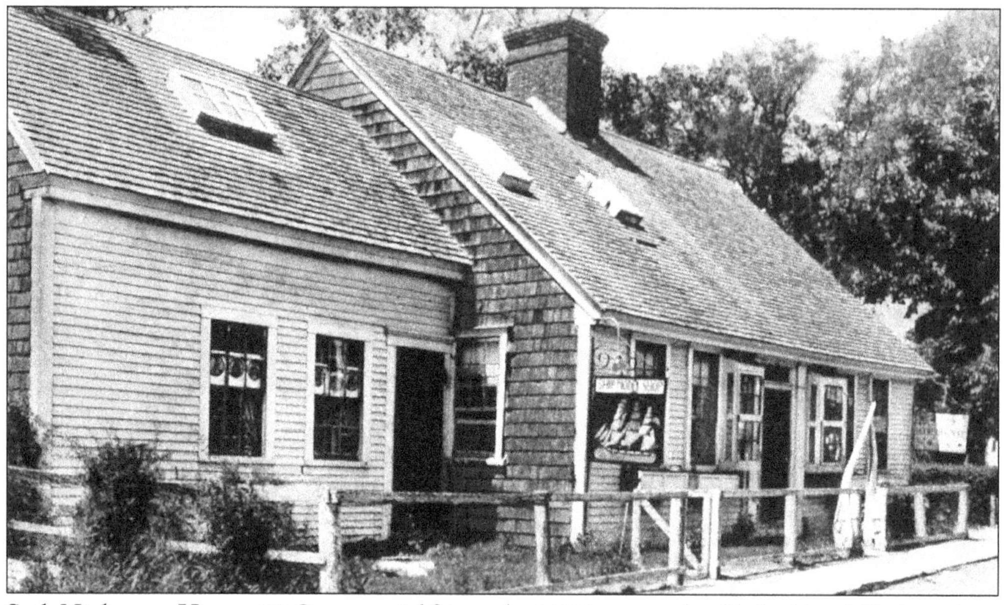

Seth Nickerson House, 72 Commercial Street (c. 1930 postcard published by C.T. American Art Colored). A whale's jawbone forms an archway over the entrance door to the cottage at the corner of Soper Street purported to be the oldest house in Provincetown. The architecturally significant, full Cape Cod-designed house contained a ship model shop and a hooked rug shop run by artist F. Coulton Waugh (1896–1973) and his wife, Elizabeth Waugh. John W. Gregory (1903–1992), another local artist and photographer, bought the house around 1945, and he and his wife, Adelaide, opened it to tourists for a modest fee.

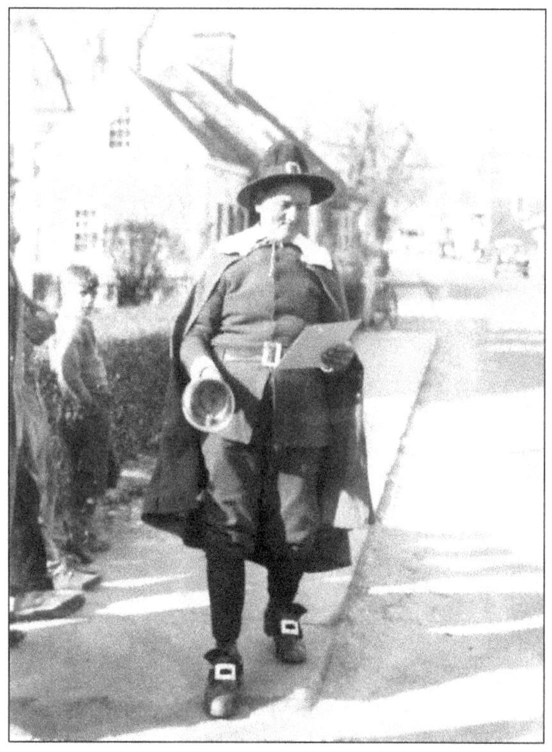

The Town Crier on Commercial Street (c. 1935 photocard; publisher unknown). Important information and trivia were both dispensed by the many town criers who served the town. Amos Kubik, the jovial fellow dressed as a "Pilgrim," has just passed "The Oldest House" and may be on his way to the First Landing Place of the Pilgrims in the far West End. A native of Bohemia, Mr. Kubik was appointed town crier in 1935, and he usually stood on Railroad Wharf where he would announce the day's activities to disembarking passengers after tolling the large bell.

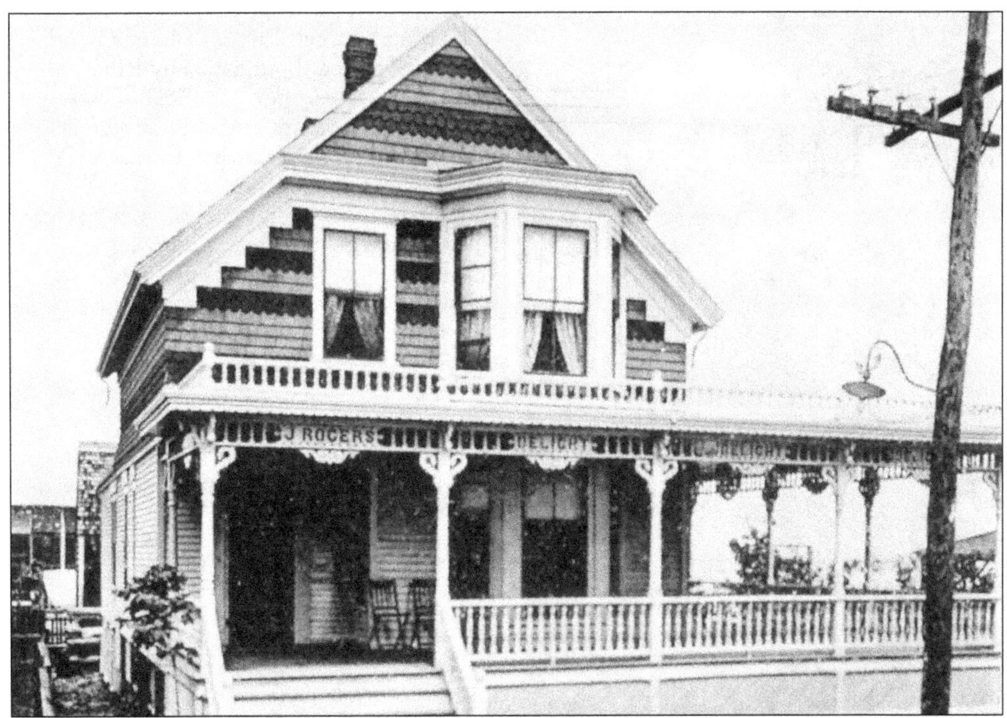

Delight Cottage, 113 Commercial Street (early-twentieth-century postcard published by *The Advocate*). The front porch of this modest Victorian dwelling was given a distinctive appearance by the owner, Jesse Rogers, a house carpenter and builder who added his name and the name of his home (DELIGHT) three times in the trim. The Rogers home was located on or near the site of the Coast Guard station where Commercial Street makes a sharp turn.

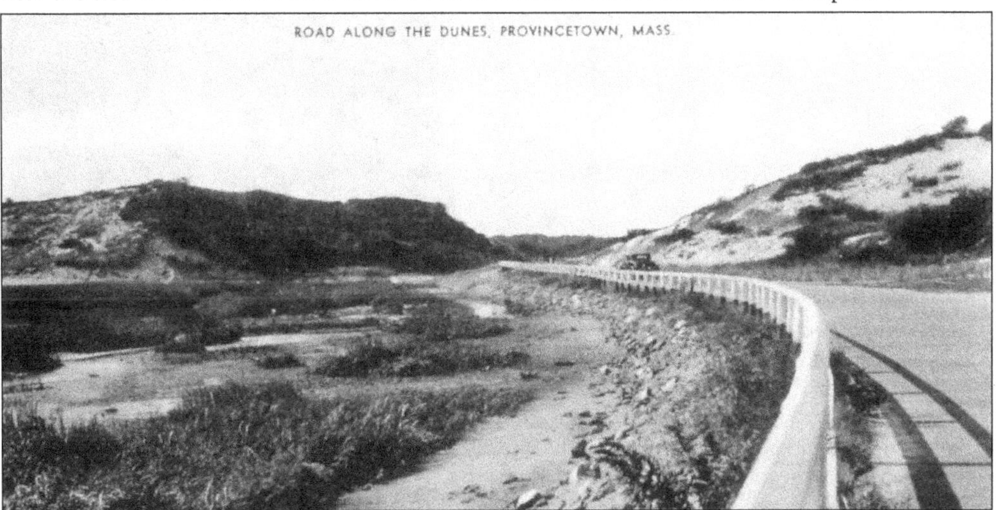

Road Along the Dunes (c. 1935 postcard published by The Town Crier Shop). The early 1930s automobile is headed away from the rotary at the beginning of Commercial Street at the right (now Route 6A South) toward parallel Herring Cove Beach and Race Point with its 1816 lighthouse. Today's driver can take a right onto Route 6 North or continue on the Province Lands Road, a part of the Cape Cod National Seashore, past the airport (built in the 1940s), and then take a right on to Race Point Road (which also leads to Route 6, Truro, and beyond).

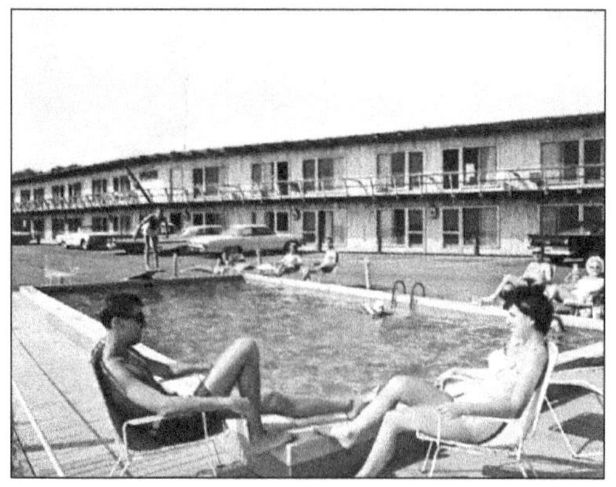

The Moors Motel, Province Lands Road (c. 1969 postcard published by Bill Bard Associates, Inc., Monticello, New York). The promotional postcard stated that the motel was "Provincetown's nicest overlooking the beautiful moors. Pool—private telephones and television, piped in music. Continental breakfast in season—Famous Moors Restaurant adjacent." These views, and the two below, appear in a vertical format on the postcards.

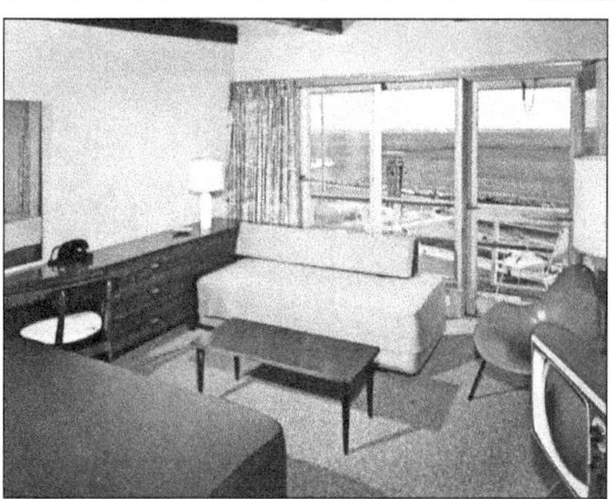

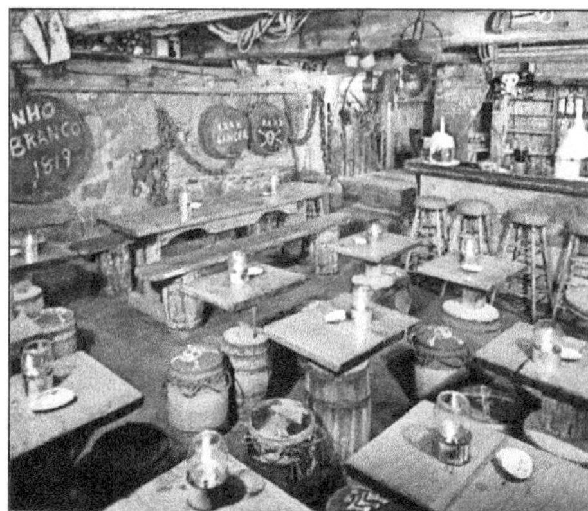

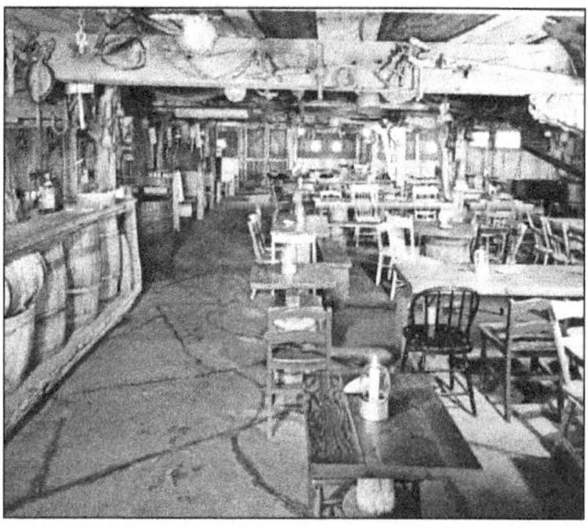

The Moors Restaurant, 5 Bradford Street Extension (c. 1969 postcard published by Bill Bard Associates, Inc.). The nautical restaurant was established around 1939 and boasted that the fresh seafood served was "combed from the Sea" and served in such a way so that "your dining and drinking pleasures are enhanced by the atmosphere of the old whaling days." Skull-and-crossbones images were emblazoned on the seat covers of wooden barrels, on the head of a wine cask, and behind the bar, setting a mysterious tone for the interior, which was enlivened by a flickering candle on each wooden tabletop.

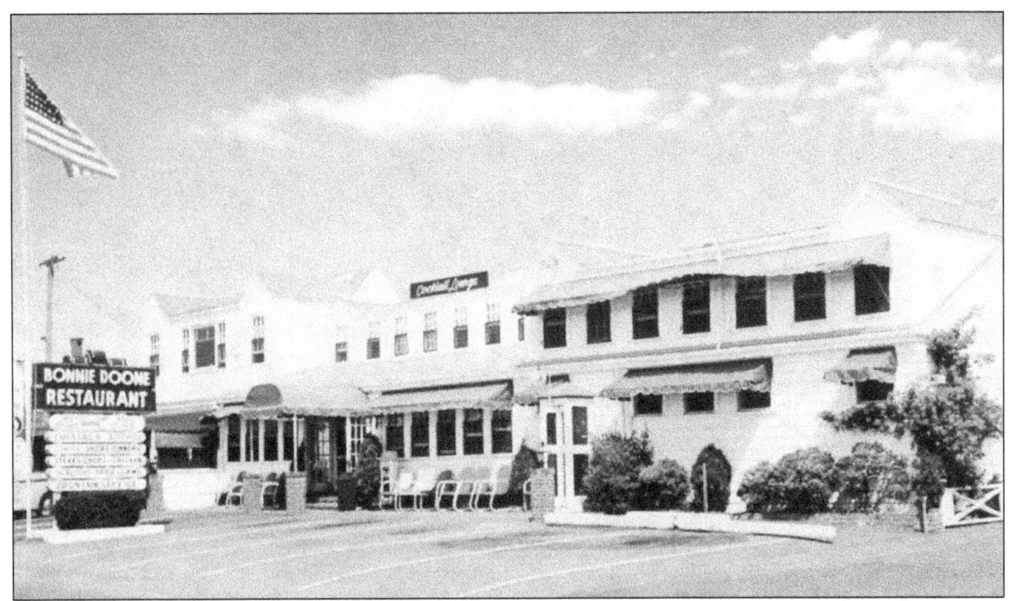

The Bonnie Doone Restaurant, 35 Bradford Street (c. 1965 postcard published by Mike Roberts). Off-street parking and lawn chairs were amenities offered by "Provincetown's Finest Restaurant. Specializing in Native Lobsters and Seafood, Steaks, and Chicken. Recommended by Duncan Hines. Approved by AAA . . . Tel. 1185. Visit Our Thistle Cocktail Lounge!" The popular eatery was in business as early as the 1930s.

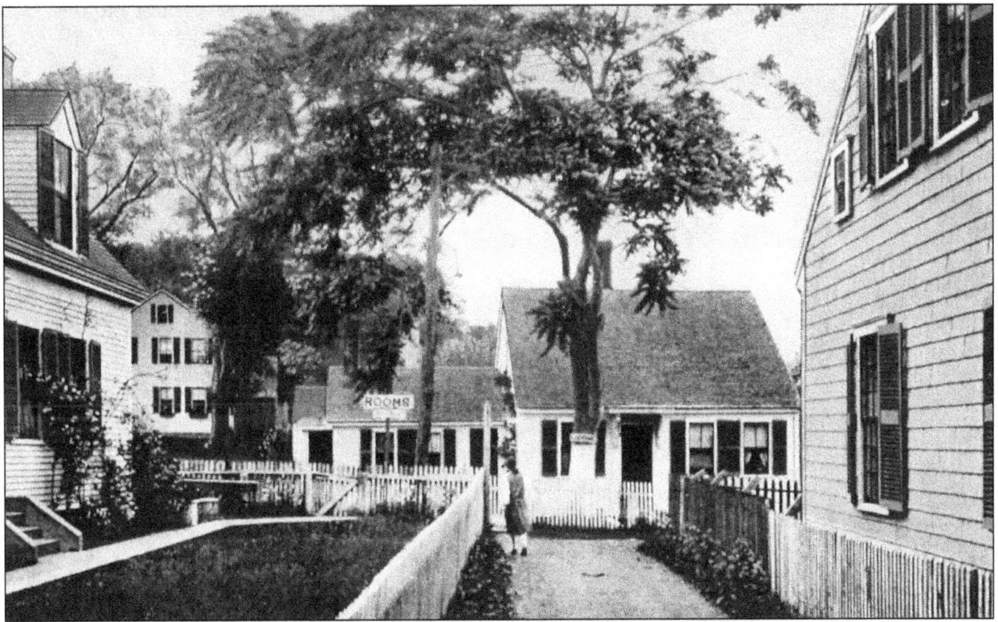

Atwood Avenue, between Point and West Vine Streets (c. 1934 postcard published by E.D. West Co.). Neat picket fences define the property lines of these residences at the intersection of Commercial Street looking down Atwood Avenue. Lodging in a quaint Cape Cod house appealed to many late-nineteenth and early-twentieth-century tourists as much as it does today. Two guest houses operating on Commercial Street in the late 1930s were the Apple Tree Cottage and Kibbie Cook's House.

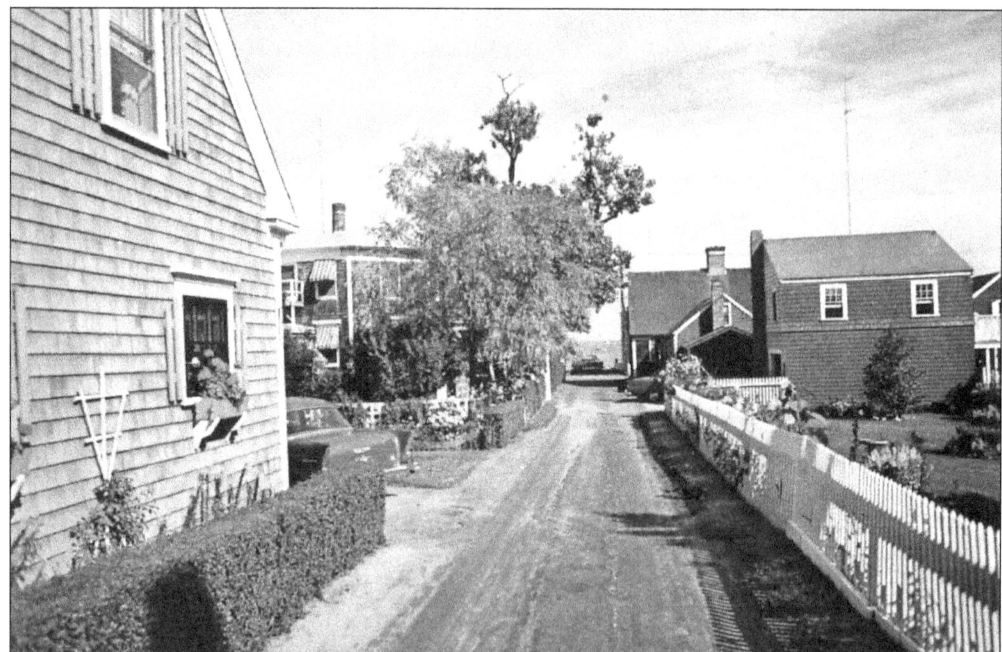

Soper Street looking toward the harbor (c. 1970 postcard published by Bromley & Co.). This narrow street lies between West Vine and Nickerson Streets and it may have been named for whaling ship captain Samuel Soper. The distinctive dwelling on the left corner of Commercial Street is the Octagon House; the smaller one on the opposite corner is the "Oldest House."

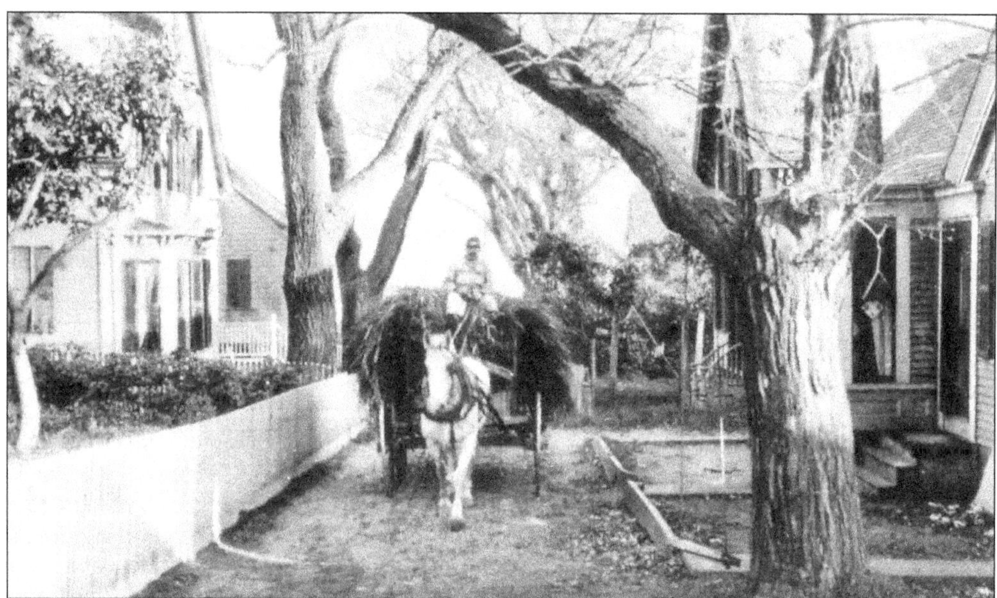

Nickerson Street looking toward the harbor (early-twentieth-century postcard published by The Town Crier Shop). A tawny-skinned salt marsh farmer navigates his horse and wagon along this former tree-arched lane in a romanticized agrarian image of an earlier time.

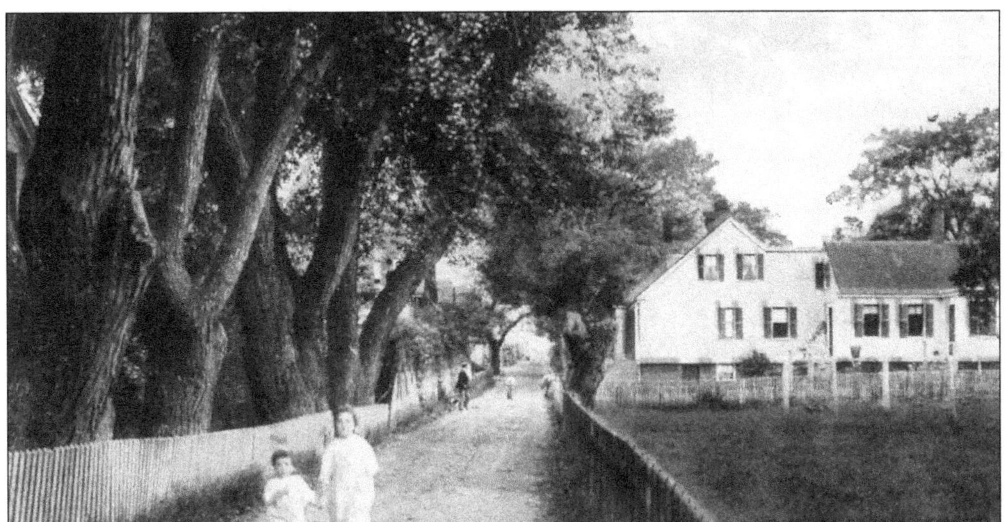

The Old Willows, Way Up Along, Nickerson Street (c. 1915 postcard published by H.A. Dickerman & Son). Nickerson Street is situated between West Vine, part of Soper, and Cottage Streets. The gigantic weeping willow trees that once lined this and other streets in town have disappeared, due to either storm damage or human hands; many residents feared they would topple onto their small homes and had them cut down, thereby changing the look of the town before the mid-twentieth century.

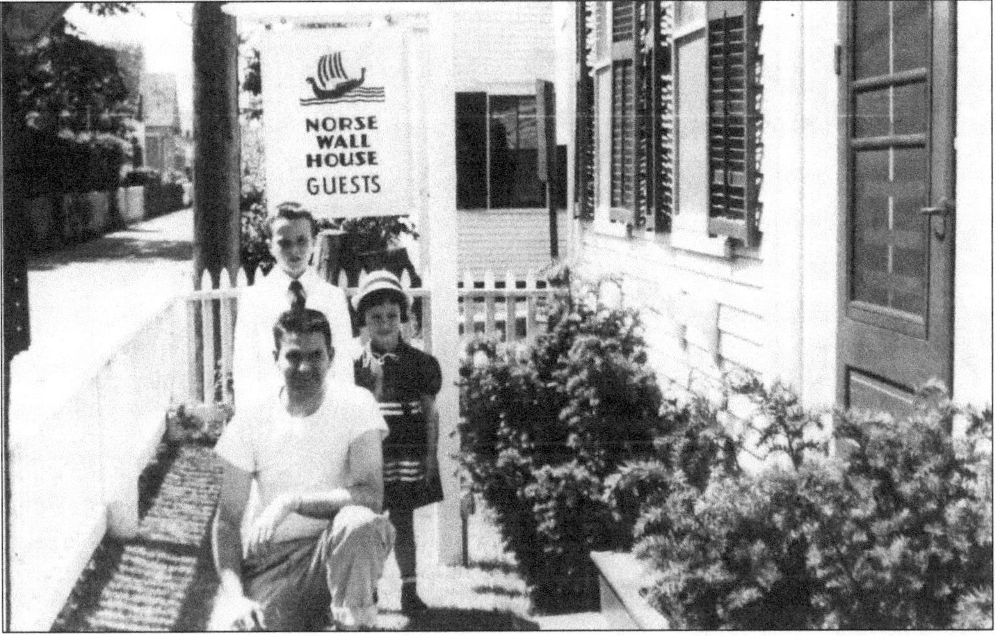

The Norse Wall Guest House, 7 Cottage Street (c. 1952 photograph). Francis E. Rogers kneels in front of his children, Francis Jr. and Joan Margaret, in a casual photograph taken by his wife, nee Eugenia Atkins. The guest house was given the fascinating name because a portion of an unexplained ancient stone foundation and a hard earthen floor were accidentally discovered about 8 feet below the ground level around 1853. Tradition has ascribed the no-longer exposed wall to Viking explorers who may have erected a shelter when they traversed this area of the cape, c. 1004. (Courtesy Eugenia Atkins Rogers.)

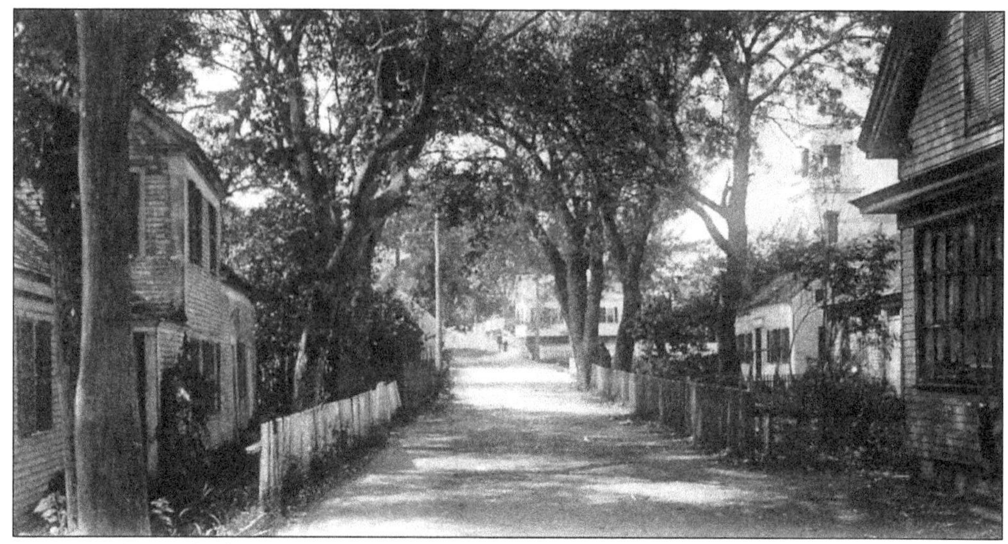

Tremont Street looking west (1905 postcard published by The Rotograph Co.). Tremont Street has remained mostly residential since it was laid out. It is a continuation of Commercial Street where it takes a left at "Lancy's Corner" (Benjamin Lancy, the nineteenth-century owner of a salt works there, would not permit Commercial Street to bisect his thriving business). The white steeple in the background is that of the former Western School, one of three schoolhouses built in town around 1844 in the Greek Revival style.

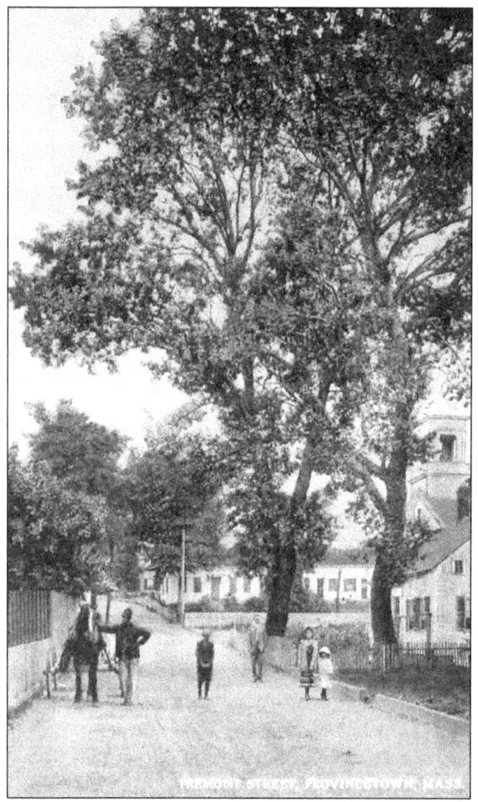

Tremont Street looking west (c. 1915 postcard published by C.T. Photochrom). A farmer and assorted schoolchildren pose near the Western School, which was located between School and Mechanic Streets. "Barshie," "Begunna," "Parchie," and "Skunchy" were nicknames given to each other by Portuguese boys who may have attended this grammar school (grades 2, 4, and 6), the Center School on Bradford Street (grades 1, 3, and 5), or the Eastern School on Howland Street (grades 2, 4, and 6).

Six

The East End

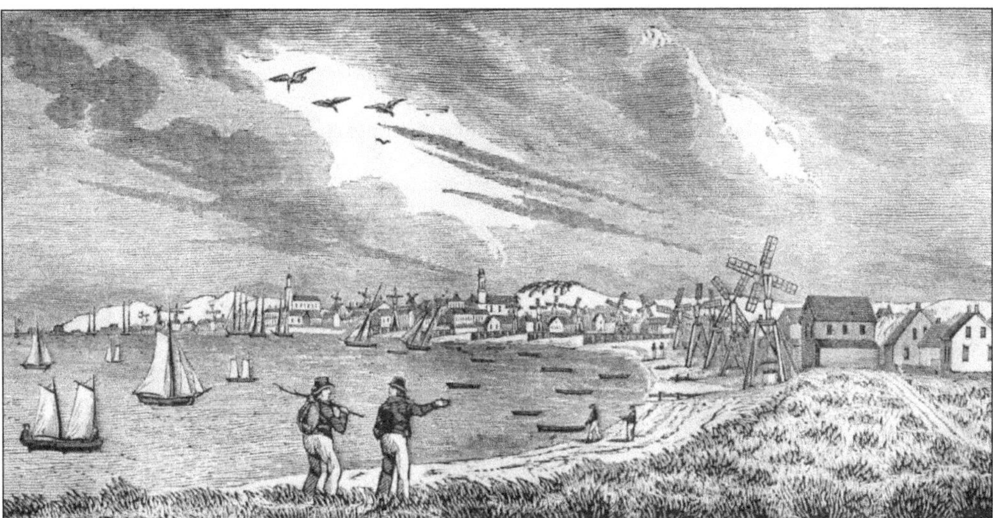

A Northeastern View of Provincetown (1839 wood engraving). An erstwhile vagabond, whom the author associates with Henry David Thoreau, asks directions from an inhabitant of Provincetown while standing "on the margin of a beach of loose sand." The numerous windmills used to process sea salt gave the town the aspect of a European village; they are dominant in this early print included in John Warner Barber's *Historical Collections of Every Town in Massachusetts*. Around 1850, in Thoreau's words, "their now idle windmills lined the shore." The windmills were so important to the local economy that Chip Hill in the West End (far left) was leveled about 25 feet in 1805 for the establishment of a salt works. The creaking windmills with their "turtlelike sheds" were only in operation during the summer months when the rays of the sun were the strongest. Salt from the summer's harvest was stored in salt bankers for the next season's use, primarily for preserving freshly caught fish. Some of the simple Cape Cod houses in the engraving no doubt exist today—"mostly situated on a single street about two miles in length, passing round near the water's edge," but the two churches, Congregational and Methodist, were replaced by later edifices of similar prominence.

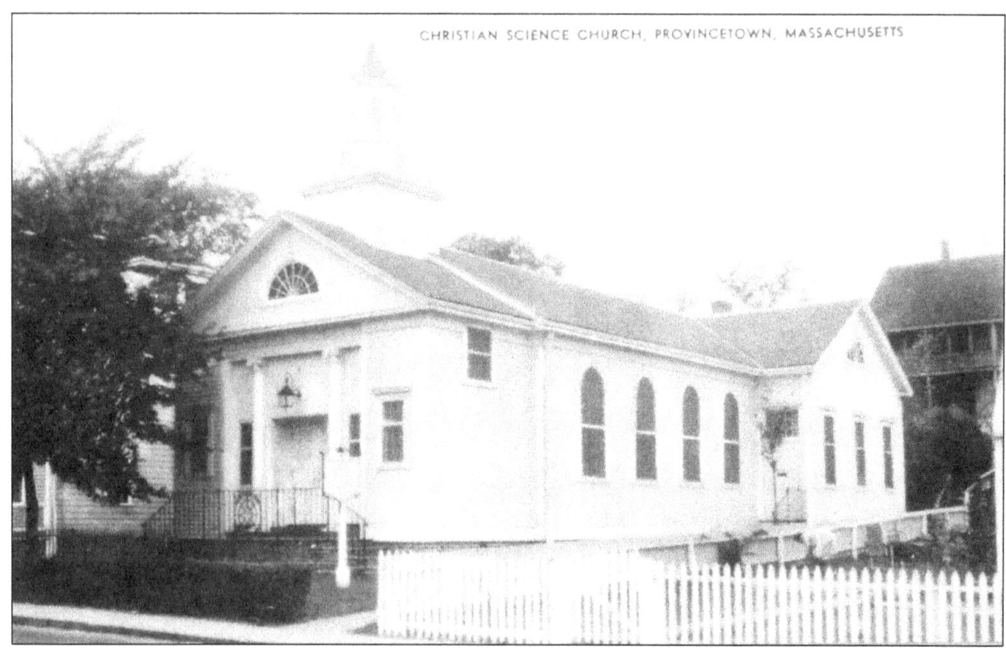

Christian Science Church, 418 Commercial Street (c. 1940 postcard published by The Town Crier Shop). An octagonal cupola with arched windows graces the modest Colonial Revival-style church attended by Christian Scientists until it was deconsecrated and later became a gallery with housing. Jose Alemany had a photography gallery behind the chapel, where he displayed and sold Provincetown scenes in the 1930s.

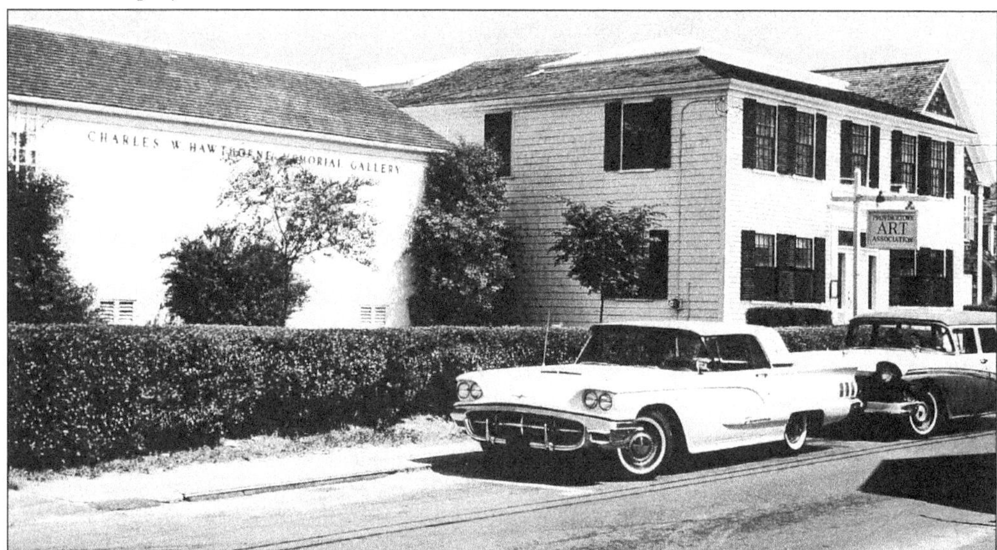

The Provincetown Art Association and Museum, founded in 1914, 460 Commercial Street (c. 1960 photograph taken by artist-member George Yater). The gallery added in 1942 to the Federal-period main building of the Provincetown Art Association and Museum honors Charles W. Hawthorne (1872–1930), the first artist to have en plein air painting classes in town—at the Cape Cod School of Art—beginning in 1899. Hawthorne's works, and those of other members of the Provincetown Art Colony, and later independent artists, are displayed in four galleries of the art association. (Courtesy Provincetown Art Association and Museum.)

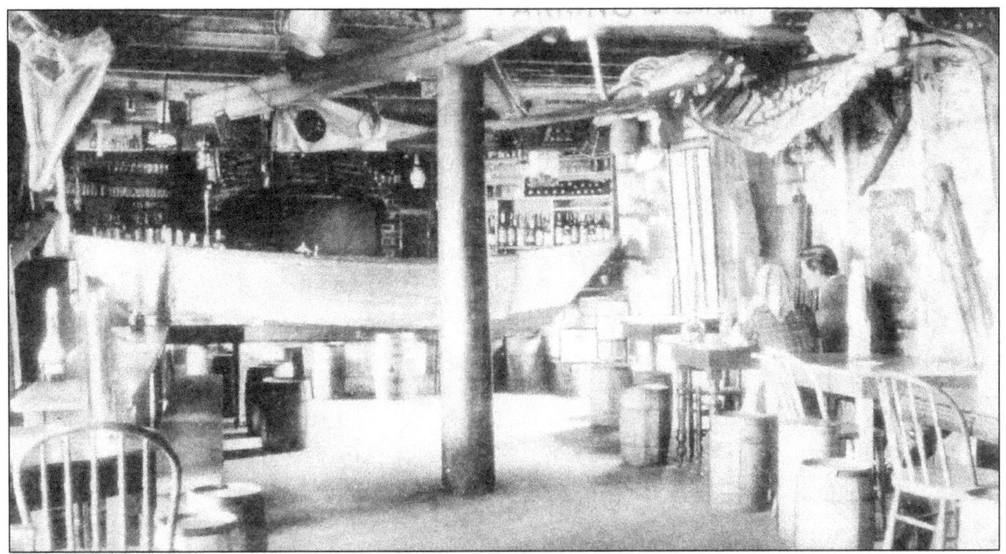

The Flagship Bar & Grill, 463 Commercial Street (c. 1940 postcard published by Art Vue Post Card Co., New York). The nautically decorated 1930s bar and grill was one of the earliest combination "eat and drink" spots in Provincetown. An advertisement in 1945 stated: "Gourmets Seek the Flagship . . . right now they're raving about the broiled sweetbreads prepared in a unique FLAGSHIP manner. Then, too, there are delicious frog legs . . . and always the delightful atmosphere . . . with its open fire of driftwood for drizzly days and seaside chairs in the cooling breezes for hot afternoons."

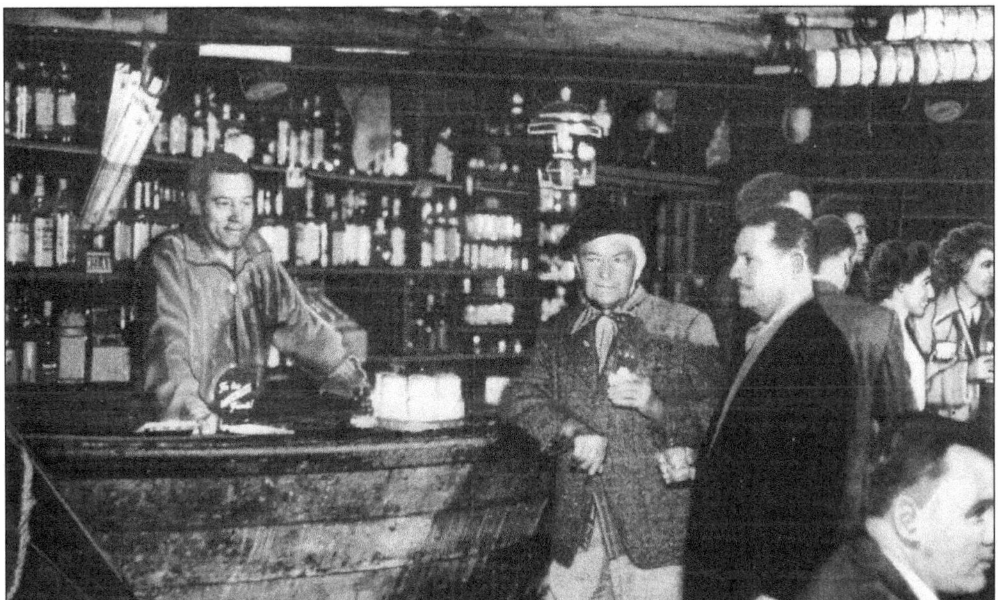

Flagship Bar & Grill, 463 Commercial Street (c. 1955 postcard published by The Mayflower Sales Co.). The Beachcombers, a Saturday night social dinner club of artists, authors, musicians, and professional men, has met in David Stull's former fish house since 1918. Attached to the Flagship Bar & Grill, the "Hulk" with its great fireplace was maintained by the exclusively male members, who sponsored auctions, costume balls, and musical shows. Flagship owner "Pat" Patrick is shown tending bar.

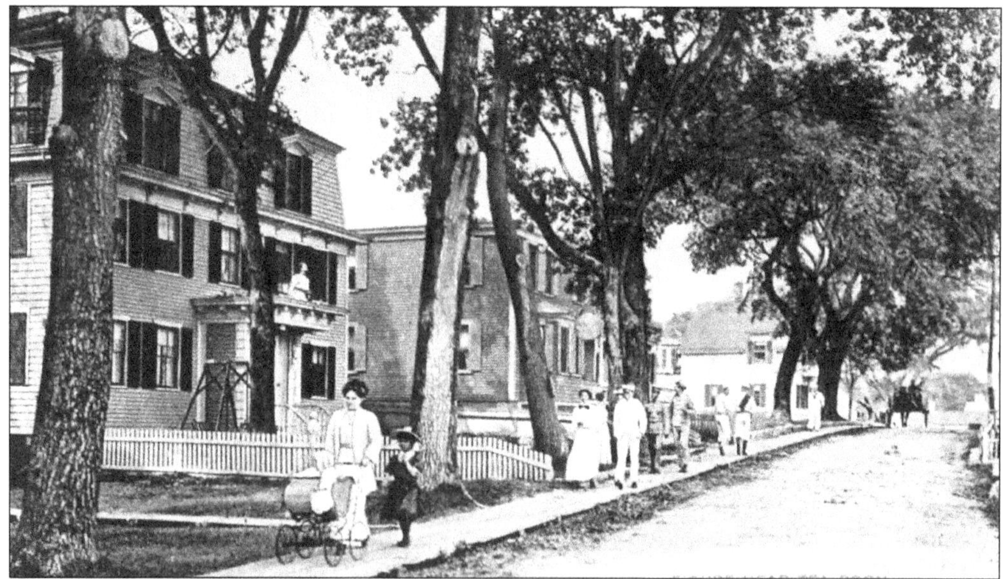

Figure Head Tea Room, 476 Commercial Street (c. 1915 postcard published by the New England News Co.). Located at the corner of Cook Street is the French Second Empire-style, c. 1850 "Figure Head House," which was operated as a tearoom during the early twentieth century. An unknown ship's female figurehead was rescued at sea in 1867—but sawn in half because of its size—and initially positioned over the door of the brothers Cook company store and wharf (the H. & S. Cook Company) opposite Henry's home. Before the store was sold, the carved and painted "Lady of Mystery" was placed over his door where she formerly beguiled passersby.

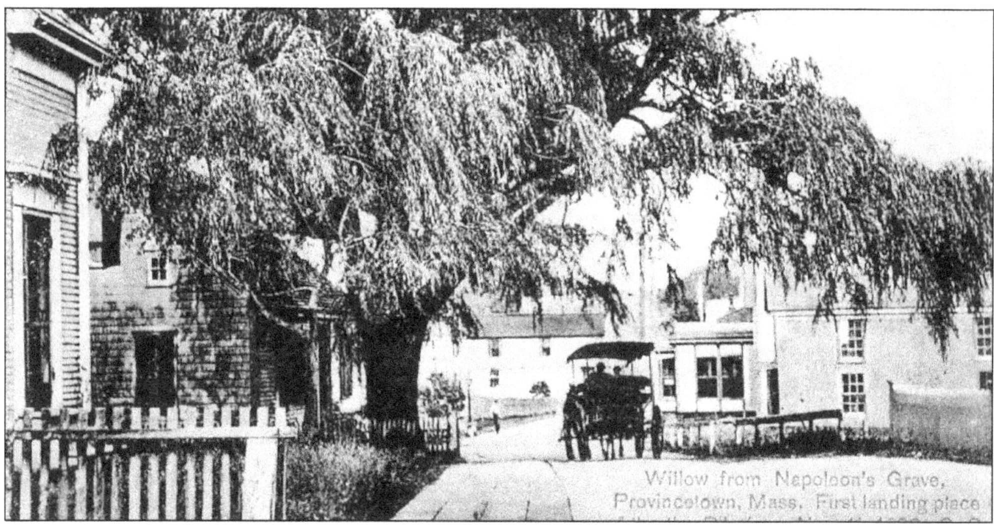

Willow from Napoleon's Grave, Commercial Street looking east from the vicinity of Howland Street (c. 1910 postcard published by *The Advocate*). It has been written that around 1827 there were only three trees in Provincetown and that they were weeping willows, traditionally thought to have been propagated from slips pilfered from Napoleon Bonaparte's grave on St. Helena and brought back by a local mariner. This long-gone, lush tree warranted a postcard with additional information about the date of the Pilgrims' landing in Provincetown "Old Style."

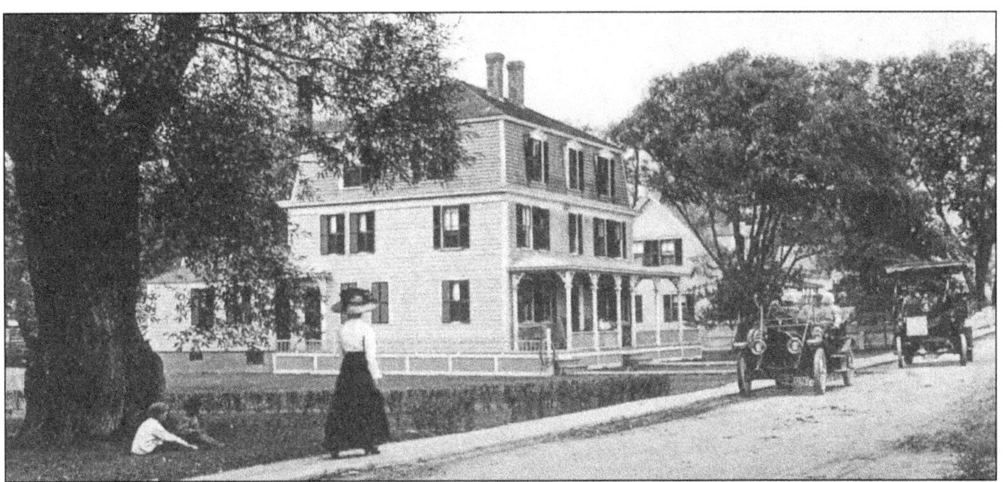

Mayo Cottage, 493 Commercial Street (c. 1910 postcard published by *The Advocate*). One of the town's accommodations is about to pass an open touring car in front of the Second Empire-style "cottage" formerly owned by Captain Edwin Mayo, a mariner. In the decade between 1890 and 1900 it was run as a guest house with the name Seaside Cottage. This stately house and Kendall Cottage at the right were razed in the 1960s for the construction of a motel.

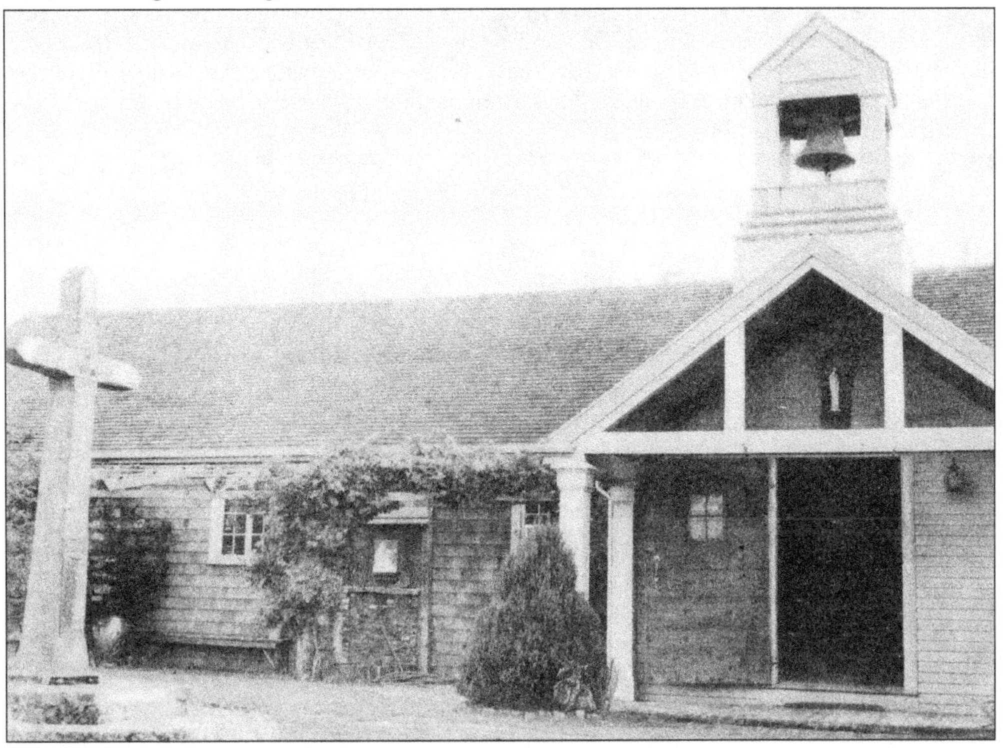

St. Mary of the Harbor Episcopal Church, 519 Commercial Street (c. 1938 postcard published by the Town Crier Shop). An old salt or fish house and part of the Sandbar Club were remodeled into a church opposite Anthony Street by local artists; the building contains works by them in different media. The wooden cross in the peaceful garden has a bronze plaque commemorating the lives of the forty crewmen of the *S-4*, an American submarine that sank off Wood End on December 19, 1927.

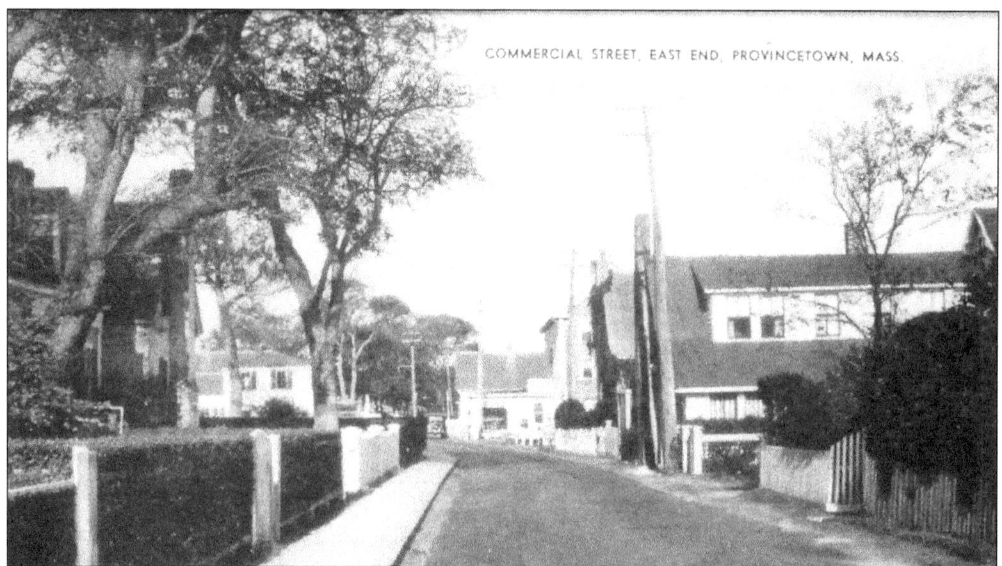

Commercial Street looking east (early-twentieth-century postcard published by The Town Crier Shop). Tilting utility poles line the harbor side of the street as seen here between Conway Street and Kendall Lane. A small monument erected in 1988 (beyond the house with the row of second-story windows at number 565 and to the left of the house at number 571 where author John Dos Passos lived) states that Mary Heaton Vorse's wharf was located there and that *Bound East for Cardiff*, Eugene O'Neill's avant garde play, was first performed there by the Provincetown Players on July 28, 1916.

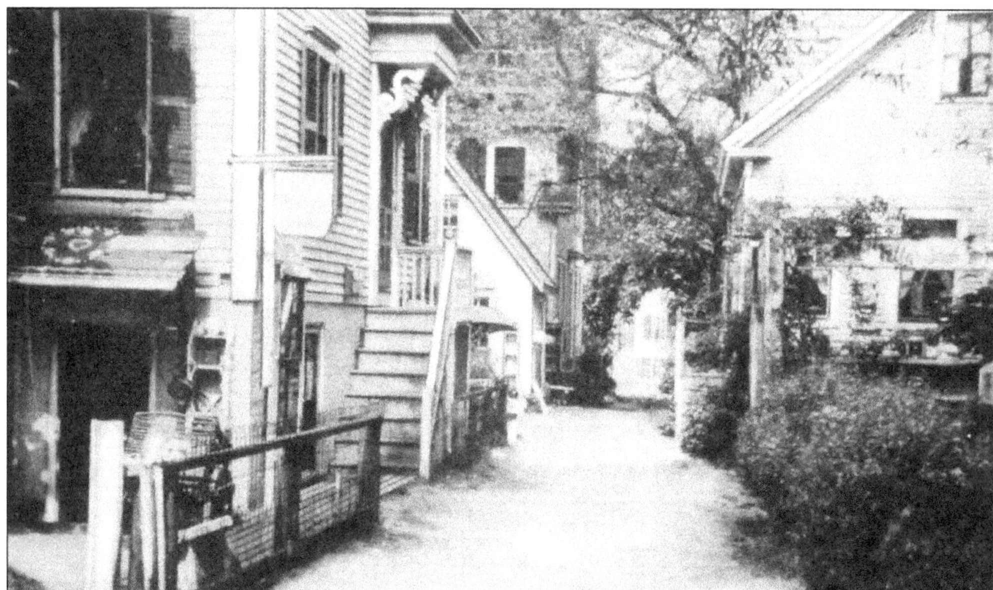

Peter Hunt Lane, a.k.a. Kiley Court (c. 1945 postcard published by *The Advocate*). Former successful New City antiques dealer Peter Hunt came to Provincetown in 1919 and began another career as a decorative furniture painter. The colorful, northern European-inspired designs that emanated from his "Pleasant Village" studio made him famous in the 1940s; he also authored the popular *Peter Hunt's Cape Cod Cookbook*. An admiring reporter wrote, "surely so much gay imagination has never been squandered on furniture and furnishings."

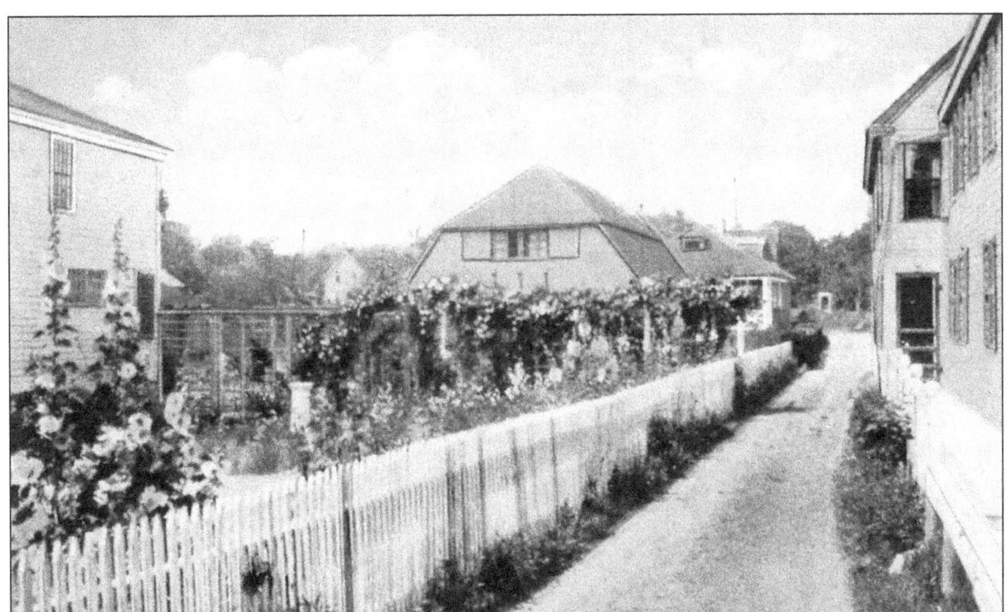

Studio Garden, Daggett Lane (early-twentieth-century postcard published by The Advocate Gift Shop). Narrow dirt roads with multi-colored, old-fashioned flowers blooming behind white picket fences elicit raves from gardening enthusiasts. When a picturesque building such as an artist's studio with a sleeping dormer is added to the composition, the scene has appeal to architectural admirers as well. Daggett Lane is located between Howland and Anthony Streets.

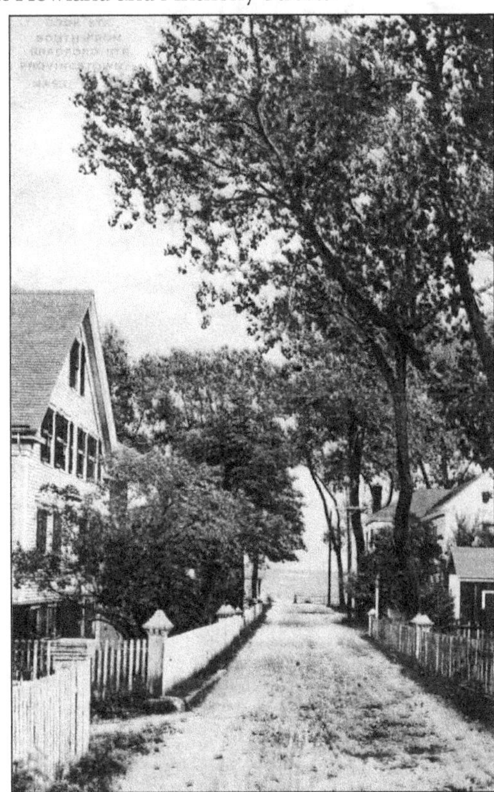

Cook Street South from Bradford Street (c. 1910 postcard published by The New England News Co.). Cook Street is the tenth road from the junction of Commercial and Bradford Streets, and was undoubtedly named for one of the more outstanding members of the seafaring Cook family.

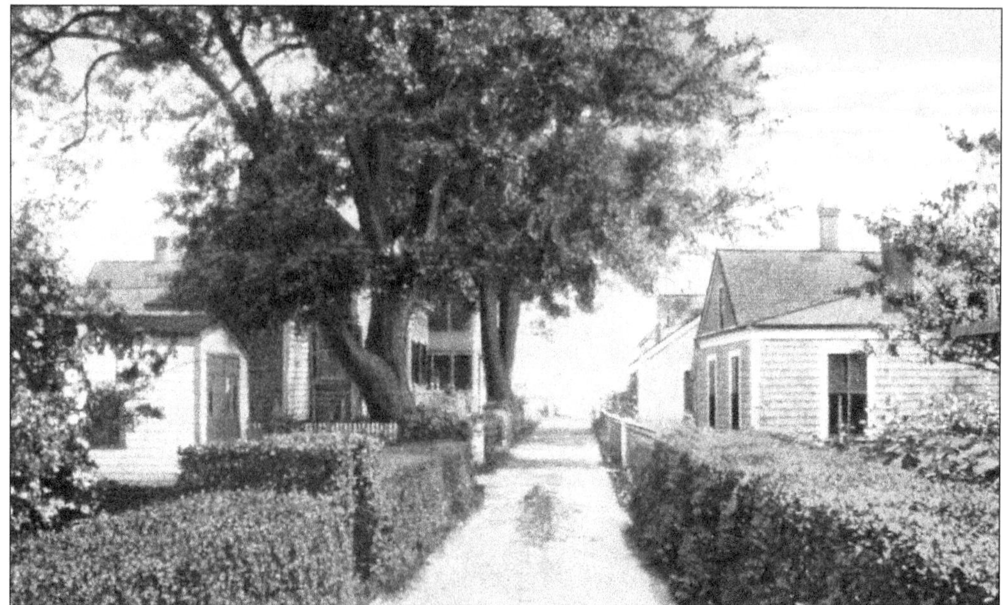

Atkins Lane from Bradford Street (early-twentieth-century postcard published by The Advocate Gift Shop). One of the narrowest lanes in town is this one between Anthony and Hancock Streets. Barely a car's width, the one-way lane from Bradford Street faces the harbor in this view.

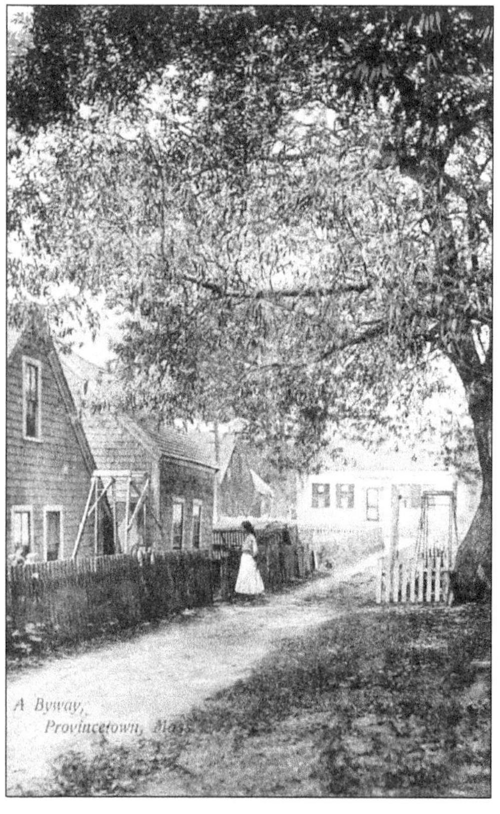

A Byway, Atkins Lane (c. 1908 postcard published by *The Advocate*). The person who sent this greeting to a friend wrote, "This card will give you a good idea of the streets of Provincetown." Swing sets in adjacent yards, under the shade of an ancient tree, provided simple relaxation for those finished with their household chores, or for children under the watchful eyes of grown-ups.

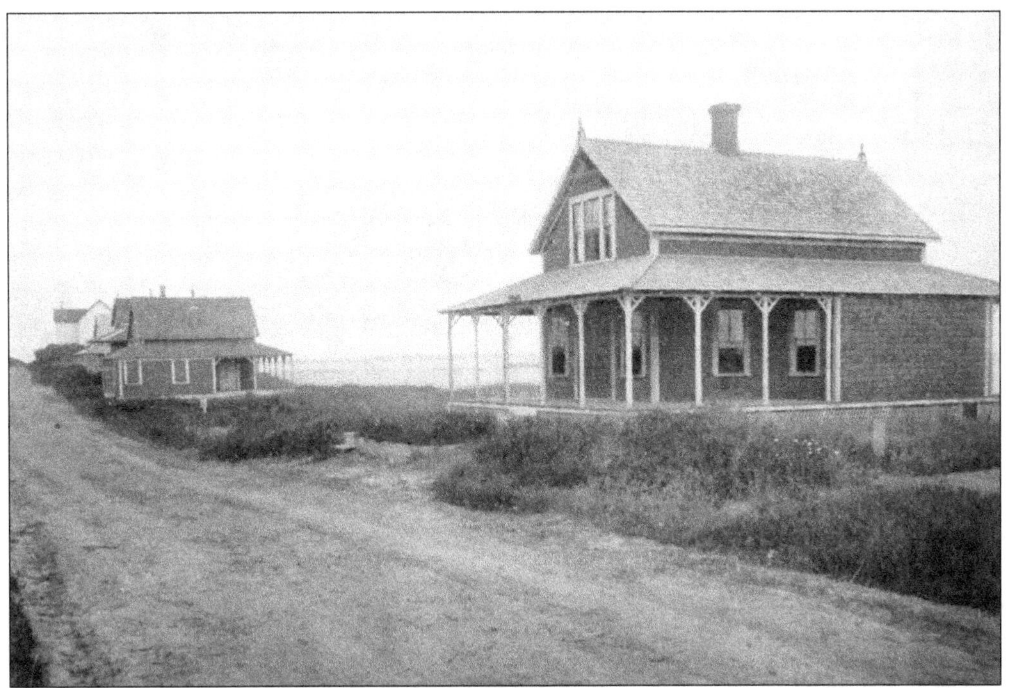

Summer cottages, probably near the intersection of Commercial and Bradford Streets (1898 photograph by The Perry Pictures Co.). The wraparound porches on these modest cottages allowed the lucky inhabitants to enjoy fresh air, sunshine, and unparalleled vistas on every side.

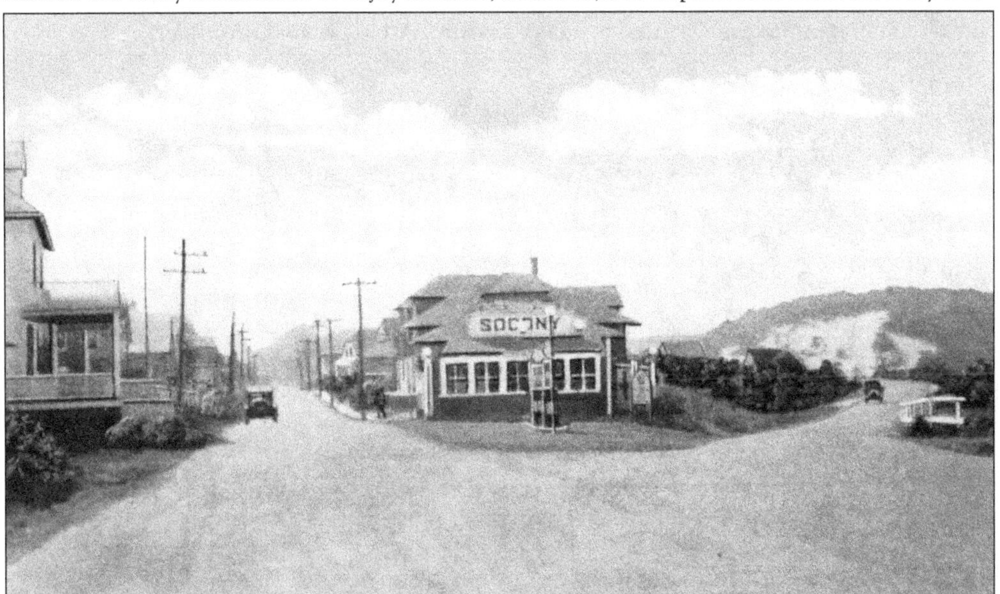

Junction of Commercial and Bradford Streets (c. 1930s postcard published by D.E. West Co.). People who drive along the shore route (6A) arrive at the junction of Commercial Street (left) and Bradford Street in the East End. Peter's Socony gas station served as a boundary marker between the area of densely-built cottages and permanent residences on the harbor side leading to the town's center, and the more open, as yet relatively unbuilt dune, or Atlantic Ocean side, which also leads to the heart of Provincetown.

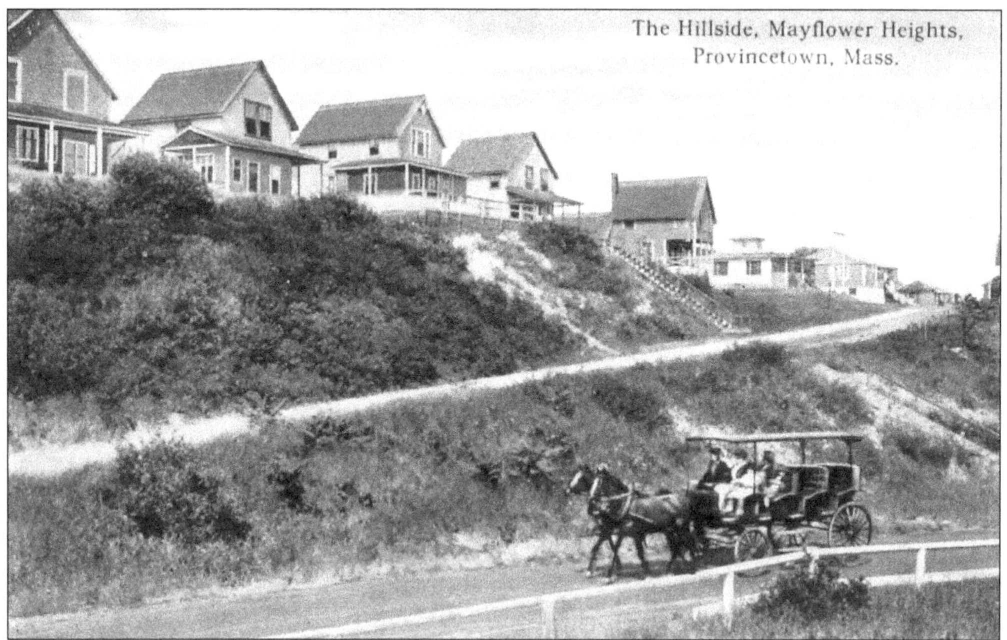

The Hillside, Mayflower Heights, off Commercial Street (c. 1910 postcard published by H.A. Dickerman & Son). Ancient Rome had seven hills and so did "ancient" Provincetown. In alphabetical order, they were Gilboa, Gull, Lothrop, Mayflower, Monument, Mount Zion, and Telegraph Hills. The summer cottages shown here on "The Hillside" of Mayflower Heights date to the turn of the twentieth century. A horse-drawn accommodation, or "barge," was the public form of transportation started by Frank Knowles Atkins around this time.

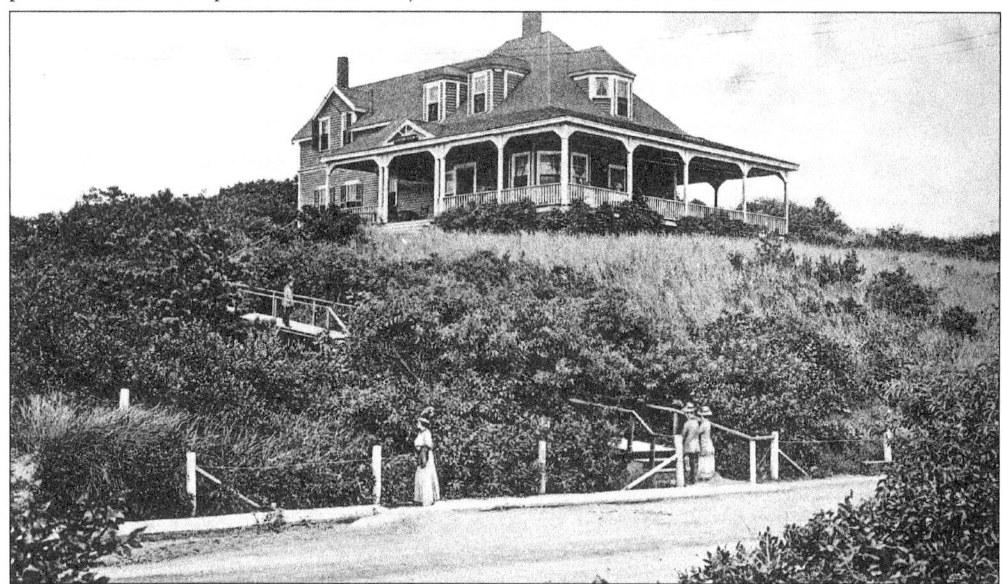

The Grand View, 676 Commercial Street (c. 1915 postcard published by *The Advocate*). This commanding residence with its wide wraparound porch and varied dormers was built around 1900 on the highest residential point in the East End. The romantic realist painter Max Bohm (1868–1923) and his family acquired the dwelling in 1919. (Courtesy Roger and Nanette Locke.)

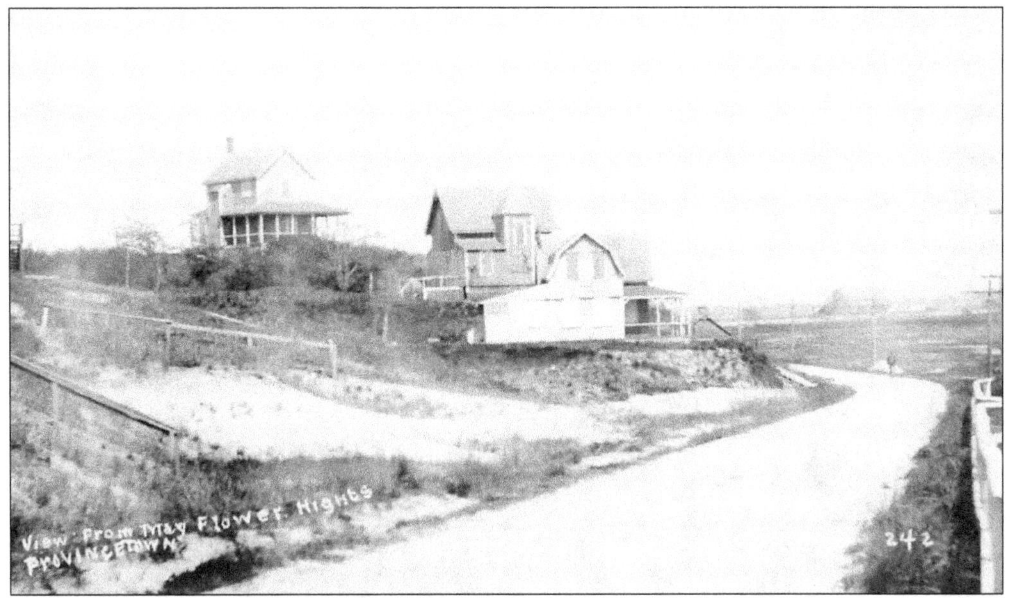

View from May Flower Hights [*sic*] (c. 1920 postcard; publisher unknown). These "Down-along" boarded-up cottages with their interesting roof shapes indicate that the summer season has passed. They and the large barn in the background are about 1/4 mile from the Provincetown-Truro town line on the shore route.

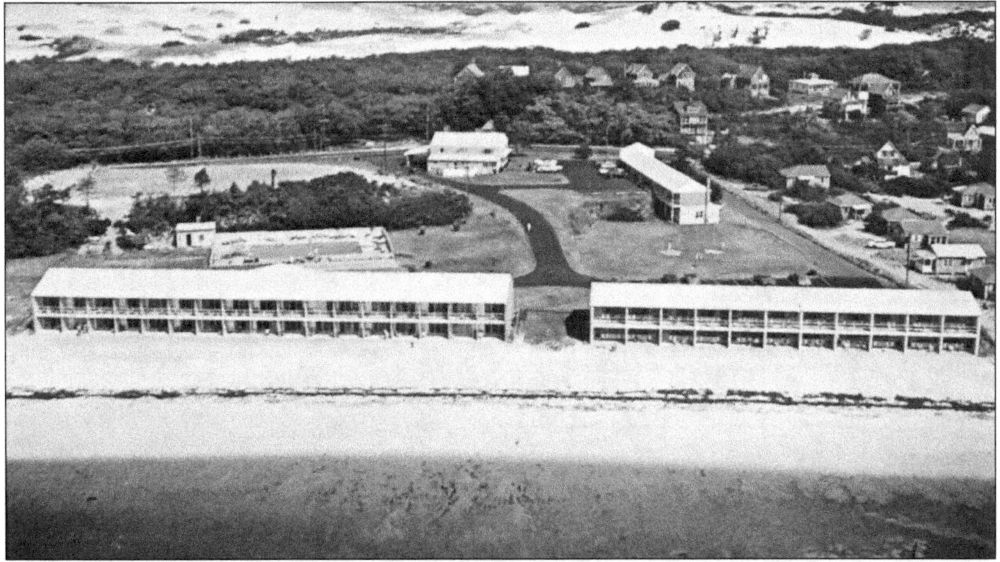

The Tides Motor Inn, 837 Commercial Street (c. 1970s postcard published by Dexter Press, Inc., West Nyack, New York). The row of cottages on Mayflower Heights is in the background of this view of the two-tiered motor inn, which is "Spectacularly located on the wide sweep of Cape Cod Bay. Beautifully appointed rooms. T-V, room phones, private sundecks, pool, coffee shop. Panoramic view of harbor and town from 500 foot beach. Convenient to shops, galleries, restaurants."

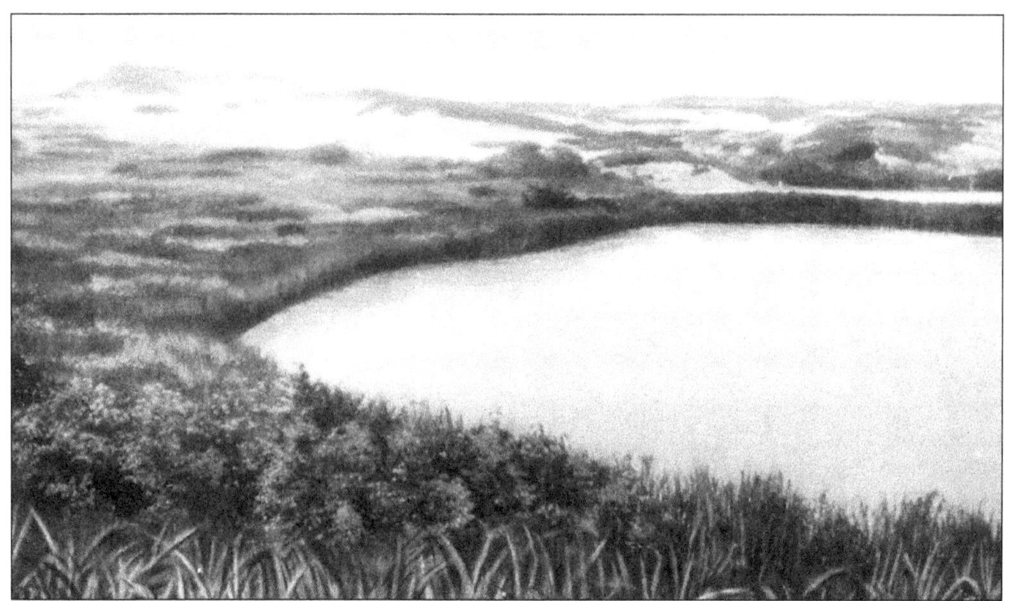

Sand Dunes, looking from Mayflower Heights (early-twentieth-century postcard published by *The Advocate*). Mount Ararat in the distance is the highest dune in the "chain of hills" overlooking Pilgrim Lake. As early as 1822 Timothy Dwight (1752–1817), the peripatetic theologian and president of Yale College (now University), enthusiastically and perceptively wrote, "The hills are of every height from ten to two hundred feet. Frequently they are naked, round, and extremely elegant; and often rough, pointed, wild, and fantastical, with all the varied forms, which are seen at times in drifts of snow . . . they are more sublime, and more interesting than can be imagined."

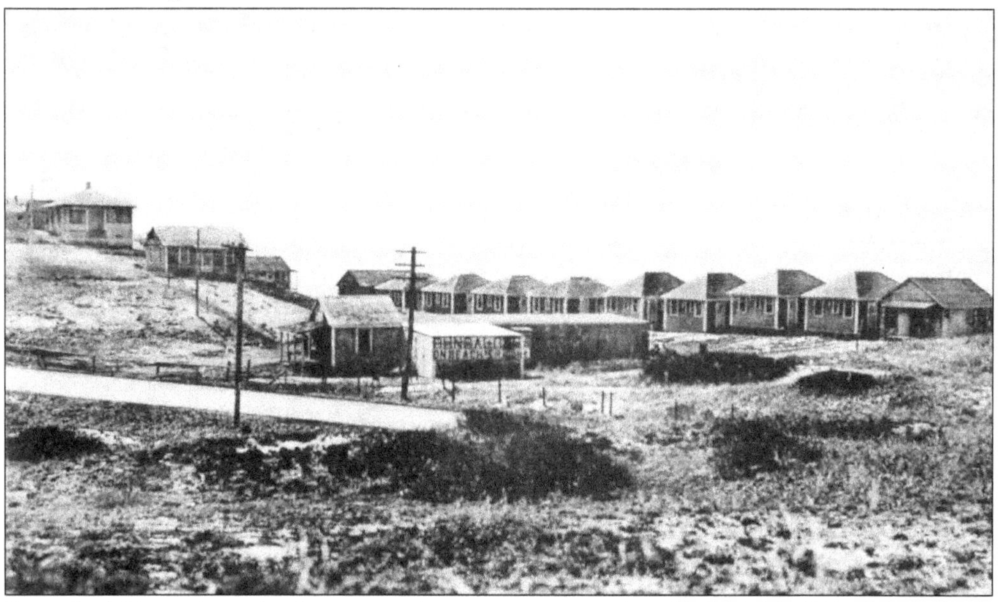

Furnished Bungalows (early-twentieth-century postcard published by E.D. West Co.). E.B. Knowles was the proprietor of the eight cheek-by-jowl, hipped-roof bungalows flanked by gable-roofed abodes. The large $5 per night sign on the end of a shed was designed to catch the eyes of passing motorists driving along the shore.

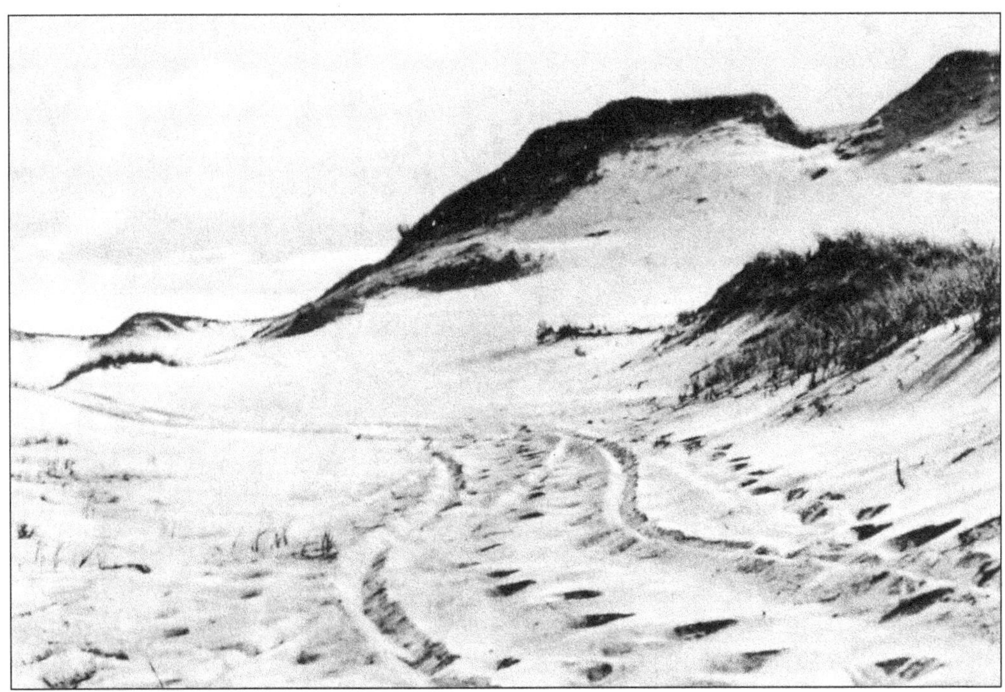

Cape Cod Dunes (early-twentieth-century postcard published by The Advocate Gift Shop). In 1839 John Warner Barber wrote that the "sand hills . . . are in some places partially covered with tufts of grass or shrubs, which appear to hold their existence by a frail tenure on these masses of loose sand, the light color of which strongly contrasts with few spots of deep verdure upon them." The dunes line the northern side of Provincetown, in the area designated as part of the Cape Cod National Seashore (established in 1961). A visitors' center, nature walk, and the Beech Forest picnic area are located off Race Point Road.

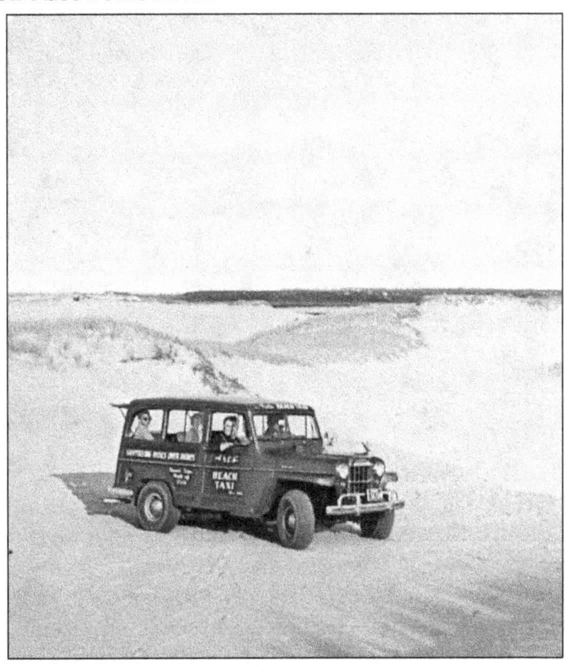

Beach taxi dune tour (c. 1955 postcard detail published by The Slate Co.). Vehicular dune tours enable those who cannot explore the vast, sandy landscape on foot, or those who want a narrated discourse, an opportunity to traverse the dunes in comfort. Dune tours were started in the 1930s; Portuguese descendant Art Costa has been giving informative tours for fifty years, since 1946.

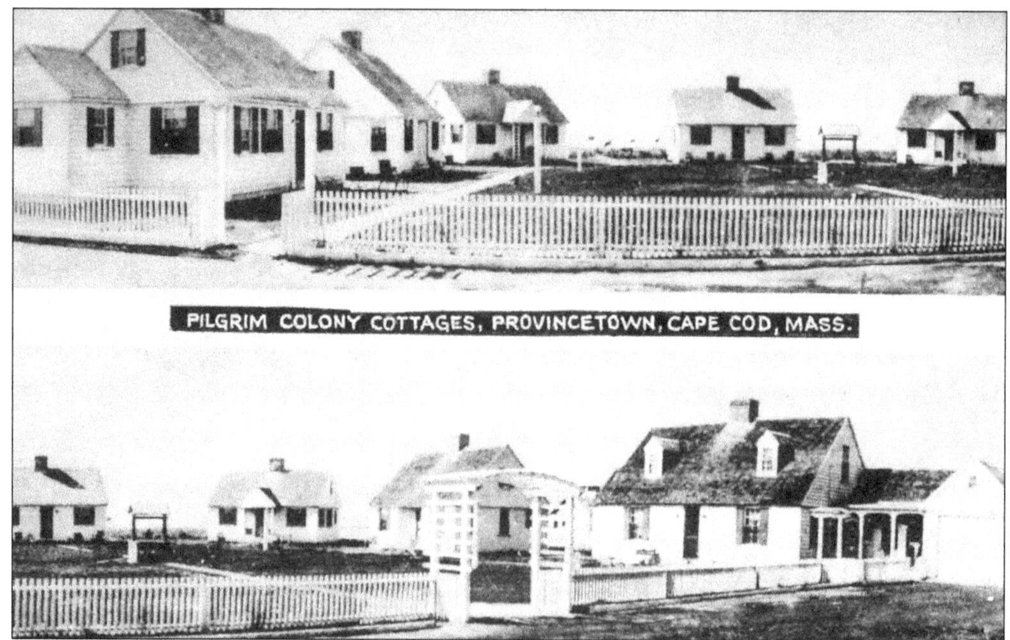

Pilgrim Colony Cottages (c. 1935 postcard published by E.D. West Co.). Separate cottages have always appealed to those who want their privacy, and yet like the proximity of other people. These charming, miniature Cape Cod cottages with their traditional well are located on the land side of Route 6A near the Truro town line, where Commercial Street begins.

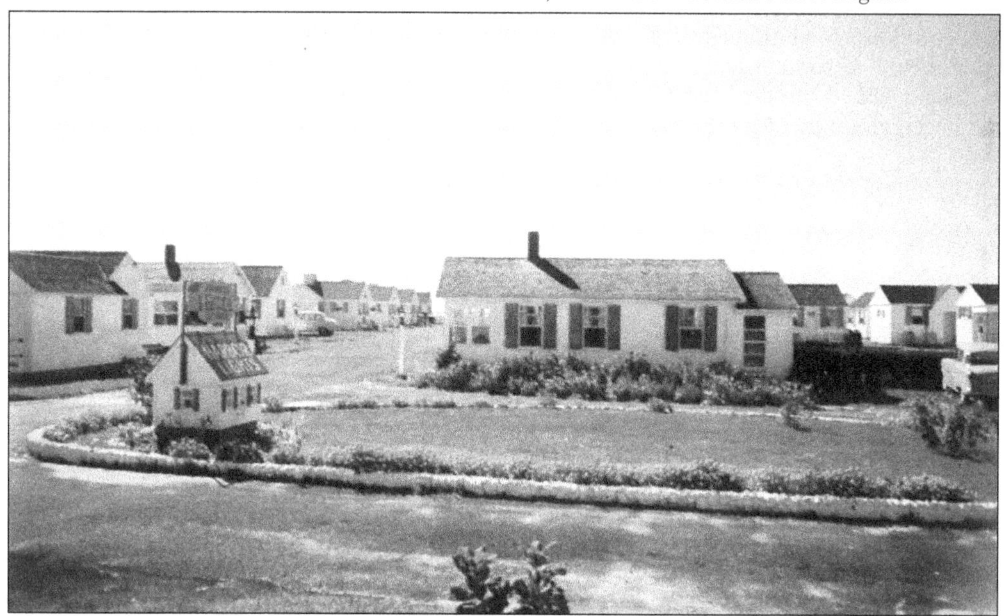

Harbor Lights Village on Beach Point (c. 1952 postcard published by Quinn Studio, Orleans, MA). Thomas O'Donnell was the proprietor at this time, and he could be reached by telephone at PROV. 1041-W in the center building. Harbor Lights Village was "Located on Cape Cod Bay with 200 feet of private sandy beach. There are 8 housekeeping cottages and 14 without housekeeping facilities. Central heat. The housekeeping cottages accommodate 2, 4, & 6 persons and all consist of two bedrooms, sitting room, kitchen, completely equipped."

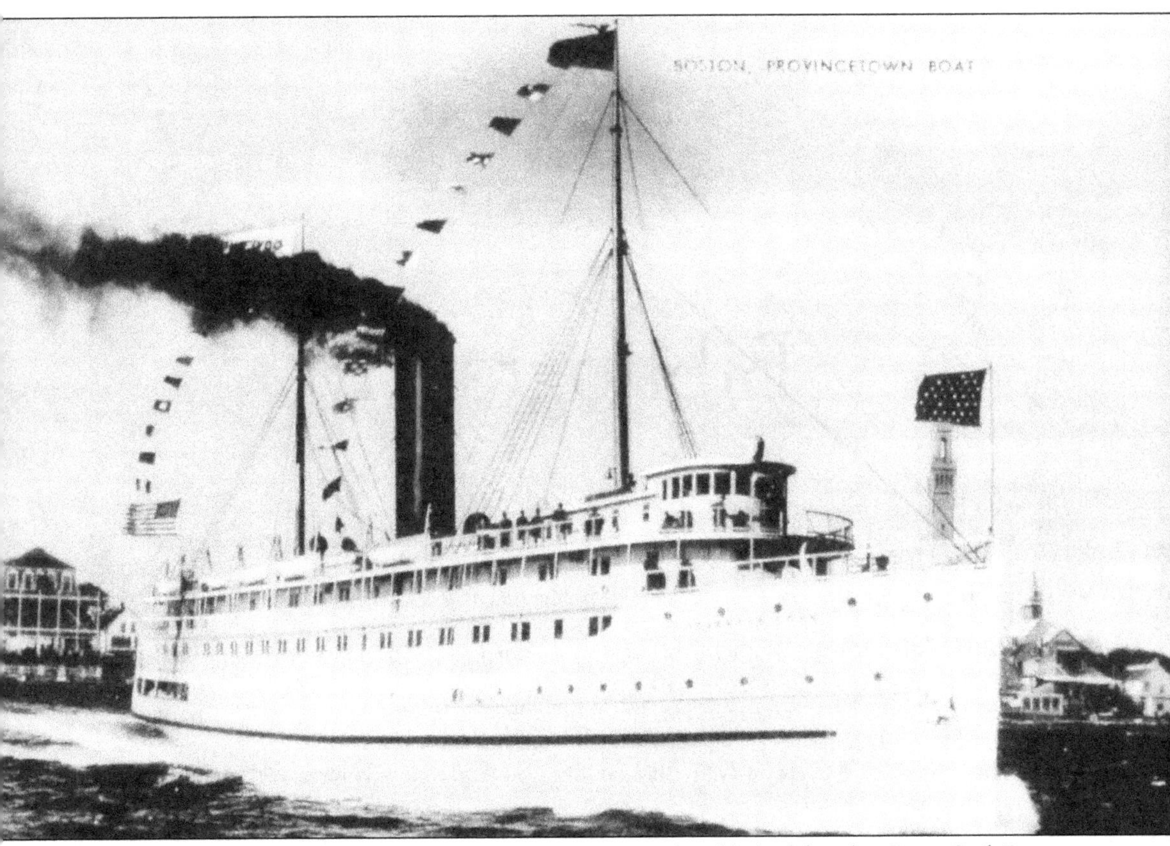

Governor Cobb Ferry (early-twentieth-century postcard published by the Cape Cod Post Card Co.). Dense smoke emanates from the tall smokestack of the Boston-bound ferry as she leaves Provincetown Harbor at 3:30 pm. Some of the passengers on board may have vacationed at the New Central House at the left, while others may have climbed to the top of the Pilgrim Memorial Monument (visible below the bow flag), and one or two may have had business to conduct in the town hall at the right. All, however, more than likely enjoyed delicious meals in the town's plentiful restaurants, took home special souvenirs, and looked forward to returning to that most special of **quaint little villages . . . You're sure to fall in love with**—Provincetown!

Bibliography

Ballou's Pictorial Drawing Room Companion, Vol. XI, 1856.

Barber, John Warner. *Historical Collections, of Every Town in Massachusetts.* Worcester, MA: Dorr, Howland & Co., 1839.

Carpenter, Edmund J. *The Pilgrims and Their Monument.* New York, NY: D. Appleton & Co., 1911.

Connelly, John. *A Century-Old Concern Business of Jones, McDuffee & Stratton Co.* Boston, MA: The George H. Ellis Co., 1910.

Drake, Gillian. *The Complete Guide to Provincetown.* Provincetown, MA: Shank Painter Publishing, 1992.

Dwight, Timothy. *Travels; in New England and New York.* New Haven, CT: published by the author, 1822.

Freeman, Frederick. *The History of Cape Cod.* Vol. II. Boston, MA: printed for the author by George C. Rand & Avery Co., 1862.

Jennings, Herman A. *Provincetown, or, Odds and Ends from the Tip End.* (facsimile edition) Provincetown, MA: Peaked Hill Press, 1975.

Provincetown Historical Association. *Walking Tours* Nos. 1, 2, and 3. 1982, 1984, 1989.

Ruckstuhl, Irma. *Old Provincetown in Early Photographs.* New York: Dover Publications, 1987.

Snow, Edward Rowe. *A Pilgrim Returns to Cape Cod.* Boston, MA: The Yankee Publishing Co., 1946.

Thoreau, Henry David. *Cape Cod.* New York: Thomas Y. Crowell Co., 1961.

Vorse, Mary Heaton. *Time and the Town.* New York: The Dial Press, 1942.

www.ingramcontent.com/pod-product-compliance
Lightning Source LLC
LaVergne TN
LVHW081553100826
845153LV00004B/373

* 9 7 8 1 5 3 1 6 6 0 1 5 4 *